H₂
BE/N

CHOSEN WORDS

by the same author

BOOK OF WORDS
I GIVE YOU MY WORD
SAY THE WORD
NO IDLE WORDS
HAVING THE LAST WORD
I BREAK MY WORD
A WORD IN EDGEWAYS

*The present volume contains extracts
from each of these titles*

CHOSEN WORDS

by

IVOR BROWN

JONATHAN CAPE
THIRTY BEDFORD SQUARE
LONDON

FIRST PUBLISHED 1955

PRINTED IN GREAT BRITAIN
BY TONBRIDGE PRINTERS LTD., TONBRIDGE
BOUND BY A. W. BAIN & CO., LTD., LONDON

ACKNOWLEDGEMENT

THE right to quote is a matter teeming with legal complexity. Authors of copyright work to whom I have appealed because I was quoting more than a phrase or a few lines have shown me the greatest kindness, and I would like to express my gratitude to Mrs. Bambridge, Mr. A. P. Watt, and Messrs. Methuen (in the matter of quoting from Rudyard Kipling), to Mr. Hilaire Belloc, to Mr. John Betjeman, to Mr. Edmund Blunden, to Messrs. Laurence Housman, Jonathan Cape, and the Society of Authors (in the matter of quoting from A. E. Housman), to Messrs. Macmillan (in the matter of quoting from Kipling and Ralph Hodgson), and to Mr. Siegfried Sassoon. I am most grateful to my friends Daniel George, John Moore, Eric Partridge, Stewart Perowne, Arthur Ransome, and J. C. Trewin for constant aid of various kinds, and to Miss Gladys Allen, Miss Margaret Catt, Miss Cecilia Becker and Miss Violet Marriott for valued secretarial assistance.

I include a list of the co-operators who wrote to me during the preparation of the Word Books. I apologize to those – I hope few – whose names have been omitted or set down incorrectly. In my prologue I made the war-time confusions of life some defence for the former fault: for the second I would plead difficult handwriting and hurried signatures (see my note on Squiggle in this collection). While some have set me problems of deciphering, all have given me a welcome incitement to continue.

FOREWORD

THE time has come, in my publisher's opinion, and also in my own, to sift my siftings or, more exactly but more cumbrously, to anthologize my word-anthologies. A series which began as a single random war-time volume had extended to eight, due largely to the goodwill of my readers who also became, in a way, my writers. They have been a kindly and a numerous team; offering, as it were, 'my word for yours', they have showered me with corrections, suggestions, and additions and have thus contributed to each new book as it came along. As my titles suggest, I was continually trying to stop and then was chased back into action. A list of these urgent co-operators appears at the end of this foreword; the roll may be incomplete because correspondence reached me at all sorts of times in all sorts of places: some of it arrived during the explosive and mobile conditions of London life in war-time when a proper regard for one's papers was often incompatible with self-regard for one's person. I did my best to acknowledge and to file these courtesies from many unknown friends as well as from a few known ones. But it was impossible to combine with a journalist's workaday existence as much response as the correspondence deserved. So I apologize for omissions on my part while I renew my gratitude for the favour of such widespread assistance.

In the course of the eight small books, published between 1942 and 1953, there was, as I have discovered on re-reading them, a certain amount of repetition and there was also inclusion of some words and notes on words which are hardly worth retention. An 'omnibus' volume, for which some have asked, would also have been unwieldy and uneconomic: the costs in the labour and material of book-production have soared so high that the 'omnibus' books, very popular and serviceable in the nineteen-thirties, have ceased to appear. The necessity now is for selection, rather than collection. So I have picked about a third of the mass for inclusion under one cover: some of the original notes on words have been cut and amended; and sometimes two or more notes have been run into one and some new notes have been included.

By this time new word-fanciers may have arrived whose appetite I hope this volume will serve: very few of my original readers will have kept up with my long, straggling output over eleven years and for those the selection here made will, I hope, include enough items that are fresh to win forgiveness if they find others that are familiar.

In making my choice I have naturally tried to establish proportion in the kinds of appeal made by the different kinds of words. When I began to collect words, it was chiefly æsthetic quality that directed my selection. I had reflected that anthologies of good writing, especially of poetry, had always given pleasure to many: good writing is the good use of good words. Surely this demands, in logic, an anthology of words that go to make anthologies of prose and verse. So I started to note the beauty of image and of sound in words that caught my eye and ear. But, after that, the oddity and the humour of our vocabulary also demanded their record. That led to investigation of meanings and origins, and when one has begun to delve in a dictionary, especially the *O.E.D.*, either in its full majesty of size and range or in its condensed, but handier, two volumes, it is almost impossible to stop: a neighbouring word comes into view and leads to delightful deviations.

To those who have plied me with problems of source and meaning, I have replied that I am not a specialist in semantics or a scholar of philology. Frequently I have passed their puzzles on to that verbal polymath, Eric Partridge, who has made word-lore his life-work, carrying on with vast energy and erudition the happy labours of Ernest Weekley and other pioneers too numerous to name. I have been the amateur and the play-boy on the fringe of this professional field, a field which I have found Elysian, rich in flowers. What I attempted was to set down, to explain, and if possible to communicate, the happiness that I discovered in these meadows.

I was amply informed by my correspondents about the wealth

of our dialects and our various types of slang. These provide not only a treasure, but a trap. If one accepted too much of racy local speech, the anthology might be overlaid with regional curios. So, while I have drawn to some extent on the good, gnarled lingo of the parish and of the shire, and, in the case of broad Scots, of the nation, I have put these elements on ration. In general I was making an anthology of English words with what might be called Dictionary Status; to wander too far into the cants and jargons of the counties, the classes, and the crafts would have destroyed my purpose. On the other hand, these oddities and rareties are useful in making a change and in contributing their special qualities of colour and vividness: so gladly I took some of them, rejecting more. I can only hope that a reasonable balance has been achieved.

In my introductions to each volume, I took my part in the campaign against the verbal pomposities and polysyllabic compositions of Officialese and Business English: nor did I overlook the appalling burdens laid on us by the learned with their own jargons of Philosophese, Psychologese and Criticese, to mention but a few. This campaign had already been widely waged by Sir Alan Herbert, and he has been ably and energetically supported by V. H. Collins, G. H. Vallins and other champions of brief, accurate, and lucid writing. The Government itself, through the excellent labours of Sir Ernest Gowers, has tried both to end the offences of the Civil Servants and to improve the usage of English everywhere. In a handy and concise book called *The Complete Plain Words*, containing in revised form Sir Ernest's *Plain Words* and *The A.B.C. of Plain Words*, Her Majesty's Stationery Office has offered the public an admirable guide to the Queen's English, at the price of five shillings. It is now superfluous for people like myself to keep hammering away at the linguistic mess which the Americans call gobbledygook and which I have described as the Barnacular in the case of bureaucrats and Pudder in the case of long-winded, muddle-headed sciolists. My third term, Jargantuan, perhaps sums up both types of offence.

9

The Word Books were intended for pleasant browsing rather than for edification or for scolding. My excursions into the Rescue of the English Language were by the way and that by-way has now become the well-covered highway of Sir Ernest and others. So I shall let that part of the subject rest and bear in mind that it is Prologue's business on the stage to state the argument and leave the actors to it.

I am deeply grateful to the owners of the following names, and deeply regret that too many are no longer here to receive my thanks.

IVOR BROWN

H. de Bels Adam
Miss H. M. Addison
James Agate
Miss Norah Airey
Vincent Alford
Miss Gladys Allen
Rev. Alex. Anderson
Cecil Andrews
H. R. Arnison
Miss Kathleen Arnold
Mrs. Janet Ashbee
J. T. Atkinson

Dr. H. Searle Baker
E. J. Bale
L. Bainbridge-Bell
J. H. Banbury
John Barbour
Owen Barfield
S. S. Barnaby
P. N. Barnard
Vernon Bartlett
T. K. Batterbury
A. W. Battersby
A. G. Bayliss

A. O. Baxter
G. J. Beaudoin
John Beavan
W. T. L. Becker
R. T. Bennett
Dr. Martin Berry
Miss F. Berryman
Frank C. Bestor
John Betjeman
Moncure Biddle
F. E. Billen
R. B. Blance
C. V. Bliss
Lady Blood
R. Bloxham
C. L. Boltz
James Bone
Stephen Bone
J. G. Booth
M. Murray Bowser
A. W. Boyd
Janies W. Boyle
Miss M. Brady
John Braidwood
C. Neville Brand

James Bridie
David Brock
Leonard Brockington
John Brooks
Miss Clara Broome
Philip W. F. Brown
W. J. Brown
Frank Buckland
Amy M. Bull
Margaret Bullivant
J. J. D. Bullmore
R. G. Bultitude
Fred Burman
E. R. Burtenshaw
W. M. Burton
E. M. Butes

Major Caillard
Bertram Carter
Denis Caseley
Miss M. Catt
C. S. Chapman
Miss V. J. Chapman
Donald Barr Chidsey
Miss Mary Child
Mrs. A. M. Clarke
Sir George J. Clerk
Miss Alice Coates
Miss V. Coldstream
Mrs. Margaret Cole
R. Coleman
Miss Phyllis Collier
V. H. Collins
Philip Conklin
J. H. Cousins
Air Vice-Marshal Cowtan

William Cox
Michael R. Crump
Dr. C. Willett Cunnington

Mrs. Dorothy Dainty
H. Ian Danby
Rev. J. A. Davidson
Gilberd Davis
Miss Margaret Denny
Alan Dent
Aubrey Dexter
A. E. Dingle
John H. Donaldson
F. E. Doran
E. F. Dow
J. G. Drummond
Mr. and Mrs. Laurence Drury
F. R. G. Duckworth
Thomas Dunbabin
Miss Janet Dunbar
L. F. Dunn
A. B. Dutton

L. Edgcumbe
Miss F. Edmundson
Miss Lucy Embury
Mrs. Monica Ewer
L. E. Eyles

Francis E. Falconbury
M. Farzaad
Mrs. Judith Foljambe
Miss Miriam de Ford
C. A. Fordyce
John Foster
Christopher Fostone

Miss Elizabeth Fraser
R. W. Frew

G. Gallie
Arthur Garnett
Robert Garrett
G. E. R. Gedye
Daniel George
Miss Phyllis M. Giles
Arthur Gleeson
Rev. P. D. Godfrey
Philip Godlee
S. Godman
J. C. Goldingham
W. L. Goodman
Miss Mabel Goss
J. E. Goudge
Reynold Greenstone
Hilton Greenwood
Miss Helen Grundy
David Gunston
Mrs. Rupert Guthrie

Sir Godfrey Haggard
A. Abdul Hakim
Lionel Hale
Mrs. Agnes Hall
G. Halliday
V. F. Hancock
Miss Anne Handley
Mrs. G. Hanmer
Miss Dorothy Hardy
H. Hardy
Miss F. Harnwell
A. B. Harrison
C. H. Harrison

Miss Agnes Hart
Miss Elizabeth Hawes
Charles Hawkins
Rex Hazelwood
David Heggie
Otto Heinertz
J. W. Hely-Hutchinson
George Hentschel
Daniel Hepburn
Denis A. Hicks
H. W. Hill
Michael Hirtzel
Miss M. E. Hobbs
J. W. Holme
Peter Holton
Patrick Home
Roy Hopkins
P. G. Horn
Valentine Horwill
W. Hough
Dr. W. B. Howell
Miss C. M. Hudson
Cecil Hull
M. N. Humphreys
F. Hurdis-Jones
E. A. C. Husbands
David Hussey
David Hutchison

Mrs. Norman Ingpen
Guy Innes
E. M. Irvine

J. Jamieson
P. S. Jeffrey
W. E. Jeffrey

John Jeffries
M. A. Jesper
E. Clinton Johnson
Miss W. N. Johnston
Mrs. Marjorie Jones
Thomas Jones

C. A. Keeble
Diarmid Kelly
C. Kent-Wright
M. Kermude
H. T. Kettle
W. Kettlewell
Lord Keynes
W. Kirk
G. Norman Knight

R. N. Lane
John T. Lawrence
Miss Mollie Leeper
S. Lees
Lord Leverhulme
C. S. Lewis
Miss Eiluned Lewis
Miss Ayleen Lorberg
Miss E. Lozena
W. E. Lucas
John Lunan
Norman Lupton
Robert Lynd

Sir William MacArthur
Sir Desmond MacCarthy
Mrs. Mary McCredie
W. S. MacCunn

Angus Macdonald
Arthur Macdonald
P. Macdonald
J. McEccles
J. W. Mackereth
Moray MacLaren
W. W. MacLellan
Mrs. D. E. MacLeod
Lord Macmillan
Maurice Macmillan
G. D. Malone
P. Maloney
Miss Mary Manson
Charles Marford
Miss Ngaio Marsh
Michael Marshall
John Mason
H. J. Massingham
Kenneth Matthews
John Mavrogordato
R. J. Medd
E. F. Meier
Miss Margaret Mellon
Miss Elma Mennie
A. F. Meredith
Francis Meres
Brian Meynell
O. E. Miles
Dr. Jane Millar
James Milne
John Morgan
Miss Moira Morley
Raymond Mortimer
E. M. Morton
E. R. Murray

Mrs. A. M. Neely
Vincent Nello
Dr. Thomas Nelson
Miss Mary Newman
Mrs. Pauline Niven
Sir Guy Nott-Bower

Thomas Ormesher
Iain Orr
Major Orr-Ewing
G. N. G. Orsini
Humphrey Osmond
J. C. Oulton
Harrison Owen

F. D. Park
C. W. Parker
Eric Partridge
Miss Pauline Peard
Michael Pearson
Dennis Peck
Sir James Peck
Dr. J. R. Peddie
J. E. W. Percival
N. S. Percival
Stewart Perowne
Derrick Perritt
J. Pimley
A. L. Plairré
James G. Platt
T. W. Pond
G. Potter
G. W. Priest
Beulah Putnam

Edwin Radford
Dr. Arthur Ransome

Donald Ratcliffe
Miss Dorothy Una Ratcliffe
E. J. Rea
J. Davis Reichard
Anthony Reiss
Miss Jane Rennie
D. Mackay Reside
Dr. G. K. C. Rettie
V. Richard
George Richards
C. B. Ricks
Rev. Luke Rigby
Hubert Riley
Mrs. M. E. Ringland
William Roberts
James Robertson
J. Harvey Robson
David F. Rodger
D. A. Rooke
Rev. John Rosie
Dr. A. Ross
Dr. W. H. D. Roose
Walter Rühemkorb
Lorne B. Russ
H. Russell-Snook

J. Leslie Sadler
Miss Gillian Sale
W. H. Sanders
B. K. Sandwell
T. H. Savory
Percy Scott
W. M. Scott
E. E. Searight
H. Dwight Sedgwick
Frank Shaw

John Shaw
J. M. Shea
W. H. Shepherd
S. T. Sheppard
Mrs. Maynard Shipley
L. R. Shore
Mrs. M. A. Simmons
Thomas H. Sims
Sir Osbert Sitwell
Dr. Edith Sitwell
Miss Y. E. Skipwith
E. Scott-Skirving
James Slack
M. L. Sloan
Dr. Harold Smith
M. H. Smith
Sir Edmund Spriggs
Alan Stark
Miss G. B. Stern
A. B. Stewart
G. E. Stevenson
Dr. Grace Stone
G. W. Stonier
Sir Ronald Storrs
Henry Strauss
Mrs. Alice Strong
Miss Dorothy Margaret Stuart
Miss Ruth Stuart
H. W. Stubbs
Theodore Sturgeon
Miss Mary Sturrock
B. E. Sutton
J. Swete-Evans
Miss Barbara Sydenham
Herbert Sykes
Douglas Symonds

J. W. K. Taylor
H. G. Tempest
Christopher Thacker
Miss Katherine Thicknesse
Kenneth Thomas
W. Thomasson
Dr. E. J. Thomson
Mrs. M. P. Thomson
Joseph Thorp
Dr. Hugh Thursfield
K. Todd
Stephen Trimen
J. C. Trewin
R. W. Truscott
D. B. Tubbs
H. B. Tunnard
Denis Turner
Donald Tyerman

G. H. Vallins
Sir Ralph Verney
Mrs. C. L. Vissen
Miss Ruth Von Phul
Judson Voyles

R. Waley
Mrs. Stella Walker
H. T. Walls
Albert Watson
Earl Wavell
Miss Mary Morison Webster
Mrs. A. M. Weesner
Miss Dorothy Weymouth
Eric White
J. F. Whitehead
C. R. Whittaker

15

Ronald Willesden
C. A. Williams
Prof. J. W. Williams
K. J. Williams
R. Powell Williams
Walter L. Williams
R. Williamson
David Wilson
Ian Angus Wilson
H. C. Withers

Miss Mary Withey
Dr. F. T. Wood
Dr. Thomas Wood
Miss Barbara Worsley-Gough
J. H. Wright
R. V. Wright

Norman Young

Miss Eleanor Zwirner

CHOSEN WORDS

ACCIDIE AND FEBRUARY

ACCORDING to a distinguished nephew of the great George Saintsbury, Oriental expert, and student of other matters, Mr. O. M. Green, incidence of accidie occurs after Christmas.

> The Christmas holiday has been spun out to its last thread. The Easter break in the daily round seems as remote as the Great Nebula in Andromeda.
> This is the time when humanity is specially prone to be attacked by Accidie, which from the earliest days of the Christian era has held a conspicuous place among the Seven Deadly Sins. 'The fourth head of the Beest of Helle is slouthe, whyche is cally'd of clerkys accidie.'

To Chaucer accidie was 'this roten-herted sinne' and Dante, as Mr. Green reminds me, described the victims of Accidie as sunk in a sea of mud. After a bout of influenza that sinking feeling is common: the world is no longer our onion; its name is mud. It is then that we join the Taoists who believe that action is the root of all evil and that to abstain from action is the principal good.

Accidie is not a handsome word. It is the Greek 'akedia' (not caring) in Latin form. But do such horrid things as the influenzal don't-care-if-I-do-die feeling and its consequent sloth deserve to have shapely and fair-sounding names?

I have linked this wretched listlessness and sloth with a certain month of the year, accepting Mr. Green's chronology, and I have deemed them to be February infections. I had carelessly and ignorantly thought that February meant the Month of Fevers, the high season of the In-flowing (or Influenzal) demon, since the Latin for fever is febris. But it does, in fact, come from februum, a cleansing or purgation and from Februa the feast of the purifications which occurred in the middle of this month. Still February in English is a word of ill-omen. Shakespeare even made it an adjective of gloom and applied it to a gloomy face.

ADIAPHORIST

In the literature of the seventeenth century you may run into an Adiaphorist, who is one showing indifference in theology; he is not in our sense an indifferent (or incompetent) theologian. Rather does he show an absence of enthusiasm, a word which originally meant divine possession and so was applied to wild forms of fervour. Pepys used the term latitudinarian for the adiaphorist, defining his friend Wilkins, Bishop of Chester, as a rising man because of his latitude in theology. The citizens of Laodicea, who ran a moderate temperature in theological affairs, have been made by one of Thomas Hardy's titles the typical adiaphorists.

I thought that the reference to Laodicean temperance came in 'The Acts of the Apostles'. But Laodicea is chiefly mentioned in the Epistle 'to the saints and faithful brethren which are at Colosse', in which the Colossians are recommended to read 'the epistle from Laodicea'. This is something of a compliment to the latter; the scolding of that place which gave it a name for ever as a home of cold (or rather of tepid) fish, came in 'Revelation'.

> And unto the angel of the church of the Laodiceans write 'These things saith the Amen, the faithful and true witness, the beginning of the creation of God; I know thy works, that thou art neither cold nor hot; I would thou wert cold or hot.
> So then because thou art lukewarm and neither cold nor hot, I will spue thee out of my mouth.

The irate 'Amen' was certainly no adiaphorist in his attitude to adiaphorism and in calling Laodiceans to 'be zealous and repent'. Now there is a cant phrase, wickedly overworked, 'I couldn't care less', to signify indifference in general. Adiaphorism and latitudinarianism have been mainly restricted to theology. But I suppose a man can be called Laodicean about any cult, even about cricket.

ADSCITITIOUS AND BEZZLE

I CAME across this Latinity amid the gay scholarship of Dr. Leslie Hotson's Shakespearean researches. This happy sifter of innumerable Rolls and Registers goes Jack-Hornering in the Record Office and, with his assistants, is generally to be relied upon to pull out a plum. The assumption that nothing more of fact will ever be discovered about Shakespeare is continually dissipated by Dr. Hotson's discoveries among the ancient files: these discoveries may not always be large, but they do link up the elusive dramatist with hitherto unknown figures of the Tudor and Jacobean scene, such as William Johnson, first apprentice and then landlord of the 'Mermaid'. Hitherto there had been no evidence that Shakespeare ever had anything to do with that favourite haunt both of the poets and the 'roaring boys'. Now it is demonstrated that the witness of one of Shakespeare's purchases of property, the Blackfriars Gate-House, was called William Johnson, Vintner. The Chancery records make it plain that the 'Meeremayd' was in the tenure of William Johnson, Vintner. This does not prove that William Shakespeare was a highly absorbent customer of Johnson's or a member of the 'right-generous, jovial, and mercurial Sireniacks' who took their pleasure there with Ben Jonson and the rest. But it does prove the existence of an interesting acquaintance in a life that has aroused and so largely defeated the curiosity of the world.

But I am slow in reaching my words. Adscititious is introduced by Dr. Hotson, who is a word-happy scholar, well dyed in the great vat of historic English verbosity. It means brought in, supplementary, additional. Evelyn the Diarist used it. Is it to be taken up now by youth attempting English style? I fancy that many examiners would be floored by it should they find it in a student's answer: and it is imprudent to be more learned than the judge. However, there it is for those who like to add imposingly to our terms for additional.

Dr. Hotson's zest for adscititious terminology is exemplified in his discussion of London breweries of the reign of Queen Elizabeth in a volume called *Shakespeare's Sonnets Dated*.

> Stow remarks, 'the Brewers for the more part remain near to the friendly water of Thames'. Friendly not only because it bore the shipping to Queenhithe and Billingsgate with sea-coal for their furnaces, and stores of hops and hard, straw-dried yellow malt, but also because they used Thames water for their 'liquor'. For in spite of Nashe's observation that brewers grow rich 'by retayling filthy Thames water', that same water was generally held to produce the best beer (Harrison, *Descr. of England*, New Shak. Soc., I. 160). More than that, English beer, with London beer made of filthy Thames water at the head, was so celebrated and sought after that despite the diligent bezzling and beer-bathing of English toss-pots, bench-whistlers, and lick-wimbles, 'like dromedaries in the caravana, drinking for the thirst past, for the thirst present, and for the thirst to come', the hard-working brewers of England made enough not only to satisfy the home market, but to supply a large export trade as well

Here is verbal plenty indeed, and sufficient toper-names to deserve the epithet of adscititious. Bezzling lick-wimbles, toss-pots, and bench-whistlers made lively company no doubt: and dubious, dangerous company too, if bezzling had then got its secondary meaning which is known to us better in the longer word, embezzle.

To bezzle was to booze and behave sottishly; and, because sots need funds and may snatch at them for lack of will to earn them honestly, a bezzler was one who not only guzzled and soaked but made away with the property of others in order to do so. So we have derived the embezzler, who may, after all, be a fanatical teetotaller; he is nominally descended from the toss-pots of the Tudor tavern: he is but a lick-wimble gone further down hill. One of the old usages of wimble was as a synonym for nimble and I take a lick-wimble to be a bezzling fellow as ready with his tongue and lips as a dog on a hot day.

ALIEN

ALIENS now are matter for legislation, ordinance, and restriction. The word has unhappy and unpleasant associations. We think of ourselves as Britons abroad, never as aliens. A dull word? Surely its adjective has immense potentialities of pathos. It rings with melancholy like a sea-bird's plaint above the waters. We all know of Ruth's sad heart,

> When, sick for home,
> She stood in tears amid the alien corn.

Sick for home! How much better than the ubiquitous 'nostalgic' of our day, the nostalgic without which no critical column can now be written. There is a short poem by Alice Meynell called 'Rivers Unknown to Song' which begins,

> Wide waters in the waste: or, out of reach,
>   Rough Alpine falls, where late a glacier hung;
> Or rivers, groping for the alien beach,
>   Through continents, unsung.

That is exquisite and its poignant picturing of wilderness is well assisted by the use of alien. 'Groping for the alien beach' is a fine phrase for the first stirrings of a great river in the hills and for the early meanderings of a mountain beck.

A long 'a' not only occurs in separation, but powerfully suggests the pains of parting. I have continually echoing in my mind various lines about this theme of alienation in all of which the same letter occurs and sets the tune. 'Over the hills and faraway', described by G. K. Chesterton as one of the most beautiful phrases in all English poetry, gains vastly by the long 'a' at the close.

The long 'a' in waste has also a rich essence of melancholy. Shakespeare's 'Richard II' cries at his end, 'I wasted time and now doth time waste me'. Did not the title of Eliot's 'Waste Land' profit greatly by the sound of it? Then, another echo tossing in the waste of waters in my memory is Matthew Arnold's

> The unplumb'd, salt, estranging sea.

Strange is such a common word that we do not pause to notice the spell inherent in this long-drawn monosyllable. It is surely worth remark that Keats, when using the word alien with such skill, followed it with a row of 'a's, including 'magic casements', and 'faery lands'. The letter does its work again in farewell. Shakespeare's infallible instinct for sending pain sounding through our hearts made him describe departure with a peal of 'a's.

> Farewell! A long farewell to all my greatness
> This is the State of Man.

The 's's at the beginning of the second line are awkward, but the repeated vowel sounds a last post with strong appeal to our compassion.

ALLAY

ALLAY is a verb of richest variety. In its time it has signified a fine assortment and even confusion of meanings, to overthrow or to appease, to dilute wine or to lay on hounds. I have also found it as one of a covey of Elizabethan verbs proper to the serving and carving of meats. These verbs run like the famous nouns of assembly, a pride of lions, skulk of foxes, gaggle of geese, and so on. Robert May, author of *The Accomplisht Cook*, thus parades them:

> Lift that Swan; Rear that Goose; Dismember that Hern; Unbrace that Mallard; Unlace that Coney; Allay that Pheasant; Wing that Partridge; Display that Quail; Unjoynt that Bittern; Unlatch that Curlew; Break that Egript; Thigh that Woodcock.

One can imagine them rolled with a sonorous rapture on a major-domo's tongue as he overlooked the ordering of his lady's table for a day of high entertainment.

To John Moore, part compiler of *The Angler's Week End Book* and author of much happily observant writing on the fruition of the English scene, I owe a similar list of Tudor fish-carving terms. So before the master of the carving-table had 'allayed' a pheasant, 'unlatched' a curlew, 'unbraced' a mallard, or 'unlaced' a coney, he had doubtless been no less exact and picturesque with the fish-slice in his hand. Here are the terms as set forth in *The Accomplisht Lady's Delight* (1719):

Barb a Lobster	Splat a Pike
Chine a Salmon	String a Lamprey
Culpon a Trout	Tame a Crab
Fin a Chevin	Tranch a Sturgeon
Scull a Tench	Transon an Eel
Side a Haddock	Tusk a Barbel
Splay a Bream	

Later terms of address to the fish course include 'frushing a chub' and 'gobbeting a trout' (1829).

To be 'accomplisht', either as Cook or Lady, involved some erudition and nice use of the dining-room lexicon. Were blunders indeed noticed? Did the host turn purple, did the hostess freeze to a glacier, if some uncouth stranger, striving for correctness, suggested unlacing a haddock, or splatting a swan?

AMARANTH

THERE are some words which ring the bell wherever they are used. How many could immediately define the amaranth? Yet, in a line of verse, it brings with such swift ease all Arcady to mind. It is first the fadeless flower, a mythical bloom, then a purple blossom, perhaps a term for our love-lies-bleeding. Milton was prodigal of amaranth:

> Bid amaranthus all his beauty shed
> And daffadillies fill their cups with tears
> To strew the laureate hearse where Lycid lies.

It is the mourning and the grave-yard petal. Browning could rival Milton in this section of the floral dance:

> Whence the grieved and obscure waters slope
> Into a darkness quieted by hope;
> Plucker of amaranths, grown beneath God's eye
> In gracious twilights where his chosen lie.

Tennyson's Lotos-Eaters were 'propt on beds of amaranth and moly'. This poet played also with amaracus, the Cretan Dittany. (And Kipling, in turn, played in delight with dittany.) This from 'Œnone':

> Then to the bower they came;
> Naked they came to that smooth-swarded bower
> And at their feet the crocus brake like fire,
> Violet, amaracus, and asphodel,
> Lotos and lilies.

A bit too easy, no doubt, for the poet of today. But I shall remain susceptible to amaranth and also to amaracus. I note that the prudent Walter de la Mare does not disdain the adjective amaranthine. And to Cowper, who thought of it as a synonym for immortal,

> The only amaranthine flower on earth
> Is virtue!

This links the word with lilies and languors, but for me it belongs to the rosy and the rapturous plantations, if roses can be undeciduous.

AMETHYST

'QUARTZ coloured by manganese or by a compound of iron and soda.' Geology makes unromantic noises of this kind, but there is often mystery in the heart of it. 'The amethist staieth drunkennesse.' So thought the Tudor folk, who knew as much about drunkenness as most. The word, in its Greek derivation, makes this explicit claim. *A*–not, *methé*–intoxication. But what, having acquired a piece of quartz coloured by manganese, etc., did the toper do about it? Did he rest it on the aching brow or grind it to powder and swallow it at some risk to his duodenum? One suggestion, that wine drunk from an amethystine goblet would be a teetotal fluid, seems definitely to libel a blameless and beautiful stone.

Anyhow the colour of this quartz is violet-purple and so amethyst has been a jewel of esteem and amethystine an adjective appealing to many minor and some major poets. Dawns especially are amethystine and the epithet rides a sounding line as handsomely as frequently. The amethyst has Biblical honours and sounds the final note of celestial architecture and also of Mrs. Browning's 'Aurora Leigh'. (Does anybody cope with Aurora nowadays? It has imposing passages.)

> Where, faint and far,
> Along the tingling desert of the sky,
> Beyond the circle of the conscious hills,
> Were laid in jasper-stone as clear as glass
> The first foundations of that new, near Day
> Which should be builded out of heaven to God.
>
> . . . .
>
> 'Jasper first,' I said,
> 'And second, sapphire: third, chalcedony:
> The rest in order: last, an amethyst.'

The order, of course, is that in 'The Book of Revelation'. After chalcedony the chosen stones were emerald, sardonyx, sardius, chrysolite, beryl, topaz, chrysoprase, jacinth, and amethyst. Of the dozen the first two, jasper and sapphire, have acquired sinister significance in our giving of names. Sir Jasper in the melodramas was never anything but a sour, black-avised villain, scheming rape and ruin, and Sapphira's vice and fate have naturally discouraged wide usage of that stone at christenings. Beryl has been moderately popular and Sir Topaz we know at least in letters. Jacinth appears occasionally. But chalcedony, sardonyx, and chrysolite would be heavy birthday presents for any infant.

These minerals appear to have much in common. Chalcedony is 'a crypto-crystalline sub-species of quartz', transparent or translucent. In lapidary work it is called variously agate, cornelian, cat's eye, chrysoprase, onyx, sard. Agate is certainly a family name and Mr. Masefield has made Sard a Christian name, but not, I think, with minerals in mind. Amethyst has been very little used as a name for girls. It would be a classic and imposing alternative to Violet. It might become Ammy – but is that worse than Vi? If contracted to Misty it could be very suitable for quite a number of scatterbrained young lovelies who never know where they are lunching, with whom or when, but arrive at two instead of one, swathed in charm and faintly cooing, 'Am I late?'

ARTICHOKE

COMING across Peacock's observations on the Italian girasol which gave us that Jerusalem which precedes a species of artichoke, I naturally reflected on the absurdity of the word artichoke. Was the thing supposed to administer crafty suffocation? Then, no sooner had I parted with Peacock's Dr. Opimian, than I had a letter from the verbally omniscient Stewart Perowne whose Middle Eastern journeyings and Arabic lore are a sure guide through the labyrinth of our lexicon.

Talking of Arabic acquisitions, I think artichoke is the most widely travelled, more even than apricot. The Arabic word for artichoke is al-kharshuf (which is probably Persian, anyway). This passed into Italian as articiocco, and so to French as artichaut, and finally came to us. No, not finally – it went back to the Levant again. But by the time it got there, the original al-kharshuf was forgotten. 'What is this?' they said. 'Artichoke,' replied the foreigner. 'Ah! Of course, you mean ardi shoki – what a good name.' And so it is, for ardi shoki means the thorn of the earth, which is a fair description of the globe artichoke. And so it is called to this day. The artichoke of Jerusalem is, naturally, not the Jerusalem artichoke. In Jerusalem, we have the globe variety. Jerusalem is an improvement of the Italian words gira alla sole, turns to the sun.

Perowne then suggests that I check 'the foreign spellings which are almost certainly as wrong as the main facts are right'. *O.E.D.* supports the spelling al-kharshuf.

It is an eventful history, this of the artichoke, brought to us with ivory and spices from the Middle East and part even of the Persian Apparatus made famous by Horace. Did Omar know al-kharshuf? Did he never sing of its consoling power?

> And evermore I went, alone, aloof,
> Beneath the blazing Heaven's burnished Roof
>   To drink the Vine of Solitude and seek
> The Peace that's rooted strong as Al-kharshuf.

Fitzgerald would not have translated the last word. Romantic quatrains could hardly absorb an artichoke.

Another vegetable named after a Near Eastern city and then confused in form is the scallion, a name for the shallot or Welsh onion known as chibol. The scallion is the tasty root from Askelon. The Jerusalem artichoke came from muddled Italian, not from the old Jewish capital; but the scallion is a true piece of Palestine. 'Tell it not in Gath, publish it not in the streets of Askelon' is a cry which has eternized the name of the shallot's home-town. Scallion makes a fine-sounding name for a savoury article. It is obviously to be imported in galleons and prepared for table by the scullions.

ATTERCOP

A LEADING authority on spiders, Dr. W. S. Bristowe, as well as some amateur entomologists, have reminded me that attercop has lingered long in the common speech, especially in Lancashire and East Scotland. There is so much in common between Danish and Scottish that attercop for spider seems natural in Fife, the Danish being Edderkopper. Attor or atter is the Old English for poison, and cop may be either head (kopf) or cup. Dr. Bristowe, who studies words as keenly as insects, likes 'a smother of spiders' as the noun of assembly when gossamer is in the making, explaining his choice thus:

> The spider population of an acre of grassland may be as much as 2,000,000. Under certain weather conditions, particularly warm sunny mornings in autumn, these spiders are stirred into uneasy wandering. They cover the grass stems, hedges and railings. Each trails a thread as they walk; so, in due course, the whole field may be covered with a shimmering silver sheet. I call this vast concourse 'a smother of spiders'. Gossamer is the result.

Gossamer, a word of flavour, is attributed to the time of year which Dr. Bristowe mentions, i.e. St. Martin's Summer, the Goose-summer. One of the best descriptions of a spider-smother morning is in Tennyson's 'In Memoriam'.

> Calm is the morn without a sound
>   Calm as to suit a calmer grief.
>   And only thro' the faded leaf
> The chestnut pattering to the ground:
>
> Calm and deep peace on this high wold,
>   And on these dews that drench the furze,
>   And all the silvery gossamers
> That twinkle into green and gold.

Dr. Bristowe adds:

> It is now too late to revive the ancient word tentbob (or taint-bob) in place of the clumsier and less descriptive harvester or harvest-mite, or to reintroduce such other attractive old English words as attercop (spider), pol-wiggle (tadpole) and oontie-tump (mole-hill), but one bids them good-bye with regret.

Tump is a word I much like. It suggests the dumping of a tumulus and has, in fact, often been applied to old grave-mounds. Hettie Pegler's Tump is a famous Long Barrow. Our archaic tumps, often so finely shaped and sited that they lie upon the summits like lions, look their best in gossamer weather. Then a smother of attercops works silken magic on these relics of the Ancient Mariners who spread their tracks and tombs across the chalky, flinty, downlands of the English coast. The dictionaries are silent about little Miss Muffet's tuffet, which I like to think is a rural diminutive of tump rather than a little tuft of vegetation, the former being a far likelier place for a whey-drinking session. It was undoubtedly a veritable attercop which so terrified Miss Muffet.

AWFUL

In *Some Miseries of Human Life*, an admirable compilation of social calamities made by 'Samuel Sensitive and Timothy Testy', there is set down as one of the main horrors of a rural ride,

> Visiting an Awful Ruin, in the company of a Romp of one sex or a Hun of the other.

It is curious to discover this use of Hun, presumably as a boorish, uncultivated fellow, with the old and good use of Awful as awe-inspiring. No word has been more foully mishandled than the latter. Romp, for a chattering, facetious adult, instead of a turbulent child, seems to be another good thing lost.

BABBLE

BABEL has been flattered by our application of it to one of the most agreeable of all sounds, that of the fall of running water on stones and boulders. We meet the old kind of Babel-babble in the old plays, in which bable is noise, chatter, gossip or the man who scatters it. 'This sack has filled my head so full of bables, I am almost mad.' Gabriel Harvey wrote of John Lyly in a fine, dismissive way in 1593,

> He hath not played the Vicemaster of Poules, and the Foolemaster of the Theatre for naughtes: himself a mad lad as ever twanged; never troubled with any substance of witt, or circumstance of honestie, sometime the fiddle-sticke of Oxford, now the very bable of London.

(Poule for lady of the town has returned to France and survived.)

Shakespeare twice united babling with gossip, once in *Titus Andronicus* and later in the familiar 'willow cabin' speech of Viola in *Twelfth Night*,

> Holla your name to the reverberate hills
> And make the babbling gossip of the air
> Cry out, 'Olivia'!

'A babled of green fields' suggests water as well as grass, some meadow by the river-side. Hence 'the stripling Thames at Bablock Hythe' brings in the perfect riparian name. Surely Bablock Hythe has never been bettered. Brooks, by now, have babbled over often and inevitably the word's quality is diminished. It reverts to prattle. (Brabble is quarrelsome babble – much anger in the 'r'.) The Greek for babble is 'Lalage' – a charming word which was turned, wittily, into a girl's name. Well, since we have Mabel, why not Babel? We all know some fair one who has earned it. Incidentally the Puritans, who made Prudence and Patience into Christian names for girls, tried to do the same for Silence. But it would not do. There was no such Miss. There are some fictions which will never work. Lalage was too often the truth.

BALDERDASH

WHEN that great figure of farce, Mr. Robertson Hare, chin up, skull and spectacles aglitter, and all the bourgeois virtues and indignations steaming from his outraged dignity, cries 'Balderdash', the audience is always in a roar. But how many know what balderdash is, except a synonym for nonsense? One (too learned) schoolboy defined it as a poem by Matthew Arnold. (He was only three letters out.) It is a verb as well as a noun. Balderdashing is, in fact, mixing your drinks. Balderdash began as beer and butter-milk mingled, which sounds sufficiently odious, and then was applied to beer and wine or to any alcoholic jumble. In this sense the punches and the cocktails are all balderdash. But they are mixed for strength, while the earliest balderdash seems to have been assembled for weakness, as in the case of shandy-gaff, and so came to signify feeble, confused ideas. The dictionaries are unhelpful about shandy-gaff (beer and ginger-beer or lemonade mixed). This is a popular summer drink and vastly improved, in the opinion of some, by being further balderdashed with a spot of gin.

Balderdash was a verb in the eighteenth century. Smollett railed at some of the stuff sold as wine in his day: 'A vile, unpalatable, and pernicious sophistication, balderdashed with cider, corn-spirit, and the juice of sloes.' Why do we always assume that those were the 'good old days' for the consumer? Any reader of eighteenth-century travels realizes that inn-keeping Boniface, as generous as rubicund, with a conscience as spotless as his apron, is a romantic dream of our own time. The inns were mainly as dirty and bad as the roads, much of the food tough and filthy, and the drinks rough balderdash. In the great Georgian

C   33

houses of the nabobs, in Brighton or in Berkeley Square, larder and cellar may have been admirable, but the ordinary visitor in town or village stood every chance of a verminous couch and of a poor medley of liquor and victuals.

BANANA

NOTICING in a Serenade by Douglas Grant Duff Ainslie the enticing first two lines

> Lady of the lovely thighs
> Curving like banana fruit

I wondered why bananas have been so little present in our poetry. They are as suave in sound as in flesh. Why should peaches and cherry-ripe and apple-of-the-eye have such powerful positions in the vocabulary of affection? Obviously one would not look for a banana-tinted cheek, but for sweetness and richness there is surely a happy image for the love-lyricist in a ripe banana. (I refer to the small, tender Malayan species, the pesang, not to the great coarse fellow that has too much and too crudely represented this noble name in the British market.)

Emerson did pass an observation on bananas,

> The highest civility has never loved the hot zones.
> Where snow falls there is usually civil freedom;
> Where the banana grows, man is sensual and cruel.

But this dubious generalization on that stalest of school-room essay themes, the Influence of Climate upon Character, does not affect the succulence of the banana or the pleasure of rolling its name, as well as its substance, on the tongue. A popular song of 1923, 'Yes, we have no bananas, we have no bananas today', could hardly have achieved its great favour with a fruit of less engaging sound. 'Yes, we have no pine-apples.' That would never do. Bananas, which, had they been known, would have been eagerly snatched by the Latin poets to end their hexameter lines demanding the syllabic close of short-long-long, have been ridiculously neglected by our minstrels. There is a fine roll about them. Stage crowds, when called on to make tumultuous and revolutionary noises, are generally supposed to mutter or shout 'Rhubarb, Rhubarb' as a suitable noise. I think the producer might throw in some bananas for variety.

In his famous and exquisite 'Song of the Emigrants in Bermuda' Andrew Marvell attributed to the island oranges, pomegranates, figs, melons, and apples; how accurately, I do not know, since I have never been able to afford a holiday in that sunning-ground of the leisured and the wealthy. While he was being as lavish as this, he might well have included bananas. Their music has been left to our barrow-boys – and the wise Mr. Ainslie. Also to fashion-writers and advertisers of 'alamodalities' for women. They sometimes employ the word banana as a colour. 'In nigger, wine, or banana.'

BANG

WHILE reading some recently published American stories I came across the employment of the word bang to mean a lock (or shock) of hair on the forehead. The usage seems more common in America than in Britain. The bang was cut square over the brow, and the term is used of a horse's tail as well as of a human being's forelock. Not only horses could be bang-tailed. There were the anglers' flies as well. ' "These bang-tailed little sinners any good?" said Drysdale, throwing some cock-a-bondies across the table.' – *Tom Brown at Oxford*. ('Cock-abondy' apparently comes from the Welsh *coch a bon ddhu*, "*red with black stem*". An angler's artificial fly.') To 'take time by the bang' would be a serviceable way of describing swift and vigorous action. But does Father Time have his tresses cut square in front?

The better-known bang was a blow long before it became a noise. Does 'bang went saxpence' refer to the Scotsman's slamming of the coin on the counter or to the explosion and consequent dispersion of that piece of property? Another kind of bang is 'a sudden impetuous movement' and so was a term for energy and what is now called 'pep'. To describe a man as full of bang is no bad way of suggesting a dynamic individual. 'Everything went with a bang' equally suggests a dynamic entertainment or a party that really was a party.

There is still another bang, that of the gipsy who means left-handed when he says bang-handed. To a correspondence in the *Manchester Guardian* I owe my information. A. W. Boyd, a great scholar of the local language in Cheshire and Derbyshire as well as of the natural life, contributed 'keggy-handed' as Derbyshire for left-handed, and while acknowledging bang-handed, said that he did not know its origin. To this J. W. Shipley replied that bang is the Romany for left and that bango wast is left hand. Swearing 'bango wast' is a phrase for perjury. He added that a woman living 'o'er t'brush' meant one living with a man and if she was living 'bang' as well as 'o'er t'brush' it meant that she was doing so in a sinister way, i.e. without marriage. The 'over the brush' phrase refers to the ritual of a gipsy wedding in which the couple jump over a besom together.

BARKABLE

THE use of adjectives ending in -able is peculiar. They are usually passive, as in lovable, eatable, drinkable, and so on. But knowledgeable, which used to mean capable of being known, has of late been commonly employed to mean 'knowing'. This I took to be an affectation or a faulty modernism, until coming across such a word as barkable for able to bark, which is as old as the thirteenth century. Eileen Power quotes this exquisite passage from a treatise of that period on Estate Management.

It profiteth the lord to have discreet shepherds, watchful and kindly, so that the sheep be not tormented by their wrath but crop their pasture in peace and joyfulness; for it is a token of the shepherd's kindness if the sheep be not scattered abroad but browse around him in company. Let him provide himself with a good barkable dog and lie nightly with his sheep.

Was John Davidson's 'runnable stag' fit to be hunted or actively fleet? In either case it might be a cause of barkability.

BARM

BARM is the foam on beer or other liquors and, by its presence, proves absence of flatness. One of the mischiefs attributed to Puck in *A Midsummer Night's Dream* is making 'the drink to bear no barm'. The fact that it is thus proved to be a Shakespearean word for froth makes attractive a proposed emendation sent me by a correspondent, Mrs. Norman Ingpen. She was re-reading *Othello* in the New Temple edition. 'I followed up,' she writes, 'a note which I have always ignored before, on Line 11 of Act II, Scene 1:

'For do but stand upon the foaming shore.'

I find that Mr. Ridley, the editor, comments:

'Foaming: This is the easy F and Q.2 reading for Q.1's obscure "banning" which probable conceals the true meaning.'

It seems to me, though I have never had a chance of seeing the Quartos and Folio originals, that it would be easy to confuse 'rm' and 'nn' in old print, and that the First Quarto's version is surely 'barming'. 'Barm' being, of course, the froth on beer or yeast, is beautifully descriptive of the creamy foam that rushes over the beach when the sea is rough enough to churn up the sand as it roars in. I notice that the adjective is applied to the 'shore', and not to the sea itself, where the 'high and monstrous mane' would appear whiter, although I seem to remember the phrase 'yeasty waves' somewhere else. I make my own bread, and the barm on the yeast mixture heaves and bubbles in a most satisfying, oceanic manner!

Mrs. Ingpen (unconsciously) remembers the yeasty or yesty waves from Macbeth's challenge to the Weird Sisters which includes the lines:

> 'though the yesty waves
> Confound and swallow navigation up.'

And she can have further confirmation of Shakespeare's comparison of sea-froth with barm in a phrase of the Clown's in *The Winter's Tale*. In describing the storm at sea he speaks of 'the ship boring the moon with her mainmast and anon swallowed with yest and froth'.

Since Shakespeare calls froth barm and more than once likens such yesty froth to the sea-foam, the emendation 'barming shore' seems reasonable to me. Why should banning have got into the First Quarto unless in the original handwriting something closely resembled that word; and foaming does not resemble banning. The First Quarto appeared a year before the Folio and the texts of good Quartos, such as this one, are supposed to be nearer to Shakespeare's own script than are the Folio versions which came through the hands of Heminge and Condell.

Barmy, a slang word for crazy, is sometimes spelt balmy. But this must be a mistake. A frothy mind gives the right suggestion of a light and bubbling person. Balm, which is an aromatic balsam, implies the very opposite; it breathes health and tranquillity. It is the biblical Nard or Spikenard and nard was also applied to the gummy essence of timber and the scent coming off a good log-fire. So it occurs in what seems to me one of the finest of English lyrics, this by Ben Jonson:

> Have you seen but a bright lily grow
> Before rude hands have toucht it?

> Have you markt but the fall of snow
>   Before the soil hath smutcht it?
> Have you felt the wool of beaver,
>   Or swan's down ever?
> Or have smelt o' the bud o' the brier,
>   Or the nard in the fire?
> Or have tasted the bag of the bee?
> O so white, O so soft, O so sweet is she!

Here are balmy things and there is nothing barmy, or crazy, about them.

BARNACULAR

THIS will not be found in the dictionary and its inclusion is a piece of vanity. While writing once of the Tite Barnacles, the great clan of office-holders satirized by Dickens in *Little Dorrit*, I had reason to mention that they are habitually cited by modern journalism to mock the Civil Service. As a matter of fact, the whole point of the Dickensian attack is that the Barnacle clan had its clutches on everything, ruled and exploited all the services and professions, and expected to have the fastest pickings of Church, Law, Medicine, etc., as well as of the Government Departments. However, one of its chief fortresses was the Circumlocution Office and so the Barnacles have become especially associated with bureaucratic dalliance and pedantry and the issue of complicated forms composed in an abominable jargon. I have the greatest respect for the British Civil Service, which recruits and retains many of the best brains in the country, but I share the general abhorrence of their 'officialese' English. This lingo I ventured to call 'The Barnacular'.

BASHAW

WE take our grandees from the East; naturally, since human grandeur is there itself most mammonlike and epicurean. The emir became the admiral. The Pasha became, for our eighteenth century, the Bashaw. Bashaws could be Indians or Anglo-Indian *nouveaux riches*, flaunting their rupees. 'The insolence of a Bashaw' continually resounds in the periods of Fielding and of the political pamphleteers of his century. If a Bashaw called up his gamekeepers, bruisers, and cudgellers, or invoked what there was of law and order, to protect his property, his enemies still looking to the East, called them his Bashi-bazouks. Bashaws have now dropped out, but I have seen our police described by a strikers' defender as 'The Bashi-Bazouks in blue'. This was good journalism in the older, full-flown style. The Bashi-bazouks were irregular Turkish troops, notorious for brutal and licentious conduct. There is plainly something of powerful attraction in the word 'bash'. Why otherwise the lately developed Service habit of calling every kind of worker a basher, e.g. stores-basher, potato-basher, etc.? 'This word,' says Eric Partridge in his *Dictionary of R.A.F. Slang*, 'is, in combination fast becoming man, chap, fellow.' It may be a sordid descent from old Bashaw to new Basher, but the word retains its fascination. 'Have a bash' (for have a shot, try, or go) is now common.

BASILISK

To basilisk, to fascinate, to conquer. This predecessor of our vulgar vamp I found in Surtees. His Mr. Rowley Rounding was a turnip-headed squire, hunting with the Heaviside. To him Facey Romford sold his lively horse Leotard. Leotard was to be ridden by Mrs. Rowley Rounding; but he was not underneath that dashing lady very long. (It needed Mrs. Soapy Sponge to get the better of Leotard.) Mrs. Rounding had begun life as Brown ('Brown Stout' to the boys) and became Madame de Normanville. Madame, widowed, had an eye for men of acres, like Rounding, whom she met on Ramsgate Pier, where 'she basilisked the booby'. 'Next day she had him as handy as a

French poodle and looking about as sensible. And widows, being generally pretty good men of business, short, sharp, and decisive, she brought him to the "what have you got and what will you do?" gate without giving him a chance of leading her over it.' Such was basiliskery.

The original basilisk was a reptile, begotten of a cock and a serpent, complete with barbed tail. Its other name was cockatrice. It suffered seriously from halitosis and its best friends would shrink apprehensively away: its enemies were either withered at a glance or overwhelmed with a breath. It could be as fatal as any blood-sucking vampire. Basilisks were cannon as well as monsters to Shakespeare and Marlowe. As such they roared and shook down turrets. But Shakespeare has the other basilisk too. When Posthumus is given Imogen's bracelet by Iachimo as proof of her infidelity, he cries,

> It is a basilisk unto mine eye,
> Kills me to look on't.

Basilisk, as well as vampire, came down in the world. But to basilisk a gentleman, instead of vamping him, is certainly a word which blondes of taste might well prefer.

The poet Cornelius Whurr has imperishably remarked,

> What lasting joys that man attend
> Who has a polished female friend!

I am sure that such a companion would never have vamped Cornelius, but she might have gone so far as to attempt a little intellectual basiliskery with well-chosen quotations from the more amorous of the classical poets.

BELVEDERE AND GAZEBO

BELVEDERE, meaning a room (or even a rock) with a view, is not commonly used. I was happy to find this formal, Italianate term in Mr. W. A. Poucher's *Escape to the Hills*. Mr. Poucher is

41

an expert photographer, and he must be a man of infinite patience as well as of rare agility in order to obtain his clear, cloudless views of our so often sodden and bemisted peaks. Belvedere is a favourite word of his for the right niche to stop at in order to look and to wonder. His use of belvedere is certainly justified by the pictures that he collects. 'Hall's Fell Tap', he writes of Saddleback, 'is an admirable belvedere', and my old experience confirms his good opinion of this spot. But belvederes have really more smack of the Renaissance than of Cumbrian crags and refer, as a rule, to turrets or to windowed rooms specially designed for those whose tranquil pleasure is to sit and stare when their fortune is to be in pleasant places. I met, in print, a Belvedere of this kind when, realizing that I have never attempted Browning's 'Red Cotton Nightcap Country', I set to work on it.

> And now the tower a-top I took for clock's
> Or bell's abode, turns out a quaint device,
> Pillared and templed-treated Belvedere –
> Prevailing safe within its railed-about
> Sublimity of area – whence what stretch
> Of sea and land, throughout the seasons' change
> Must greet the solitary.

A full definition.

Gazebo (three syllables with the 'e' long) is the same article as a Belvedere. There are two theories of its origin. One is that Gazebo is a jesting alternative to the Latin *Videbo* – I shall see. The other assumes a corruption of some Oriental word, because the earlier uses of Gazebo associate it with Eastern oddities. Where the scholars disagree I shall modestly withdraw, surmising that Gazebo is perhaps better applied to such an alien-spirited niche as the Pagoda summit in Kew Gardens, while Belvedere is kept for classic architecture. What then of Nature itself? One most exquisite place of this kind in my acquaintance is a shelter built of rock, with ample windows. Contrived upon the coast of the Isle of Jura it looks south to the Paps and east to the coast of Argyll: behind that and sweeping away

to the north-east is the huge tumble of the Western Highlands.

There are books within and a peat fire for the days when the
rain drives in across the bare and beautiful island. A Gazebo for
all weathers.

BIFARIOUS AND AMBIVALENT

TWOFOLD, but especially possessing a twofold stance and so
facing both ways. 'A cogging, bifarious politician' is a sounding
term for the rhetoric of contempt and the creature can be
trifarious too, should there be three parties or causes which he
seeks to appease, cozen, or support.

The bifarious type can also be dismissed as an 'anythingarian',
i.e. one who will believe or accept or affirm anything, so it be
to his advantage. I noticed this in a quotation from the *Works
Serious and Comical* of Thomas Brown (not Urn Burial Browne,
but one of the same century). The forthright and resonant
Brown had a good, wordy way with 'those bifarious any-
thingarians that always make their interest the standard of their
religion'. Anythingarian was a word that survived. Swift employed it. Bifarious has somewhat faded. Trifarious likewise.
Quadrifarious or Quintifarious, if they ever appeared, did not
stay. But multifarious, of course, has been well established,
though rather with the general sense of manifold than with a
particular reference to the slippery mind or character that faces
many ways. In strict accuracy, of course, the anythingarian
should be multifarious rather than bifarious. Meanwhile what
hope for reanimating the somewhat moribund state of bifariety?
I think it would go well at Westminster. 'The contemptible
bifariety of the Opposition' might yet be hurled in the timidly
chattering teeth of statesmen willing to wound and yet afraid to
strike.

Ambivalence has now supplanted bifariety in literary criticism.
It does not appear at all in my two-volume *O.E.D.* A long-
established Scottish-English Dictionary, that of the house of

Chambers, knew nothing of it until its most recent edition when it admitted the term with the bracketed explanation (Psych), suggesting that some psychologist hath done this. Psychology is now a leader in word-making and journalists use ambivalent with a wide variety of meanings. It should, apparently, signify possessing contrasted emotional states, but it is applied to such notions as neutrality and facing both ways. Even sex-and-murder novelists now have it on their list of favourites. Here is an extract from *Something for Nothing* by H. Vernon Dixon, a tale of a beautiful racketeer at large among the Californian rich; it is a fiction on which every vice has its grip. 'She threw herself about and into his arms and clung to him fiercely. "You're no good," she whispered, "but I'm crazy about you. I loathe you and I–I guess I love you too. There's a word for it–ambivalence".' To this display of erudition by the amorous lady the terse and masculine answer was 'Yeah'.

The lady later remarked, somewhat unnecessarily, that she was 'all wild and physical' and that she had no shame. To which the racketeer replied, with good sense but something less than courtesy, 'Stop yapping'. No ambivalence about that. He believed in the deeds of love rather than in lavish concessions to its psychological terminology. But why blame him? He was in the highest and most reverend literary company. Dr. John Donne, destined Dean of St. Paul's, had given quite as vigorous expression to the 'Stop yapping' sentiments of Mr. Dixon's libidinous racketeer when he began a poem to a lady, 'For God's sake, hold your tongue and let me love.'

BLAZON

THE whole peacock world of tabards and trumpets is blazoned in a single word. Blazon begins as a shield or banner, heraldically marked, and then comes to mean a description of such things: at last, a description or report of anything. As a term for tidings it has the full sonority of powerful brass. The Ghost of Hamlet's father, having threatened to 'harrow up the soul' with his news of life beyond the grave, remembers that such hair-raising information is not for the living.

> But this eternal blazon must not be
> To ears of flesh and blood.

This is, as I interpret it, a magnificently condensed phrase to signify report of the long hereafter. George Russell used blazoned in the commoner sense in a quatrain of uncommon quality in his lines 'On behalf of Some Irishmen not Followers of Tradition'.

> No blazoned banner we unfold –
> One charge alone we give to youth,
> Against the sceptred myth to hold
> The golden heresy of truth.

Shakespeare was fond of blazon. Cassio calls Desdemona 'One that excels the quirks of blazoning pens'. Words dear to the richest wordman of them all must surely command the general affection.

BOANTHROPY

BOANTHROPY is the curious malady which befell Nebuchadnezzar, namely that of believing oneself to be an ox. But Nebuchadnezzar did more than believe; he became.

'The same hour was the thing fulfilled upon Nebuchadnezzar: and he was driven from men, and did eat grass as oxen, and his body was wet with the dew of heaven, till his hairs were grown like eagles' feathers and his nails like birds' claws.'

According to the poet:

> He murmured as he chewed the unwonted food,
> 'It may be wholesome, but it is not good.'

If Nebuchadnezzar did have these doubts, the king was only a half-hearted boanthrope, for a true ox-man would have tucked in with avidity. All-in boanthropy is not, I think, very common nowadays. The profounder psychologists may argue that the assumption of the name of John Bull as a national symbol proved the presence of subconscious boanthropic tendencies among the English, but John Bull has ceased to be either an accurate or popular figure-head for our policy and mood. There are a few people who eat mainly grass and many who are content with salads and such; but there is no reason to dub them boanthropes on that account; they might as well be labelled hippanthropes. Boanthropy was practised of old by some legendary deities for purposes of amour.

BORBORYGMY

WRITING on 'Poetry in Scotland' recently Mr. Hugh Macdiarmid alluded to the

> immense 'dish o' whummle' – this vast wind-pie – upon which successive generations of Scots have been 'nourished' to the exclusion of their proper pabulum. No wonder the result has been an Anglo-Scottish literature of little but flatulence and borborygmy.

Whummle I could, as a Scot, place. It is, I believe, confusion. But borborygmy? As a one-time classic I should have been able to define this imposing Grecian, but was driven to the dictionary. It appears to be a rumbling in the bowels and for that sounds gastrically right. (The word is much rarer than the ailment.) Hence comes borborology for the rumblings of unclean talk and one expects an adjective borborygmatous for rumblers. 'The profound silence of Fogeys' Club after luncheon was disturbed only by the occasionally audible distress of borborygmatous old men.' But the epithet has no authority save my own. On the other hand there is Borborite, 'One of the names or nick-names given to certain Ophitic Gnostics, according to Epiphanius, because of their unclean living' and so applied in the sixteenth

46

and seventeenth centuries to any holder of filthy opinions or bestial doctrine. Ignorance of the Ophitic Gnostics and their nasty habits need not bar us from use of the word. To call your opponent a Borborite would certainly be a relief. This is the kind of term much affected in his early days by Aldous Huxley who loved a long Grecian noise, especially for physical matters. Surely he must somewhere have written of Steatopygous (broad-based) victims of incessant borborygmy.

BOSKO

A FRIEND, having called my attention to Bosko Absoluto in Kipling ('The Janeites') for drunken, set me reflecting on the number of terms which alcohol has evoked from the ordinary man's metaphorical resources. Here is a sample list of terms used during several decades as variations on the solemn words intoxicated and inebriated. Many of these are derived from the kitchen and the larder and are as dull as flat beer.

Blotto	Lush
Boiled	Oiled
Boozed	Pie-eyed
Bosky and Bosko Absoluto	Plastered
Bottled	Soaked, Soused, Sozzled
Canned	Squiffy
Draped	Stewed
Fried	Stinking
Glazed	Tanked
Half-seas over	Tight
Lit up	Tipsy

The last is now antiquated and most are crude. One naturally looks to America for help. The alternating austerities and orgies of Prohibition should have stirred the creative fancy to some altitudes of word-making. But did they? Delving into H. L. Mencken's first supplementary volume to his vast and famous treatise on the American language, I find allusions to most of the above, also to:

Cock-eyed	Lordly
Corned	Moon-eyed
Curved	Nimptopsical
Lappy	Staggerish
Limber	In the suds
Loose in the hilt	

There is a little poetry here, but, on the whole, Dionysos should have won better service from the tongue that lapped his stimulant gifts. I do not appreciate the significance of nimptopsical. On the whole, I would rather be fried or stewed, little as I like those terms for the consoling, encouraging and uplifting influence of the grain or grape. During the last war some Americans used the simple word high for the elevation of strong liquor, adding to it such similes as 'high as a kite'. Certainly 'loose in the hilt' and 'high as a kite' are an improvement on the melancholy suggestions of oiled, plastered, and so on. When all has been swallowed and said, I return to the Italianate romanticism of Bosko Absoluto with the reflection that the practitioners of absorbency have often done themselves far worse in the matter of vocabulary.

BOSS

A BOSS, as we all know, is a protuberance, a knot, a jutty decoration. It is several other things as well, but I like it best as a protuberant person, especially a lady, 'grasse et grosse'. So, gloriously, it occurs in Marlowe's 'Tamburlaine' (Part I, III, 3). Zabina, wife of Bajazeth, says to Zenocrate,

> Base concubine, must thou be placed by me
> That am the Empress of the mighty Turk?

whereupon Zenocrate counters with a straight jab to the jaw,

Disdainful Turkess and unreverend boss,
Call'st thou me concubine, that am betrothed
Unto the great and mighty Tamburlaine!

The first of these lines is, in my opinion, a knock-out.

BRAINBLATHER

Mr. J. L. Bailes, a specialist in northern English dialects, is
not hopeful about the future of the native terms and idioms on
the farm, since we are all State-instructed in our agricultural
techniques as well as in reading and writing and arithmetic.
Writing in the Journal of the recently formed and much needed
Lancashire Dialect Society he remarked:

> Already I have found that the various official pamphlets on
> how to build a cowshed have resulted in young farmers
> forgetting the names of parts of 'byres' such as *fothergang,
> skelboose, slatherstone*. The 'cowleech' gives place to the
> veterinary surgeon, and sheep die of liver fluke instead of
> *turnsick, stackers, stoddy* or *brainblather*.

Brainblather must never die; rather should it pass far beyond
the farmyard. Surely some of the talks delivered to the more
intellectual Conferences at Summer Schools might be classified
so. And turnsick could well be the adjective in front of it.

BRAXY

Braxy is a strange and ugly matter, splenetic apoplexy in sheep.
So braxy mutton is the flesh of sheep that have fallen dead and
then, less accurately, of sheep that have been killed by accident.
So the hungry shepherd might not always despise a bit of 'braxy'
and in war-time, on the hills where there were no restaurants
or canteens and only the pressure of keen air upon hard-working,

hungry bodies, there were sometimes, I fancy, more sheep that had accidents than might have been expected from the peace-time figures. Much of this war-time braxy would be good feeding, coveted and well-earned. I was reminded of braxy by coming across some lines, still well known in a phrase or two, but rarely remembered in full. Written in 1901, they referred to the vast possessions of the Marquis of Breadalbane, now, I think, much less vast.

From Kenmore
To Ben Mohr
The land is a' the Markiss's;
The mossy howes
The heathery knowes
An' ilka bonnie park is his.
The bearded goats
The toozie stots,
An' a' the braxy carcasses;
Ilk crofter's rent,
Ilk tinkler's tent,
An' ilka collie's bark is his,
The muir-cock's craw,
The piper's blaw,
The gillie's hard day's wark is his;
From Kenmore
To Ben Mohr
The warld is a' the Markiss's!

The author was James Mactavish of Waterside Doune, a re-nowned breeder of black-faced sheep. He and his father were tenants of Waterside for close on a century.

BREASTSUMMER

To the local builder, it is more commonly bressomer or bressumer. Not that we have such bravely sounding woodwork nowadays. The breastsummer was a large beam over a large opening and supporting large walls. It needed to be of enduring wood and oak was its usual constituent. The beam itself is scarce now. (Tudor-style villas of our time often have their poor little beams laid on externally, like milady's pencilled eyebrows.) But the word bulks finely when one comes across it. Half corporal, half climatic, it seems to proclaim a happy mixture of strength and sunshine.

This set me wondering whether the word summer is itself adequate to the natural splendours of its subject. Spring is simple and lively and summer has the heavy, stagnant air of a July afternoon. But it lacks in sound the exhilaration which it possesses in idea. It makes the perfect noise in such lines of drowsy murmuring as,

> On the idle hill of summer,
> Sleepy with the flow of streams,

but is it radiant enough for the clear, blue sky of a June day in all its sparkling pride? Sometimes it seems to fail us.

> Now is the winter of our discontent
> Made glorious summer by this sun of York.

'Winter of our discontent' is supposed to be the conquered thing, but here it is the conquering phrase. 'Glorious summer' is weak beside it. Besides, there are too many s's in the second line. Their tendency to weaken effect is notorious, though not inevitable. Yet the noise of summer can sometimes be magical and not just a lullaby.

> And now to these unsummer'd skies
>   The summer bird is still.
> Far off a phantom cuckoo cries
>   From out a phantom hill.

That vaguely suggests Chesterton to me. It is, as a matter of fact, Tennyson. (Prefatory Poem to my Brother's Sonnets, Midnight, June 30, 1879.) But talking of summer will outlast a winter night, so back to the builders. Tennyson was the breastsummer of the great fabric of English Victorian poetry; Browning abundantly added its gables and its gargoyles.

BRICK-BAT

DURING the height of the Calcutta riots of 1946 a letter reached me from New Delhi. It was vice-regally papered and enveloped, almost meriting the high title of 'missive' so dear to Victorian dramatists and novelists. That insatiable lover of words, Lord Wavell, was, in fact, inquiring, 'What is a brick-bat and why?' He observed that far worse things than brick-bats had been flying about, but that allusions in the Press to this mysterious article continued, as ever, to appear and also to puzzle him. Brick we know and bat we know. Is a brick-bat really a brick at the end of a stick or piece of wood? No. Apparently not. Bat is a very old word for a lump or piece and the brick-bat is ancient English for the 'arf-a-brick of the violent Cockney's fancy. Brick-bats are as old as Foxe's Martyrs and are Miltonic too.

Brick-bat, accordingly, is a more sensible term than bombshell. Dealers in ordnance know bombs, which are dropped or thrown, and shells, which are fired. But popular writing has linked the two. Bomb-shells continued to be dropped, by journalists, in political circles, with far less justification than brick-bats are thrown across the reports of a street riot.

BRIGANDINE

WHY have our poets made so little of Brigandines? 'Furbish the spears: put on the brigandines', cried Jeremiah (in our biblical English) when calling to battle against the Gentile with a preliminary advice to harness the horses. (He had more faith in cavalry than Isaiah, who was a champion of infantry and stayed not on steeds.) Brigandine is body-armour, made up of metal rings sewed on canvas, a primitive form of corselet and, incidentally, a powerful adjunct to iambic verse. Milton's armoury was a music-box indeed and he made weapons the powerful ministers of his verse as well as of his Samson, when challenging the champion of Gath.

> Then put on all thy gorgeous Arms, thy Helmet
> And Brigandine of Brass, thy broad Habergeon,
> Vant-brace and Greves and Gauntlet. . . .

(Habergeons are sounding bits of armoury too,

> 'The sword of him that layeth at him cannot hold: the
> spear, the dart, nor the habergeon'.)

Shakespeare missed a chance by neglecting brigandines: they would have clanged well in some of his battle-pieces. Brigandine is explained as the proper martial outfit for a brigand and there we link up with brigands and brigadiers and even with the maritime brigantine. Since briga or brigue meant strife and contention, the contending parties became brigades or brigands (wearing brigandines) on land or sailed on brigantines or brigs at sea. The origin of the word brigade is noticeable in Milton's usage, for he pronounced it as if it were bríggad, with pioneers also accented on the first syllable.

> Thither, wing'd with speed,
> A numerous Brigad hastened. As when bands
> Of Pioners with Spade and Pickaxe arm'd
> Forerun the Royal Camp, to trench a Field,
> Or cast a Rampart. Mammon led them on.

The military brigade was early formed and the rough 'brigad' of contentious persons was organized into the section of an army even in Milton's lifetime. Then the brigands parted from the brigades and went their lawless way: though verbally brothers, the two became frequent enemies as representing Law

53

and Disorder. Meanwhile the resonant brigandine was relegated to the museum and foolishly forgotten by the bards in need of a thumping noun wherewith to strike the drums of martial verse.

BUG

THE kind of bug which interests me is the bogy-bug. When Hamlet, his sea-gown scarf'd about him in the dark, 'finger'd the packet' of those commissioned to grind an axe upon his head, he discovered many counterfeit pleas of State why this should be done. The dispatch was,

> Larded with many several sorts of reasons,
> Importing Denmark's health and England's too,
> With, ho! such bogs and goblins in my life.

Bug is here our bug-a-boo, a source of false alarm. Posthumous in *Cymbeline* has a striking phrase for those who strike terror in a battle. They are 'the mortal bugs o' the field'. Again in *3 Henry VI*, v, 2 there is a line which might be misunderstood:

> For Warwick was a bug that feared us all.

This does not mean that bugs could be fearful as well as fearsome; the verb fear is obviously transitive here and means frighten. *O.E.D.* quotes this line to prove that bug meant a fellow and was the source of the American usage 'Big bug' for a tycoon or 'big shot'. Bug may have been slang for chap in Elizabethan times, but far more commonly it is a bogy, fetch or wirrikow.

BUMBASTE

BOMBAST, which is now used exclusively in this form and for a swollen kind of speech, is much more persuasive in its old spelling and might have retained its old meaning. Bumbaste was cotton-stuff used for stuffing garments and the heavily-quilted Tudor folk were bombastic indeed: still more so, James I, who bumbasted himself all over and wore immensely padded clothes in order to defeat the dreaded assassin's dagger. The word was then common as a verb. Greene accused the 'prentice Shakespeare of 'bumbasting' blank verses and Heywood wrote of plays bumbasted out with all manner of noisy irrelevance and mummerish titivations. He boasted his own austerity.

A Strange Play you are like to have, for know
We use no Drum, nor Trumpet, nor Dumbe Show:
No Combate, Marriage, not so much to-day
As Song, Dance, Masque to bumbaste out a play.

In the same way Shakespeare spoke of certain kinds of wit as 'The bumbaste and the lining of the time.' Our bombasine, a magnificent word considering the type of lady once addicted to this fabric, comes from the same origin, and might with point have kept the old spelling. This leads to the further and scholastic usage of bumbaste, 'to beat the posteriors'.

BUNGALOW

DEAN INGE once wrote in characteristic melancholy of the bungaloid rash disfiguring England: I do not know whether he coined the adjective. Bungaloid might simply mean Bengali, for bungalow is our form of an imported Hindu word and signifies 'of, or pertaining to, Bengal'. Nowadays the bungalow is one of our commonest words and sights. It has, unjustly, become the symbol of suburban and quasi-rural ugliness. It is usually a far less aggressive article than the two-storey, mock-Tudor villa. Bungalows, being so low, have less chance to sprout absurd excrescences, like Little-Baronial turrets. The English have been great importers of housing words and the citizen of to-day inhabits his bungalow (Hindu) or villa (Roman-Italian) with its veranda (also Indian but used, too, in Spain). If it be storied, there may be a balcony (Italian). His windows may be French, his blinds Venetian. If his bungaloid garden is at all ambitious there will be a pergola (Italian). If at the end of all this the owner or tenant calls the place 'Mon Abri' instead of 'The Nook', Paradise Park, S.E.57, he is continuing the alien tune. But he probably will not look to France and his Indo-European nest is more likely to go vastly Celtic about the gate, whose label will announce 'Glengarry', 'Killarney', 'Poldhu', or 'Afonwen'.

BUSY
AND OTHERS

BUSY is an Old English word which has come into a state of grace in our new English civilization. In making this ascent from disrepute it reflects man's opinions about the nature of work. It is only since the Reformation that the idea of labour as a social obligation has afflicted mankind. Previously toil was the curse of Adam, not his duty or his opportunity. Wise gentry got slaves or serfs to work for them while they followed the wars, the arts, and the ladies. Then came this all-conquering notion of honourable toil, a Puritan conception, which has endured; nowadays to proclaim yourself above all claims of drudgery and a careless fleeter of the time is to be regarded with disfavour even by the lordly ones. Consequently to assert that one is busy is now to make a claim to virtuous living; but busy at one time was frequently used with an unkind suggestion of meddling and officiousness. It was implied that only a fool, a knave, or a mischief-maker would busy himself. Oberon talks of the meddling monkey and the busy ape, while Emilia, in *Othello*, cries:

> I will be hanged if some eternal villain
> Some busy and insinuating rogue
> Some cogging, cozening slave, to get some office,
> Hath not devised this slander.

Again, Hamlet, having stabbed the eavesdropping Polonius and dismissed him as a 'wretched, rash, intruding fool', adds:

> Thou find'st to be too busy is some danger.

Busy here obviously means over-busy by our standards. We preserve the usage in talking of a busy-body.

Henry Vaughan sang to

> Dear Night, this world's defect,
> The stop to Busie Fools, Care's check and curb.

Busy was a favourite word of John Donne. Did the daylight interfere with his amours? Then would he protest,

> Busy old fool, unruly Sun,
> Why dost thou thus
> Through windows and through curtains call on us?
> Must to thy motions lovers' seasons run?

In that frankest of poems, his Elegy xx – odd that a future Dean of St. Paul's should have given us the most pagan and precise acclamation of sensual raptures – he bids his beloved,

> Unpin that spangled breast-plate which you wear
> That th' eyes of busy fools may be stopped there.

The hour of Judgment occurs for Donne 'at the last busy day'. He obviously hated business. He saw no goodness in occupation. But the Puritans and the Business Men have altered all that. No longer does the busy ape or lecher set the meddlesome example. The busy bee has become our tutor in morality. Yet the old notion of busy lives still in the slang of thieves and criminals. For them a detective or a policeman is 'a busy'. Raging against their enemy in the cell, they may in fact be echoing English poetry and cursing with the language of Shakespeare and of Donne.

Busy has come up in the world; pragmatical has not. First it was practical: then busy; then over-busy. It has a good classical weight for the description of an interfering creature. With it

Pepys truncheoned a too zealous constable encountered on a vinous and vagrant occasion.

> Home in a coach round by the wall; where we met so many stops by the watches, that it cost us much time and some trouble, and more money, to every watch to them to drink; this being encreased by the trouble the prentices did lately give the City, so that the militia and watches are very strict at this time; and we had like to have met with a stop for all night at the constable's watch at Mooregate by a pragmatical constable; but we came well home at about two in the morning.

Plainly, a busy.

Obsequious and Officious have both changed their meanings. The latter used to mean useful and dutiful. Marvell sang of

> Ye glow-worms whose officious flame

showed the way to wanderers in the night. Now it signifies the over-zealous and the busy-body. To Milton the stars were 'officious luminaries'. Obsequious used also to be dutiful and obedient in a good sense. George Wither wrote of the obsequious Marigold, since

> Duly, every morning, she displays
> Her open breast, when Titan spreads his rays.

Now the obsequious man does his duty so humbly as to fawn upon and cringe before authority.

BUZZ

Buzz has more meanings than the usual one of humming and droning. To Shakespeare it was an exclamation of impatience or disgust; to Thackeray it was a verb for to empty, applied to a bottle. That, perhaps, links up with the slang usage of to buzz as to rob. Chariot-buzzers was an old term for those who snatched

purses in public vehicles. When Marie Lloyd sang her famous
song of a home broken up

> My old man said, 'Follow the van
> And don't dilly-dally on the way'

she used, during the patter, to look in her purse, find nothing
there, and say, 'Girls, I've been buzzed'. Coming from one who
was already on the tramp, this was, on the lips of a genius, as
terrible as a line in *King Lear*.

The meaning was obvious, but the word was quite new to me
when I heard it. It is likely that the phrase 'buzzing a bottle of
port' meant robbing it of its contents: table-buzzers, not chariot-
buzzers, would be responsible for that. I never hear the word
buzz connected with stealing in the slang of today, but it may
linger on in the relics of the Cockney language.

The word has also been used as an adjective meaning swollen.
In *A Supplementary English Glossary* (1881), by T. Lewis O.
Davies, M.A., Vicar of S. Mary Extra, Southampton, I find: 'The
Anti-jacobin having spoken of P—r's [Parr's] *buzz* prose, adds
in a note: "The learned reader will perceive that this is an
elegant metonymy, by which the quality belonging to the outside of the head is transferred to the inside. *Buzz* is an epithet
usually applied to a large wig. It is here used for swelling, burly,
bombastic writing."'

CANTRIP

CANTRIP, for a trick of witchery or piece of mischief, is mainly
Scottish, but found its way into Tennyson. Burns's 'Tam o'
Shanter' of course has cantrips, the poem being packed with all
such Satanic manifestations. Cantrip in the lighter sense of fun
and games I found in a novel by William Black. Does anybody
read William Black now? According to the London Library,
there is little raiding of the shelves which hold his ample range
of romantic Anglo-Caledonian fiction. Black's late Victorian

Scotland was full of English Stag-parties (in the sporting sense), Inverness capes, whiskers, deer-stalker caps, spatter-dashes, yachts, millions of money, handsome ghillies 'profusely bearded' and given to mournful piping at odd moments, and lovely Highland daughters of the native, proud, and impecunious lairds and chieftains. These always had blue eyes and enormous reserves of purity. Such an one was the heroine of his 'Wild Eelin', a Miss Macdonald of Kinvaig, much given to cantrips as well as to Jacobitism and works of charity. Her cantrips included swimming dangerous rivers and falling out of boats, which antics she practised when not taking tea and eggs to the aged and infirm of Glen Garva. Thus she gave admirable opportunities for gallantry to the Canadian millionaire (a Macdonald returned from exile) and the local journalist, both of whom equally worshipped the frolic Miss Eelin: the more cantrippery she displayed, the greater the devotion. (Tactfully she solved the problem of their rivalry by dying at about p. 450 as the result of a cantrip.) Black graced his novelettish plots with a Roman grandeur of style. His books are like tartan-covered sofas: one sinks easily into them. The cantrips of his Wild Highland lasses were a convention, but the mountains of which he wrote are real—save that it is hardly ever raining on them.

CARAPACE

'THE upper body-shell of tortoises and crustaceans.' So fair a sound deserves a gentler meaning. Since Cara is the Latin for dear one, then surely a darling who covers a lot of grass, as the comedians say of the fast feminine, might seem to be indicated by a carapace. The 'cara' words are so handsome and have such alien charm that this rough and tough invader of their niche in the lexicon distresses me. Steeds of mettle caracole and may have dashing carabineers upon their soaring and unrestful backs. Travellers to the gorgeous East would in past centuries thread the coral islands in Caracores or Caramoussals; to read of such journeys is an occupation made the sweeter by the suction of caramels. I discover that a cannon at billiards was known of old by its Spanish name of Carambole. This was applied both to noun and verb so that caracoling horses might carambole in the process. Amid so much of romance the stiff and shelly meaning of carapace is indeed disappointing.

But I was brought to it by a glorious passage in a Paper on the Navel (more correctly 'A study of the Umbilicus') by the late Dr. O. H. Mavor ('James Bridie' to the playgoer). Mavor's argument, which will be congenial to most of us, was that man's natural function is repose. He explained that the word navel means the hub of a wheel, and round it we rotate. We are both centripetal and centrifugal and his discourse, he admitted, was of the latter kind, a random and outward-flying matter. In the course of these centrifugal observations he noted that Man

> can lie on his back, a posture long sustained by no other uncarapaced animal except in death. It is little wonder that his sleep is the amazement of the animal kingdom. It is superior to the long unconsciousness of hibernating animals. They curl their vegetative organs into the smallest bulk and lie in an uncomfortable tight knot in a condition near to death. How different is man! Man's great lungs heave and blow, his noble heart thuds merrily, and his marvellous bowels continue in gentle peristalsis, his brain is the house of a thousand lovely fancies, his liver, his blood, his glands, transform the dead cells of his food into the living elements of his body and slay his myriad of airy foes. He is badly constructed for locomotion by road or by tree. The slowest fish swims faster. He is adapted primarily for rest.

> This and much more to the same purpose we can learn from the contemplation of the umbilicus or navel.

So let all of us who are torpid, indolent, and little given to violent motion take heart. Inertia is an important aspect of our natural genius. Among the great host of the Uncarapaced we are the master-sleepers, and in reclining we do but comply with our destiny.

Having become entangled in the umbilical cord, which is Latin, we can hardly escape without a glance at the omphalos, which was the Greek word for the same, and held by Dr. Mavor to be the nobler of the two. He gave his reason.

> Professor Popochik, the etymologist, tells us that omphalos means the drawing together of the band of the helmet that held the crest or plume. The pleasant picture of a spray of feathers springing from the umbilicus of each of us need not detain us. I wish to draw your attention to the sonority of the word 'omphalos', and to regret, in passing, that Celsus thought fit to change the noble-sounding name of a noble organ to the pedestrian word 'umbilicus'.

It is well known that the navel has powers of mystical fascination. An Omphalopsychite is 'one of a sect of quietists who practised gazing at the navel as a means of producing hypnotic reverie'. (Presumably it was his own navel at which the omphalopsychite stared so rewardingly.) This centralized concentration is part of the Yogi practice and may lead to calm and wisdom. But for a sheltered life a good strong shell may be helpful. It is not only the crustaceans who have discovered that. Not so long ago Britons scuttled, in their tin hats, to a Morrison or Anderson shelter, precious carapaces of their metallic kind.

CATZERIE

CATSO was Italianate-Tudor-English for a scamp. 'Nimble-spirited Catsos' play their tricks in Ben Jonson. The abstract noun is Marlowe's and occurs in a grand piece of description (*The Jew of Malta*, Act IV):

> He sent a shaggy, tatter'd, staring slave,
> That, when he speaks, draws out his grisly beard,
> And winds it twice or thrice about his ear;
> Whose face has been a grind-stone for men's swords;

His hands are hack'd, some fingers cut quite off;
Who, when he speaks, grunts like a hog, and looks
Like one that is employ'd in catzery
And cross-biting; . . .

The trick of extracting a beard and then looping it round the
ear seems bizarre, but attractive.

Cross-biting is another term for swindling. Marlowe's contemporary, Robert Greene, writing on 'Coosnage', explained that
sometimes 'a nip, which the common people call a cutpurse, hath
a crossbite by some bribing officer'. He also spoke of 'the leger-
demaines of nips, foists, conycatchers, and crosbiters'. Greene
had a magnificent lexicon of knavery. But he seemed to miss
catzerie.

CHAPPIN

SOUP tickets one associates with the poorer parts of ugly cities,
bleak houses in hard times. I was surprised to receive from a
relative an article of this kind which emerged from the fine-
sounding township of Old Meldrum of Aberdeenshire; it was
an ancient and a beautiful card. One also expects a soup-ticket
to be a mean-looking chit. But this was a handsome, substantial
docket beautifully scrolled about the border. The Victorians
took trouble with such trifles and did these things in style; I
fancy that the broth for which it stood must also have been a
good substantial liquor. The card announces,

Old Meldrum, Soup Kitchen, One Chappin

Chappin or chopin (French chopine) is a term for a liquid
measure containing, in France, half an old French 'pinte', in
Scotland a Scottish half-pint, which is equivalent to an English
quart. 'I hae had chappins enough,' said Inverashalloch (in *Rob
Roy*), 'I'll drink my quart of usquebaugh or brandy wi' ony
honest fellow, but deil a drap mair when I hae wark to do in the
morning.' Other times, other thirsts – and other chances.

The Scot is ever more lavish than the niggardly Englishman. Consider his whisky measure. In Scotland the measure is a half-gill or a quarter-gill and that means a definite and, in the larger dose, a satisfying dram. The English have whittled the tots down to 'doubles' and 'singles'. These are much smaller and also vary according to place – and also according to inn-keepers' fancy. I have a Scottish inn-keeper's measure, a finely-shaped glass phial, which records the true half-gill and therewith, when stocked, I help myself; an English licensee, on being confronted with this noble vessel, would faint with dismay at the sight of such a companion to his contemptible little 'doubles'.

And so with soups. The English idea of charity was a pint of soup; Scotland's a quart. The Chappin, so decoratively ordered on the card sent to me, would have been a meal of some value if its contents were a true Scotch Broth. Chopin is not a Scottish usage only; but it became an old Scottish term for quart-addiction of all kinds: again, the English show themselves the less capacious nation, with their talk of pint-snatching. Jamieson remarks gravely, 'To "tak a chappin" is a circumlocution commonly used to express an attachment to intoxicating liquor'. (In the circumlocutory art Jamieson himself seems to have been a considerable performer.)

This chopin or Chappin of Scottish absorbency has nothing to do with Hamlet's chopine, the high-soled shoe of the actor seeking to enlarge himself, an article which came to England by way of Italy and Spain.

My friend, who gave me the half-gill measure, Mr. Park of the Moulin Hotel, Pitlochry (Advt. – as they say in newspapers – which I freely bestow because he never needs it), wrote to me, since I had expressed my gratitude for a decent-sized tot, 'Apropos of good measure; is it not astounding and an odd reflection on our times that we can be agreeably surprised, and even glow with satisfaction, merely by receiving what is justly due to us?'

Agreed.

CLICKITTING
AND OTHERS

'THERE was', wrote the Rev. W. B. Daniel in 1801, 'a peculiar kind of language invented by sportsmen of the Middle Ages, which it was necessary for them to be acquainted with.' One expects sportsmen to be strong and silent; but few classes of society have been more articulate in the creation of vocabulary. Mr. C. E. Hare's volume on *The Language of Field Sports* runs to 276 pages; it reveals not only the extent of the hunters' vocabulary but that linguistic snobbery which has so long prevailed. In the sporting field you must not only do the right thing, you must say the right word. The distinctions available are countless and must be observed. It is not only the nouns of assembly, or of company, many of them now widely familiar, which had to be correct; right down to an animal's droppings there has been a curious insistence on differentiation. There is even a special chapter on 'Ordure or Excrement' which lists the Crotels of a Hare, the Fiants of a Boar, the Spraints of an Otter, the Werdrobe of a Badger, and – quaintest of all – the Billeting or Waggying of a Fox.

One of the early authorities on the lingo of sport was Edward, Duke of York, first cousin to Henry IV, who was 'Master of Game' at Court and wrote a book of that title. Hare says of this Master:

> For 'stinking beasts' he gives the term 'drift' and he is the only authority to give that term waggying for the billets of a fox and werdrobe for the fiants of a badger. For the hare, Halliwell gives Buttons.

This, no doubt, may fairly be called an unsavoury subject, but the fact that such a diverse and picturesque vocabulary was employed by the trackers of game, to whom fiants and the like were valuable evidence, is typical of the extreme care lavished by the early hunters and fowlers on the jargon of their exercise.

Every phase of animal life was given its special list of names, including mating. When the Otter 'hunteth for his kind: the Fox goes clickitting'. Not long ago the English pavement slang spoke of young people 'clicking', i.e. getting-off. I fancy clicking is no longer heard: I only mention it because of its resemblance to the clickitting fox.

To the terms of assembly there is no end. Hare quotes many not hitherto known to me, he cites: a Trembling of Goldfishes, a Murder of Crows, an Unkindness of Ravens, a Rafter of Turkeys, a Nye of Pheasants, a Siege of Bitterns and a Pitying of Doves (or, much the same, a Dule of Doves). The cries, too, had their own verbs in abundance: there is an especially notable list of them in Pantagruel's description of the noise to which Gargantua was exposed. Urquhart includes: 'Mioling of tigers, bruzzing of bears, sussing of kitlings, clamouring of scarfes, whimpering of fulmarts, booing of buffaloes, warbling of nightingales, quavering of meavises, drintling of turkies, coniating of storks, frantling of peacocks, clattering of magpies, murmuring of stock-doves, crouting of cormorants, cigling of locusts, charming of beagles, guarring of puppies, snarling of messens, rantling of rats, guerieting of apes, snuttering of monkies, pioling of pelicans, quacking of ducks.' (Scarfes are cormorants and messens are lap-dogs.)

And so with this drintling of a rafter of turkeys and with the frantling of so many peacock-terms we can leave the complicated matter. But the niceties of sporting terminology had to be observed. It 'was necessary' as Parson Daniel firmly said.

CLOGDOGDO AND TITIVIL

WHAT is a clogdogdo? The *O.E.D.* knows that it occurs, but is not otherwise helpful, mentioning clog and dog, but carrying the puzzle no further. But Captain Otter, in Ben Jonson's play, *The Silent Woman*, apparently knew a clogdogdo when he saw or heard one. Here are the Captain's views on holy wedlock:

Wife? Buz! *Titivilitium*. There's no such thing in nature! I confess, gentlemen, I have a cook, a laundress, a house-drudge, that serves my turns and goes under that title. But he's an ass that will be so uxorious to tie his affections to one circle. Come, the name dulls appetite. Wives are nasty, sluttish animals ... a wife is a scurvy clogdogdo, an unlucky thing, a very foresaid bear-whelp, without any good fashion or breeding, *mala bestia!*

Yet the lady in question was obviously of fashion, since Otter, not a consistent scold, next observed of his helpmeet:

A most vile face! She spends me forty pounds a year in mercury and hogs-bones. All her teeth were made in the Blackfriars and both her eyebrows in the Strand and her hair in Silver Street. Every part of the town owns a piece of her. She takes herself asunder when she goes to bed into some twenty boxes and next morn is put together again like a great German clock.

A lively guide to the ways of London ladies in 1609. But what is a clogdogdo? I must leave it to my readers.

Titivilitium is the Plautine Latin for a trifle. It was Anglicized as 'titivil' which came later to mean any knave or tale-teller as well as a trivial piece of gossip. In Hall's *Chronicles* appear

Certain Catchpoules and Parasites, commonly called titivils and tale-bearers, who sow discord and dissension.

Captain Otter's allusion to a hair-factory in Silver Street is particularly interesting because that is where we know that Shakespeare lodged for a time with Christopher Mountjoy, who was a maker of tires (head-dresses) and wigs.

CLOUD

A COMMON climatic word, but no longer commonly employed, in its old and beautiful usage, to mean hill. At the southern base of the Pennines, in Cheshire and Derbyshire, it still is so applied and there you may climb a Cloud. That sounds magical and lyrical, but, as a matter of fact, cloud is, in origin, the same as clod. It is a mass. First a clod of earth or rock, then a clod of air . . . but, with a stroke of genius or by accident, those designating clods of air started to use the far more gracious form cloud. And what an exquisite word it is, almost creating poetry with no more said!

> Like far-off mountains turnèd into clouds

is not one of the best-known lines in a very well-known play of Shakespeare, but it is certainly one of the loveliest, being most simply descriptive as well as musically perfect. Demetrius, if you are curious, says it to Hermia. (*A Midsummer Night's Dream*, Act IV, Sc. 1.) It unites the two meanings of cloud and for me has an enduring suggestion of mist over Dovedale, where some of the fells are Clouds.

When I was a schoolboy at Cheltenham we spoke of the highest Cotswold ridge, which rolled smoothly above us, as Cleeve Hill. But since then one of the senior masters has told me that in his early days it was Cleeve Cloud.

COMFORT

THIS is one of the admirable words which have turned soft and needs to be re-stiffened to its proper shape and value. It is, by origin, the giver of strength and valour. But the ubiquitous advertisement of 'All Modern Comforts' hints mainly at central heating and other niceties of plumbing. 'Comforts for the troops' would once have been allies and reserves: in Berners's Froissart we read of companies 'on a wyng in good order, ready to confort the prince's batayle'. Now such comforts are mainly chocolates, cigarettes, and woollies. One is not depreciating the pleasures and utility of these latter in wishing more substance and dignity for the grand old word. This has become so dwarfed and so insipid that the unlettered Christian of today may easily think of the Holy Ghost, the Comforter, as a rather sickly source of sentimental consolation, a celestial crooner almost, instead of as an ally in the good fight and bringer of mettle and resolve. Gerard, the herbalist, used comfortable to imply a tonic and strengthening power. 'If odours may work satisfaction, they are so soveraigne in plants and so comfortable that no confection of the apothecaries can equall their excellent vertue.'

The common use of the adverb comfortably to mean easily can result in some surprising judgments. A medical witness went into the box at a particularly revolting murder trial. The corpse had been sliced up for concealment. The doctor laid it down in giving his evidence that 'A human body could be cut up comfortably in about an hour'.

CONVALLARIACEOUS

THIS seven-syllabled giant suits the subject of Gracie Fields's well-known song, 'The biggest aspidistra in the world'. For convallariaceous is just what the aspidistra is. John Moore, who has acquired in England's Middle-West a treasury of native names for plants and beasts and insects known by more solemn titles, told me recently that the aspidistra is a lily. Much-loved for its tenacity, much-mocked for its Suburbanity – yes, this is a dictionary word – the aspidistra endures all our facetiousness with no bowing of the head. It sounds, with that Grecian spear (aspis) in the forefront of its name, far better than it looks. In its kinship it has distinction. Its convallariaceity comes from Lilium Convallium, lily of the valley. The Tennysonian 'lily-maid of Astolat' might as well have been called Aspidistra as Elaine. But there must be no abbreviation, if this is to become a favoured Christian (or given) name. Lady Aspidistra Vale will pass: 'Aspie, darling' is altogether too serpentine.

Our lily of the valley may ring a gentle bell and look like a poet's pet, but in essence it is severely medical, yielding Convallarimin, 'an acrid purgative glucoside'. Those feeling seedy and dumpish might profit internally by chewing the landlady's

darling pot-plant and so taking a serviceable dose of Convallarimin. If you can imagine yourself seeing Aspidistra in
print for the first time, it might strike you not as a joke but as a
handsome addition to the catalogue of floral felicities.

CORYZA

IT sounds so romantic. Surely the lady must be a Tragedy
Queen. She murders her husband and flees from one lover
to another, poisons her children, and is destroyed at last by
Nemesis? Not a bit of it. She is just your constant companion,
as little romantic as a dish of gruel. Coryza is a running of the
nose, the common cold. Does it comfort you to know that, when
you sniffle and sneeze and feel your whole being to be at once
ice and lead, hot shivers and cold sweat, you may claim to be
Coryzantic. Corybantics are religious enthusiasts, demonically
rapt and revelling. Coryzants have nothing but rheum, despite
the romance of this name.

Another old word for the nose-drip is the Pose or Poose. This
is Chaucerian. 'He speketh in his nose . . . as eke he hath the
pose.' Was Poosy Nancy an Ayrshire lady with catarrh?

> But running through the nose,
> 'Tis called Coryza: others say the Pose.

I prefer Coryza. There is certainly no imposture about the
matter when I become a coryzant. Some people get slight colds
and 'shake them off'; others, of whom I am one, get colds that
are really colds. You could no more shake off Coryzas than you
could a ton of coals. You just work through them, preferably
alone.

COSSET AND TANTONY

COSSET was a noun before it was a verb. It was the pet lamb,
the shepherd's favourite in the flock, and so any loved one. As
moppet, a little fish, became a little darling (human and feminine)

70

so cosset became the sweet and spoiled one. And then, for some reason, it was forgotten as a noun and kept alive as a verb. People now cosset anything, not fair ones only, but their children, their health, their whims. We have moved a long way from the usage of Stephens, the Jacobean essayist, who liked to see his 'cosset wanton', i.e. his pet lamb frisk.

Tantonies were in the pigsty what cossets were in the sheep-fold. Since St. Antony was the patron of the swine-herds and was often pictured with a pigling in attendance, the tantony became a name for the smallest of a sow's litter. It was then employed as a symbol of faithful or obsequious following. The verb to tantony, i.e. to fawn, was next introduced, like Shake-speare's 'To spaniel'. Tantony was rarely, if ever, a term of genuine affection, like cosset, and sometimes both were used in a depreciatory manner. The *O.E.D.* gives an instance of the two words in company. 'Some are such Cossets and Tantonies that they congratulate their Oppressors and flatter their Destroyers' (1659). It is odd that tantony never became a synonym for darling, for it is a darrlin' word, as Sean O'Casey's Joxer Daly would have said. If men could turn a moppet (little fish) into a term of affection, why not tantony, for little pigs are easy conquerors of the human heart?

COTQUEAN

COTQUEAN occurs in that queer, not obviously needed, little scene of *Romeo and Juliet* (iv. 4) in which Capulet is hurrying on the preparations for the marriage-feast. The Nurse, with her usual frankness, bids him keep clear of larder and pantry matters. 'Go, you cotquean, go,' she commands. A cotquean, for her, was a man who busies himself with women's affairs. Why? The word meant originally a cottage woman, therefore a rough-and-ready housewife. So a masculine hand at work on feminine concerns suggested a conversion of the term and Restoration comedy bandies cotquean as a term of mockery. Addison, who would have been no admirer of the feminine M.P., wrote: 'A states-woman is as ridiculous a creature as a cotquean: each of the sexes should keep within its bounds.' The husband who must show his hand as a cook (usually less enthusiastic when there is need for the hand of the scullery-maid in washing-up) is the cotquean of today. Jonson used the noun cotqueanity.

COY

WHAT parson nowadays would beseech the Lord to make him coy? Yet George Herbert did so, for coy to him meant quiet, unassuming. The word has come to designate someone, usually a girl, pretending to be much more innocent and demure than he or she really is. When Herrick, bidding Virgins to Make Much of Time, wrote:

> Then be not coy, but use your time
> And while ye may, go marry:
> For having lost but once your prime,
> You may for ever tarry

he was using coy, as Herbert did, to mean retiring in an un-affected way.

Then came Andrew Marvell to give the word that pure and shining magic which he bestowed upon so many others. His 'coy mistress' is his chaste beloved:

> Had we but world enough, and time,
> This coyness, Lady, were no crime.
> We would sit down, and think which way
> To walk, and pass our long love's day.

and this leads on to the magnificent plea for the satisfaction of love:

> But at my back I always hear
> Time's wingèd chariot hurrying near.
> And yonder all before us lie

Deserts of vast eternity.
Thy beauty shall no more be found;
Nor, in thy marble vault, shall sound
My echoing song: then worms shall try
That long preserved virginity:
And your quaint honour turn to dust;
And into ashes all my lust.
The grave's a fine and private place,
But none I think do there embrace.

The coy mistress has indeed been warned!

By the time we have reached Sir Walter Scott, coy has altered its meaning and come to suggest a teasing quality:

O Woman! in our hours of ease
Uncertain, coy, and hard to please.

Wordsworth also seems to imply a readiness feigning reluctance in these dreadful lines from that dreadful poem 'Hart-leap Well'. Here the Knight, after triumph in the chase, announces:

I'll build a pleasure-house upon this spot
And a small arbour, made for rural joy;
'T'will be the traveller's shed, the pilgrim's cot,
A place of love for damsels that are coy.

Coy has never recovered from that sort of blow. It has become a nasty little word to signify the mock modesty of a flirtatious miss. Yet it evoked prayer from Herbert and turned the Puritan Marvell to epicurean argument and to a praise of immediacy in love which is matchless in its grave urgency and power of phrase. So we must ever be grateful to the once dignified but now poor, vulgarized and diminished coy.

CRAPULOUS

WE have abandoned the classic crapula for the Anglo-Saxon hang-over. Both words have their merits; an image of somebody sea-green, catarrhal and peevish is well suggested by the adjective crapulous. Hang-over is a simpler statement of oppressive and depressive consequence. The eighteenth-century writers made frequent allusion to this unpleasant aftermath, and I have been reminded that Charles Cotton used it earlier still in his *Night Quatrains*.

> The drunkard now supinely snores,
> His load of ale sweats through his pores,
> Yet, when he wakes, the swine shall find
> A crapula remains behind.

Nowadays we treat the condition with aspirin, alka-seltzer, and other cooling alkaline swills. Mr. Pepys, after coming home 'foxed', drank chocolate in the morning, a frightening thought. But he, too, should have learned by experience.

The elegant English nobleman of the eighteen-eighties, if we accept the authority of Oscar Wilde, was not roused with a cup of tea but with chocolate, which is in the Pepys tradition. Lord Arthur Savile, after his nocturnal perambulation of the West End and Bloomsbury, 'sick with horror' at the prospect of the murder he must commit, woke at twelve.

Then his valet brought him a cup of chocolate on a tray. After he had drunk it, he drew aside a heavy *portière* of peach-coloured plush, and passed into the bathroom. The light stole softly from above, through thin slabs of transparent onyx, and the water in the marble tank glimmered like a moonstone. He plunged hastily in, till the cool ripples touched throat and hair, and then dipped his head right under, as though he would have wiped away the stain of some shameful memory. When he stepped out he felt almost at peace. The exquisite physical conditions of the moment had dominated him, as indeed often happens in the case of very finely-wrought natures, for the senses, like fire, can purify as well as destroy.

Much power in onyx, marble and a cup of chocolate!

CRAVAT

THE Cravate was originally a piece of Croatian neckware, sometimes of lace. I would think of it, more recently, as a large, showy kind of neck-tie, but to Conan Doyle and Sherlock Holmes it was a muffler. 'It was a wild tempestuous night towards the close of November. Outside the wind howled down Baker Street while the rain beat fiercely against the windows.' The inevitable cab came down the empty street. Enter 'that promising young detective', Stanley Hopkins, to whom Holmes showed a sympathy rarely granted to others of Scotland Yard. Hopkins was introducing the case of *The Golden Pince-nez*. 'My poor Watson,' cried Holmes, scenting immediate work on the pince-nez trail, 'we want overcoats and cravats and goloshes.'

Fifty years later the Cravat of this kind has been much on view, worn without overcoat or goloshes by the Student Class. To wear a school, club, or college scarf or muffler, thrown about the neck is, I suppose, economy's bow to foppery. The 'fancy vest' has made a brief reappearance, chiefly in buff; but those who want to 'peacock it a bit' find that ties and mufflers—the Holmesian cravats—are the easiest and cheapest means with which to show one's colours. They are sported without relevance to weather. On the coldest days I have seen undergraduates at large and even watching football matches with no overcoat; they only wreathe the throat with what some of our fathers called, as well as a cravat, a comforter. This same garment is also visibly favoured in days of considerable warmth. The muffler now is a ubiquitous and an all-weather decoration as well as a thoracic defence. But does anybody call it a cravat?

Holmes was fond of writing monographs on this or that obscure topic – indeed, he was unravelling a palimpsest when Hopkins came in from the hurricane and the deluge – and many a monograph has been written upon him. Has any such treatise been written on his use of the English language? His conversational prose was formal and orotund; he loved a cliché as dearly as he loved tobacco and once, alas, cocaine. (But his creator cured him of the last.) How many a case did he describe 'as not entirely devoid of interest'! How often did he say to one of his more distressed clients, 'Pray compose yourself', and even to his life-long ally and companion – can the solid Victorian Watson be called a 'buddy'? – 'Pray, continue'! Indeed, it is with something of a shock that we find the latest Holmes of all – him of *The Retired Colourman* – suddenly snapping at Watson, with no 'pray' at all, 'Cut out the poetry!' Watson's poetry had been no more than the description of a garden-wall in Lewisham as 'sun-baked, mottled with lichens and topped with moss'. But that was too much for Holmes. Yet the Master continually set an example of periphrastic verbosity. When there was every need to be up and away upon the heels of villainy he would prose away to Watson like this, 'I admit to you that the case, which seemed to me so absurdly simple as to be hardly worth my notice, is rapidly assuming a very different aspect. It is true that, though in your mission you have missed everything of importance, yet even those things which have obtruded themselves upon your notice give rise to serious thought'. Suggested translation: 'I thought it was too simple a case for me, but it isn't. You missed what mattered at Lewisham, but what you did manage to see was something important.'

Did Doyle give Holmes this kind of fireside style as part of a literary convention? Or did gentlemen of the 'nineties really talk like that? At any rate, Holmes rarely, if ever, described a criminal as 'getting away'; he was always 'effecting his escape'. But I deviate from cravats.

CRIMSON

WHEN I first read, in a fine Scots ballad,

> When we cam in by Glasgow toun,
> We were a comely sicht to see:
> My love was clad in the black velvet
> And I myself in cramasie,

I would have answered any question about the nature of cramasie by saying that it was a species of gay cloth named after some foreign place, as cretonne is named after Creton in Normandy. But cramasie is the old Scots form of crimson, itself a comely word, but no aboriginal, however native it may sound. It is, in fact, a Middle-Eastern import and one of our many Arabians. It is also, like other arrivals from the gorgeous East, an insect. Cramasie and cremosin, later crimson, came from the Arabic Qerinasi, the cochineal insect which, on being crushed in quantity, yields a reddish-purple dye. Out of this sordid mush comes our rich and romantic name of crimson, a name which always reminds me of one of the most strangely beautiful Shakespearean passages. When Iachimo is standing over the sleeping Imogen he spies,

> On her left breast
> A mole cinque-spotted, like the crimson drops
> I' the bottom of a cowslip.

The next time you pick a cowslip, look within, not only to appreciate the imperial mixture of crimson and yellow, but the exquisite sharpness of Shakespeare's eye that went to the making of this simile.

CRINKUM-CRANKUM

IN its earliest use this word stood for poor stuff or naughtiness. This of Dr. Kettell, the President of Trinity, when John Aubrey went up to Oxford just before the Civil War.

> Mrs. Howe, of Grendon, sent him a present of hippocris and some fine cheese-cakes, by a plain country fellow, her servant. The Dr. tastes the wine:—'What, sayd he, didst thou take this drinke out of a ditch?' And when he saw the cheese-cakes—'What have we here? Crinkum-crankum?' The poor fellow stared on him and wondered at such a rough reception of such a handsome present: but the Dr. shortly made him amends with half-a-crown and a good dinner.

Hippocris or hippocras was a cordial made of wine with added spices. Chaucer speaks of it as a source of courage.

Later on it became a contemptuous word for all the fussily over-decorated things. Lord Ogleby in Coleman's comedy, *The Clandestine Marriage*, thus dismissed the vogue of Gothic which, in the middle of the eighteenth century, was beginning to fill the grounds of an English Nobleman's Seat with sham ruins and twisty ponds. At that time canals, not yet industrialized, were still channels (the words are really the same) and the gardens of a great mansion had to be rich in such ornamental waters. Fashion continually made the canals more bizarre, equipped them with a false façade of bogus bridges, and even introduced the fantastic Italian style of grotto with curious fountains, vivarium, aquarium, and so forth. All, of course, to be designed 'with knobs on', as the modern slang so expressively describes a certain kind of architecture. In short, crinkum-crankum.

CRISPS

WE all eat 'crisps' on occasion, for these potato-wafers accompany the cocktail party at the Grand Babylon as well as being freely purchased in the packet at the Red Lion or Black Horse. They are so called, presumably, because they are so hard, brittle and crunchy. But crisp, before it got this connotation of a crackling substance, had a strange variety of meanings. Shakespeare used it twice of water and once of the sky. The River Severn, affrighted by the conflict of Mortimer and Glendower,

> Ran fearfully among the trembling reeds
> And hid his crisp head in the hollow bank.

Crisp there probably means wavy and curly. Chaucer had used it so of hair. In the masque in *The Tempest* Iris bids the Naiades, 'nymphs of the wind'ring brooks', leave their crisp channels. Wavy again? Or clear? In *Timon of Athens* the raging outcast speaks of

> The abhorrèd births below crisp Heaven
> Whereon Hyperion's quickening fire doth shine.

This is generally interpreted as meaning bright and lucent. For crisp does mean shining elsewhere. But Shakespeare may have been thinking of white, wavy clouds like the ripples of the Severn and of Iris's channels.

From these heights we descend to crisp as a noun of the kitchen, signifying the crackling of pork. So we move on to the potato crisps of common delight. A correspondent informs me that in West Cornwall it is common to misplace consonants. The word pixie, for fairy, becomes pisky (it used to be pisgy in Devon) and he assures me that 'in any inn around St. Just local inhabitants can be heard asking for a picket of crips'. I fancy that the smoothing out of crisps is not limited to St. Just or even to West Cornwall. Familiar words are apt to lose a letter or soften one. Trumps at cards are often called trumphs in the

Glasgow area, where the player of an ace might exclaim 'Here it's' rather than 'here it is' when he puts it down. The Cockney is supposed to say srimps for shrimps and may very well ask for a packet of crips too. Crisps is a something of a nuisance to lazy speakers.

The potatoes sold in this slender form remind me of the name Smith. In the pictured 'comics' of my boyhood the Londoner's Smith was Smiff. Smith's Crisps, though familiar, invite some slurring from the eager or slightly fuddled consumer. 'A packet of Smiff's crips' might come easier. Shakespeare, writing before Sir Walter Raleigh's importation had become popular, kept crisp for larger matters. Falstaff would certainly have disdained such trifling companions for his sherris-sack. The man who disdained eggs with his liquor ('I'll no pullet-sperm in my brewage') was not to be regaled with a sliver of a tuber. But Bardolph and the Page might have welcomed such a nibble when larger fare was lacking.

Mincing, who is Millamant's maid in *The Way of the World*, when explaining that her lady curled her hair only with letters written in poetry, wished to describe the result as crisp, but she called it crips. On being laughed at, she retorted, 'You're such a critic, Mr. Witwoud.' So the crisp-crips confusion is an old one.

CRONY

THE crony comes in with Pepys. The age of Charles II, says Bernard Groom in his *Short History of English Words*, was prodigal of brevities. The Restoration dramatists liked some stately terms too, but it seems that

> Short informal words are the characteristic contribution of the time to our language. Banter and crony are first recorded in the reign of Charles II. Sham appears about 1677, and was much used during the excitement of the Popish Plot. The abusive term Whig was applied to the

promoters of the Exclusion Bill in 1679 and was soon the accepted badge of a great political party. Prig came into use as 'a vague term of disrespect' about the same time. Chum is first recorded in 1684, fun in 1685, mob in 1688. Swift protested against the spread of new popular words,[1] especially against the 'barbarity which delights in mono-syllables'. But there seems to have been small opposition to the movement until the great campaign against 'low' language in which both Johnson and Chesterfield played an energetic part.

Crony I find particularly fascinating. It suggests a certain snuffling guile, a companionship in mischief, a joint pottering over the cups and glasses; it smells of gossip and of 'another one for the road'.

Burns so used it to perfection.

> His ancient, trusty, drouthy crony:
> Tam lo'ed him like a vera brither,
> They had been fou for weeks thegither.

Drouthy, so much better than thirsty, and fou, so much more suggestive than full, run nicely with crony. The *Oxford English Dictionary* calls it University slang, but the crony soon widened his social range and I think of the Dublin soaks, saloon-bound fellow-travellers, as cronies. Was not Joxer Daly a perfect crony for the Peacock?

Cronies appear to be exclusively male and have nothing to do with aged crones. There is no reason, except chance association, why they should be spoken of as old. May we not have young cronies? Surely a University word should have some relevance to the friendships of one-and-twenty. Nowadays the young appear to have their buddies; and cronies are getting scarcer too. But they must not disappear.

---

[1] 'I have done my utmost to stop the progress of Mobb and Banter' (Swift).

CRUMPET AND MUFFIN

THE late Lord Asquith of Bishopstone appealed for more muffins to ease the strains of the afternoon and indeed of life itself. (And why should not a Lord of Appeal do a little appealing as well as being appealed to?) When told that Britain lacked butter to make his desired confections and so to refill the tray of the old-time muffineer and set the hand-bell ringing in the streets again, he asked why crumpets should be able to defy that shortage. He did not like crumpets. To him they were 'limp, lardaceous, pock-marked parodies of muffins'. With that he may be said to have put the crumpet in its place, which, for him, is out of the window.

I thought lardaceous must be an Asquithian creation. But the dictionary gives it protection, telling us that it means 'containing lardacein', and lardacein, defined, is certainly no matter for the queasy. It is 'a nitrogenous substance deposited under morbid conditions in certain minute arteries and tissues of the body'. Those 'morbid conditions' immediately avert my appetite: also I am surprised to find *O.E.D.* writing 'under' conditions: my instructors in English composition had always made it plain that we were in or amid certain conditions, not beneath them.

But let us return to our crumpets. They mean curved or curled up cakes, since to crump is to bend into a curve. But they are no more curvaceous – to use an adjective dear to the advertisement-writers for lingerie and such – than any other kind of circular bun. However, to crump has another meaning, 'to eat with an abrupt but somewhat dulled sound applied to horses and pigs'. And why not to the human crumpeteer, for surely we may munch abruptly but in a muffled way our lardaceous muffin-substitutes?

Incidentally, I surmise that Lord Asquith may have been inclined to this rage by a surfeit of crumpets in his youth. I remember that, at the Oxford College of which we were simultaneous members, it was customary to send out from the buttery at tea-time large piles, hot or lukewarm under a metal cover, of the extremely limp, lardaceous and pock-marked enemies of his palate. These were often accompanied by an equally rich pile of banana sandwiches. The banana was so long away from our English menu that few now are aware that a sliced, well-ripened banana makes an excellent wadding for two thin slices of fresh, well-buttered bread. Teas were gigantic then, banana-bountiful and crumpet-lardy. But they came after exercise and lunch was scanty.

Slang has promoted crumpet, Lord Asquith doubtless dissenting, to the honour of representing the human head. This signification of the brain-pan it has shared with boko, napper, noggin, and nut among others. The nut is in the list for obvious reasons of shape, and the napper presumably because it is the site of one's nap or hair. Boko sounds like something attractive to bashers and crumpet, for skull or sconce, can be explained by yet another meaning of the verb to crump, that is to hit or slog. The crump as an explosive missile is a further product of that. It is a melancholy fact that we should regard the seat of intelligence chiefly as something to be bashed: but that, unfortunately, is what our slang terms for it do imply.

Daniel George, in *Pick and Choose*, quotes from Boswell's *Johnson* a story told by Topham Beauclerck: 'Mr. ——, who loved buttered muffins, but durst not eat them because they disagreed with his stomach, resolved to shoot himself; and then he ate three buttered muffins for breakfast, before shooting himself, knowing that he should not be troubled with indigestion.'

In *A Peck of Troubles* Daniel George retells another muffin story – Crabb Robinson's: 'I have heard of a lady, by birth, being reduced to cry "muffins to sell" for a subsistence. She used to go out a-nights with her face hid up in her cloak, and then she would in the faintest voice utter her cry. Somebody passing by heard her cry – "Muffins to sell, muffins to sell! Oh, I do hope nobody hears me."'

CURIOSO

CURIOSO may be well-nigh extinct, but he is as good a fellow, surely, as the virtuoso who survives almost in abundance. A curioso took care, inquired, studied, was expert. He practised curiosity in Dr. Johnson's sense. 'Curiosity is, in great and generous minds, the first passion and the last.' The curioso loved that into which he probed. He was a lover of the rare and queer as well as learned therein, the true amateur. The usage of 'curious' to describe books of an abnormal or indecent kind – as the bookseller judges indecency – is a common feature of certain literary catalogues. This links, in a one-sided way, with the activities of a curioso. But the true curioso had a wider range of taste.

Curiosity has declined in status. It is now a synonym for tiresome inquisitiveness; nursemaids – when there were such – used to observe, for what reason I do not know, that 'curiosity killed the cat' and so implied that small people practising the first and last passion of great and generous minds were reprehensibly engaged and well on the way to the everlasting bonfire, in short Nosey Parkers (who, by the way, was this Prodnose Parker that he should have become immortal?).

I must admit a liking for Nosey as an adjective of dismissal. It is an expressively odious term for those extremely odious people who must ever be reading postcards, looking over shoulders, poking into desks and drawers, and badgering one with a flow of why's and where's and when's. The Curioso I visualize standing silent upon a peak of Helicon, viewing, discerning, subtly exploring. He is at the top of that high school in which the gabbling Nosey Parker is bottom of the lowest form.

Curious nowadays means, nearly always, strange or queer. Chaps and happenings of no importance are often curious. The word has lost quality and one is visited by a shiver of delighted surprise when it is once again met in exalted places, lurking, for example, among Marvell's greenest shades in the garden of Nun Appleton:

> What wondrous life is this I lead!
> Ripe apples drop about my head;
> The luscious clusters of the vine
> Upon my mouth do crush their wine;
> The nectarine and curious peach
> Into my hands themselves do reach:
> Stumbling on melons as I pass,
> Insnar'd with flowers I fall on grass.

Why 'curious peach'? Was the peach seeking something in the poet's hands or just a rare, unusual fruit? In either case Marvell became, in the tranquil Fairfax home near Tadcaster, the curioso and virtuoso of all orchard thoughts or lawn philosophy.

CURMUDGEON AND MECANTODOR

ACCORDING to an anonymous correspondent of Dr. Johnson's, curmudgeon is a Scottish term, created by the Scottish habit of appropriating and telescoping the French phrases, with which the Old Alliance had made people familiar. (Gardyloo for gardez l'eau is the common example.) Curmudgeon, on this model, is cœur méchant. This explanation is not generally accepted, but there is an interesting parallel. I have been told that old leases of houses, in the east of Scotland, used to guarantee the purchaser or tenant against mecantodor, this being méchant odeur. But I have never had confirmation of this from a lawyer. At any rate it is nice to believe that satisfactory plumbing once led to so handsome a title. Leading articles about housing (and lawyers' leases too) would be far easier reading if they were aflame with such Norman decoration as this. Indeed, a Sonnet of Real Estate could properly soar to some such concluding line as

A Messuage without Mecantodor.

DAEDAL

DAEDAL is pure classicism, deriving from Daedalus, the inventive one, and used both of the contriving hand and of the multiplicity of things contrived, especially by Nature. *Natura naturans* is daedal in one sense, *Natura naturata* in the other. Evelyn, the Diarist, wrote of 'a Daedale' as a complicated device in the laying out of gardens. Landor liked the word with its suggestion of multitudinous and glittering growth or movement. To him a dance was daedal. Robert Louis Stevenson implied a gloriously daedal world in his famous

> God's bright and intricate device
> Of days and seasons.

To Lord de Tabley, that gifted as well as baronial bard, looking out over Tabley Mere in Cheshire, a county which long remained lordly in a quiet way, the month of May and the pinguid scene ('Earth's royal aspects of delight') suggested the classic epithet. He saw

> The serene domes of mounting lime
> The meadow's crest of daedal May
> And deep-eyed morning ere the time,
> Sleeking her curtain clouds away.

I am indebted to Sir William Beach Thomas and his rustic anthology 'The Squirrels' Granary' for being reminded of de Tabley's excellence.

DAFF AND DAFFODIL

THERE are two Daffs, apart from the abbreviation of Daffodil. There is the Scottish Daff, which is to talk or behave sportively. In Jane Elliot's *The Flowers of the Forest* when 'The English, for ance, by guile won the day', the melancholy has reached the sheep-folds and there is sad silence at the milking-pails.

> Lasses are lonely and dowie and wae
> Nae daffin', nae gabbin' . . .

A dowie, i.e. dismal, lass may be the opposite of a daffin' one in meaning, but she is equal in felicity of phrase. The English Daff is to put off, cast aside. Clothes are both daffed and doffed. Daffing may be applied to far larger matters than a doublet. 'Canst thou so daff me?' cries Leonato when Claudio is pushing him away. Henry V was once the Mad-Cap Prince who 'daffed the world aside'.

Daff I have claimed to be twice virtuous, once on each side of the Tweed. But it becomes abominable when used as an abbreviation of Daffodil, a word so fair that truncation is a vile malpractice. Daffodil itself is a childish creation (daffadowndilly still more so) and a nursery version, as it were, of Affodil, which, in turn, is our conception of Asphodel. Poetry is for ever candled with the light of Asphodel, as Elysium was carpeted with its blooms. When I was introduced to Asphodel on the Greek mountains beside Mycenae, I was as much disappointed by the first as staggered by the majesty of the second. Presumably I was shown the wrong article, for it bore no resemblance to our 'lamp of beauty', Shakespeare's brave anticipator of the swallow. Asphodel shall remain for me a lyric love, a flower laid up in fancy, frequent in the grounds of Castle Bunthorne – as well as in the classic meadows. English lyric poetry sways and shines with the windswept gold of daffodils. They are summoned to a lamentation by Milton.

> Bid amaranthus all his beauty shed
> And daffadillies fill their cups with tears,
> To strew the laureate hearse where Lycid lies.

But for the most part they are vessels of rejoicing.

DANDER

DANDER has a strange assortment of meanings. It can be a cinder or a piece of scurf or a show of temper. But it is also, and far better, a wandering or stroll. The Scots have retained this usage, and wisely – for what more expressive of an easy walk at dusk than 'a wee bit dander in the gloaming'? The very slowness of the movement is in the word. The English have preferred saunter, which is also happily expressive. But I always have the sense of the right noise for a slow and pleasant vagabondage when I read in a Scots book of a dander in the glen. The Mearns on a summer night, the Mearns so richly and rhythmically described in Lewis Grassic Gibbon's tremendous novels of the eastern Scottish coast and its dwindling crofter life, *Sunset Song* and *Cloud Howe*, is rare dandering country, as it ripples between the Grampians and the sea. When you read of such crofts and villages as Kinraddie and Blawaerie and Peesies' Knapp and of the peewits and curlews above them, it's a dander that any wise man would be having in 'the lithe' of the hills, as Gibbon would say, lithe here meaning cover or recess.

DANDIPRAT, ETC.

A DANDIPRAT suggests at first a prattling dandy, a gossiping fop or macaroni. But it is nothing so substantial. It merely means anything little. It began as a small coin and ended as a small boy.

This form of urchin lurks in the by-ways of Elizabethan drama and makes one of his last appearances – for where is the imp now? – in Calverley's glorious piece of mock-Browning, 'The Cock and The Bull'. Speaking of his pebble-stone the poet proclaims:

> Well, to my muttons. I purchased the concern,
> And clapt it i' my poke, having given for same
> By way o' chop, swop, barter or exchange –

'Chop' was my snickering dandiprat's own term –
One shilling and fourpence, current coin o' the realm.

This chop, term so dear to the snickering dandiprat, is cousin
to chap and cheap, the market terms which gave us chapman,
Cheapside, and the several Chippings of our English countryside, Chipping Norton, Chipping Sodbury, Chipping Ongar, and
the like. Dandiprats, especially of the snickering kind, are much
given to a crude form of chop-logic, which means exchange of
argument. 'Chop and change' did not originally, I suppose, mean
veer about or waver, but swop and barter.

Calverley, having introduced his dandiprat, continues to spray
the reader with a rich jet of the 'classicalese' so dear to Browning:

> I shoved the timber ope wi' my omoplat;
> And *in vestibulo*, i' the lobby to-wit,
> (Iacobi Facciolati's rendering, sir,)
> Donn'd galligaskins, antigropeloes,
> And so forth; and, complete with hat and gloves,
> One on and one a-dangle i' my hand,
> And ombrifuge (Lord love you), case o' rain,
> I flopp'd forth, 'sbuddikins! on my own ten toes,
> (I do assure you there be ten of them),
> And went clump-clumping up hill and down dale
> To find myself o' the sudden i' front o' the boy.
> Put case I hadn't 'em on me, could I ha' bought
> This sort-o'-kind-o'-what-you-might-call toy,
> This pebble-thing, o' the boy-thing? Q.E.D.
> That's proven without aid from mumping Pope,
> Sleek porporate or bloated Cardinal.

Omoplat is shoulder-blade and ombrifuge umbrella. Antigropeloes are water-defiers, and so are galligaskins, which were
trousers or gaiters of the Grecian mode. Nowadays, those who
wish to see ombrifuge, antigropeloes and galligaskins in their
most protective, voluminous, and even colourful form should
watch our leading golfers plodding through the downpour in

some grim competitive event, from which none may flinch, however terrible the 'on-ding' of the elements, as a Scot would say. Golfers of this calibre know all about antigropelistic wrapping up.

What is the mumping Pope? Mumping can be either muttering or spongeing and cheating. Porporate I had to hunt out in the larger *O.E.D.* It is 'clad in purple'.

Of all these terms I would most like dandiprat to return to us. It is a darling word.

DARKLING AND DIMPSY

Darkling began life as an adverb meaning 'in the dark'. 'Out went the candle and we were left darkling', says the Fool in *King Lear*.

'Wilt thou darkling leave me?' is Helena's protest to Demetrius. Cleopatra, as she beholds the dying Antony, cries to the heavens:

> Oh sun,
> Burn the great sphere thou mov'st in! Darkling stand
> The varying shore o' the world!

In Milton:

> the wakeful Bird
> Sings darkling and in shadiest covert hid
> Tunes her nocturnal note.

Keats also kept this, the correct, usage in his 'Ode to A Nightingale':

> Darkling I listen: and for many a time
> I have been half in love with easeful Death.

(This does not mean that he is going black in the face: merely that he is standing in the dark.) But before Keats's time darkling had come to be regarded as the participle of a verb 'to darkle'. (This error was natural enough. If day sparkled, why should not night darkle?) Ever since the beginning of the nineteenth century, all sorts of things from minds to moonless landscapes have darkled for the poet's benefit.

'When matter darkles or when spirit beams' is a line of Moore's, and night often darkled for Byron. If you wish to be learned, you can call darkle a 'back-formation'. It is certainly useful and decorative. The same process can be seen in 'sidle', a verb 'back-formed' from the adverb 'side-ling' or 'side-long'. Old writers went 'side-ling'. Later on they sidled, as the nights darkled.

Several West Country correspondents have advised me that dimpsy is still in use for twilight in their localities. I was more surprised to hear that the same is true of Lincolnshire, where duskling (pronounced 'doosling') is also in use. Our word 'dusk' follows the adjective dusky (for dark) and only came to be a noun and to mean the dark time at a later stage. Shakespeare, for instance, would not have understood what we mean by dusk. He would have called it the dusky hour. (Nor, incidentally, did he use twilight, a word dear to Milton):

> As when the Sun . . .
> In dim Eclips disastrous twilight sheds.

This use of disastrous will remind Shakespeareans of Horatio's lines in *Hamlet*:

> Disasters in the sun: and the moist star
> Upon whose influence Neptune's empire stands
> Was sick almost to doomsday with eclipse.

(Disaster originally meant something wrong with the stars and so an ill-starred occurrence.)

True twilight or dusk could hardly be thus disastrous, except amid the cursed necessities of war-time 'black-out'. To dusk for to make dark is as old as Chaucer, while the verb is used intransitively with superb effect by A. E. Housman:

I see the air benighted
    And all the dusking dales,
And lamps in England lighted
    And evening wrecked in Wales.

Dusking goes well with Clee and Severn, dimpsy with the lush grass of South Devon.

DAYLIGONE

An Ulster correspondent kindly sent me this word (short for 'daylight-gone') as a local usage for twilight or eventide. It is certainly a nice one and it seems that it has found its way into print in Lynn Doyle's *Ballads of Ballygullion*. It is not a dictionary word, but investigating the lexicon led to the discovery that English words for daybreak have indeed been many and charming. Over and above day-break and day-dawn, there are day-peep, day-rawe, day-red, and day-rim. More abiding has been the day-spring, which the Church of England has preserved in Tindale's phrase about our visitation by 'the day-spring from on high'. Milton had it too, showing 'the breath of heaven' to be fresh-blowing and 'with day-spring born'. From day-spring to dayligone suggests long, basking hours in a warm and lucid air.

DAZE

It is right that the North should have the best terms for cold. The South has lost the use of daze for numb, narrowing its usage to strong effects on eye and brain, just as it has limited 'starve' to matters of appetite. The Yorkshire child who, when settled in an air-raid shelter of the dank and draughty kind, cried out to his mother, 'Ee Moom, ba goom, ma boom is noom', might have called his posterior dazed had he lived a little earlier. In Scotland the use of daze does, I believe, linger. How well it sits in Gavin Douglas's sharp, clear, and tingling description of a Scottish winter:

In this congealit season sharp and chill,
The caller air penetrative and pure,
Dazing the blude in every creature,
Made seek warm stovis and bene fyris hot.
In double garment cled and wyliecoat,
With michty drink, and meatis confortive . . .

The last robust and reassuring word surely amplifies and justifies
my earlier note on the original implication of comfort.

DECREPITUDE

DECAY does well for decline and withering, no doubt, and can
be magically used. There is Vaughan's

> My days which are at best but dull and hoary,
> Mere glimmering and decays.

But, for weighty expression of corruption by age, it is beaten
by decrepitude, whose grave Latinity awesomely rings the bell
for parting vigour. In his defence of the Art of Painting as
an admirable solvent of care for the busy, fatigued or ageing
intellectual worker, Sir Winston Churchill has used decrepitude
with characteristically rhetorical effect.

> Painting is a friend who makes no undue demands, excites
> to no exhausting pursuits, keeps faithful pace even with
> feeble steps, and holds her canvas as a screen between us
> and the envious eyes of Time or the surly advance of
> Decrepitude.

Gibbon himself could not have bettered that final cadence, to
which the last word so well contributes. The envious eyes of
Time may be drawn from the cliché country; but the surly
advance of Decrepitude is glorious and essential Winston.

Lovers of a full-sounding prose naturally welcome decrepitude into their lexicon. John Buchan cited this of the world-

mood or world-opinion at the beginning of the seventeenth century.

> There prevailed in his (Milton's) time an opinion that the world was in its decay, and that we have had the misfortune to be produced in the decrepitude of Nature. It was suspected that the whole creation languished, that neither trees nor animals had the height or bulk of their predecessors, and that everything was daily sinking by gradual diminution.

He also quoted John Donne.

> We have a winding-sheet in our mother's womb, which groweth with us from our conception, and we come into the world wound up in that winding-sheet, for we come to seek a grave.

The unthinkableness of eternity haunted their imagination.

> Methusalem with all his hundreds of years was but a mushroom of a night's growth to this Day, and all the four Monarchies with all their thousands of years, and all the powerful Kings and all the beautiful Queens of this world, were but as a bed of flowers, some gathered at six, some at seven, some at eight, all in one morning, in respect of this Day.

Buchan who wrote finely of that period in prefacing his life of Montrose, quoted many instances of the devouring pessimism, the dark conviction of a general decrepitude, even of a swift and common doom, which followed the Tudor blaze. Donne's sermons are a continual reminder that we are less than the grass and await no more than a divine trampling.

We, who live in the atom-bomb age, have surely better reason for all this parade of sackcloth and display of ashes. But it was more than three centuries ago that the sermonist of St. Paul's saw only

The seasons of the year irregular and distempered; the sun fainter and languishing; men less in stature and shorter lived. No addition, but only every year new sorts, new species of worms and flies and sicknesses, which argue more and more putrefaction of which they are engendered.

Decrepitude indeed!

DECUMAN AND DECIBEL

THAT unflagging Latinist, Francis Thompson, wrote of

> The lover whose soul shaken is
> In some decuman billow of bliss.

The decuman is the tenth or largest wave and the word has accordingly been used to express unusual size or strength. Decibel, presumably a tenth of something, has been recently used as a unit of sound. It is an attractive word, but one finds it applied rather to the more odious clangours and screechings of modern life than to sweetness of music or song. It is the thudding, mechanic, road-ripping drill and not the nightingale that is considered in terms of decibels. So, when tanks are 'sounding through the town' with grimmer justification for that splendid verb than was ever provided by the bonnie Earl of Moray, one thinks of a new participle, decibelligerent. One can fit the almost delicate word decibel into many agreeable rhythms and metres. However, it must be reserved mainly for tumult and braying and clatter of all kinds. A Muscovite victory-salvo, for example, might be compiled in terms of decibellic output and described as a veritable decuman of din.

DEMERGATURE

I AM reminded that officialese of the formidably Latin type is not merely a modern invention. A man might have been 'hospitalized', as we now say, for attempting demergature, as they once said. Mr. Wanklyn, the historian of Lyme Regis, and a great student of old West Country journals, left this note on an entry in *Pulman's Weekly News* of that district.

> ... One of the most curious entries in the list of burials is a case of suicide by drowning in 1802. The story is told by Roberts, and the victim was one John Crookshanks, and the entry in the Register is as follows: 'March 25th, 1802, John Crookshanks, bachelor, late of London, demergature.' Now, no English dictionary, old or modern, admits the word 'demergature'. As a substitute for 'death by drowning' it deserves to rank with our old friend 'defenestration' of Jezebel, which described another form of death. ...

My correspondent, who told me of this, added:

> This example of 'early-Darset' officialese has the advantage of supplying a single word to describe death by drowning – criminal, self-inflicted, or accidental – where at present no single word for it is in use.

The value of such safe words is obvious, especially to journalists who have to be extremely careful not to anticipate the verdict of a coroner's jury (or any other jury) by their choice of terms. Hence the constant usage of, and favour shown to, the word fatality, which covers accident, suicide, manslaughter, or murder without any risk of prejudging the issue. Fatality properly and originally meant the condition of being predetermined by destiny, but it came to mean anything to which fate condemned a man. So, lastly, it was an accident or disaster. Journalism, which finds fatality protective and useful, might consider reviving demergature, which is equally non-committal. I note that our

Board of Agriculture and Fisheries, in its officialese, writes of 'demersal fish', by which it presumably means those which keep to the bottom.

DEMIREP

It is a nice point of charitable courtesy to allow half a reputation to her who has none. For the demirep is, in fact, a no-rep, i.e. the owner of no reputation at all. Somebody has defined a demirep as 'one whom everybody knows to be what nobody calls her'. But must demireps be always feminine?

I was reminded of demireps during a return to that richest of Browning's conversation-pieces, 'Bishop Blougram's Apology', so full of

> truth that peeps
> Over the glass's edge when dinner's done
> And body gets its sop and holds its noise
> And leaves soul free a little.

In the debate we meet

> The honest thief, the tender murderer,
> The superstitious atheist, demirep
> That loves and saves her soul in new French books.

Demireps are not altogether new arrivals in the language. They were preceded by the Tudor 'demi-lass' another gently evasive word for a trollop.

DIACODION

In Congreve's bawdy piece 'Love for Love', which surprisingly had recent status on the British stage as being cultural and educational, Diacodion is coupled with Cowslip-water among remedies prescribed. It was a favoured night-cap of our forefathers, acting like mandragora and other drowsy syrups, whose names are as beguiling as their nature. William Bullein, 1564, recommended the following diet for good health:

> Eate good broth made of chickens, leane Mutton, roste a little Partriche, eate light leavened breade; beware of grosse meates, Beefe, Porke, &c, and salletes, strong wine, Spice, sweete meates, and rawe fruites. I praie you remember this, and drinke your Diacodion at night to reconcile slepe again, and be somewhat laxative.

It sounds reasonable, much more so than many of the salves ordered at that time. (But notice the distrust of fruit, shared by Swift.) Daniel George has collected many startling prescriptions in his rich miscellany called *Alphabetical Order*. The philosopher, Bishop Berkeley, for example, recorded this:

> Seely told me that he has drunk ten young vipers taken out of the womb, all living, as big as large pins, in one glass of wine. Takes powder of vipers dried in the shade, a drachm a day during the months of May and September. Sweetens the blood above all things.

The Tudor therapy seems the better to me.

The release of suppressed feelings was a salve in Tudor and Jacobean medicine, long before it was discovered by our modern psychologists. Here is a nice list of Sir Francis Bacon's remedies for maladies, including the secular confessional, which psychoanalysis now provides. He wrote of Friendship:

> A principall *Fruit of Friendship*, is the Ease and Discharge of the Fulnesse and Swellings of the Heart, which Passions of all kinds doe cause and induce. We know Diseases of Stoppings, and Suffocations, are the most dangerous in the body; And it is not much otherwise in the Minde: You may take *Sarza* to open the Liuer; *Steele* to open the Spleene; *Flower* of *Sulphur* for the Lungs; *Castoreum* for the Braine; But no Receipt openeth the Heart, but a true Friend, to

whom you may impart, Griefes, Ioyes, Feares, Hopes, Suspicions, Counsels and whatsoeuer lieth vpon the Heart, to oppresse it, in a kind of Ciuill Shrift or Confession.

Diacodion opened the gates of sleep, whose stopping is so constant an affliction to many.

DICKY

WHY should a word which so obviously implies perkiness mean also feeble, falling to pieces, or out-of-sorts? (Out-of-sorts, when you come to look at it, is, like well-to-do, a very queer combination.) The dicky-bird is not one that feels dicky: he is a chirruper. Dicky has, indeed, an astonishing number of meanings, chiefly as a noun. This, I suppose, has occurred because various people called Richard have, at various times, had various characteristics or pet decorations or specially allotted seats in a carriage.

Dicky has kept the lexicographers in full employment, detecting him as a male-donkey or 'an officer acting in commission'. He has been bird, petticoat, skirt, apron, bib, oil-skin and overall. Most familiar perhaps was the dicky which small boys, on formal and formidable occasions, used to attach to the collar as a starchy breastplate, concealing their common and possibly grubby flannel shirts and giving, it was hoped, an air of dressiness. This dicky flourished most, I think, when young gentlemen were habited for Sundays, Speech Days and the like, in 'Etons'. That repulsive outfit, at once gloomy to the eye and chilly to the rump which had no protection from the pert, abbreviated coat, was a proper companion for the pretentious bit of humbug that was the linen dicky masquerading as a dress-shirt.

At some period or place Richard was a coachman: at another a footman. The dicky seat could either be the driver's or one at the back for the manservant in attendance. In our humbler days it became the open back-seat of a two-seater car, a detestable perch except in heat-waves or for those who revel Spartanly in the wind and rain as conditions of their travel. Many a dicky-traveller in winter-time has dismounted feeling very dicky indeed.

DILETTANTE AND DILLITANT

SIR MAX BEERBOHM has written: 'Well, for my own part I am a dilettante, a petit maître. I love best in literature delicate and elaborate ingenuities of form and style. But my preference does not keep me from paying due homage to Titanic force and delighting, now and again, in its manifestation. I wonder at Ouida's novels and I wonder still more at Ouida.' We, too, may wonder sometimes at the extent to which 'Max' would carry his dilettantism and his cult of verbal elaboration, as, for example, when he described the racing of jockeys on the turf, as 'the scud-a-run of quivering homuncules over the vert on horses'. It was astonishing that, having striven so industriously not to use an ordinary word, he should at last have mounted anything so normal as a mere horse. What has so common a beast to do with 'the vert'? Surely the homuncules might have been poised on palfreys! (The palfrey, so dear to the romantic author of my youth, was a light saddle-horse contrasted with the heavy war-horse.)

The dilettante is, properly, one who delights, and who more delightful than such a man in our world which is so often either a dormitory of the lethargic or a cock-pit of the captious? But the name was diminished to mean one who took delight in trifles, a finical fellow, an amateurish idler among the arts. Indeed, it has become, unfortunately, a word of abuse. Pronounced in various ways by the enthusiasts of energy, it is now employed to hint at disgust with the play-boy. I have heard a public speaker announce, with regard to politics, 'We want no dillitants in our movement.' (That was his version of the term.) Dillitant, with its suggestion of dilly-dally and hesitant, has surely a claim to incorporation, with honour, in the English language. The idea of delight and self-indulgence is still vaguely there along with that of inertia. Yes, on the whole, dillitant is an admirable word, and I fancy that 'Max' might gratefully accept it.

Carlyle had a good smack at the dillitants when he thundered:

> Midas-eared Mammonism, double-barrelled Dilettantism, and their thousand adjuncts and corollaries, are *not* the Law by which God Almighty has appointed His Universe to go.

Carlyle was uncommonly sure of himself and of his comprehension of God's Will. What exactly he meant by the adjective double-barrelled in this connection is hard to say. But at least we may surmise that Sir Max Beerbohm was never more than single-barrelled in his dillitancy.

DIM

SHORT, simple dim, source of emotion in many a moving line, has had radically different meanings. To Shakespeare it mainly conveyed the idea of darkness. Tombs are dim, cloudy skies are dim, and 'violets dim' (magical phrase, as only Shakespeare could make magic of the simplest words) must refer to darkness of hue. Yet the notion of faintness was also implicit in his use of the word at times. 'As dim and meagre as an ague's fit', he says of a dying child. Milton's 'dim, religious light' perhaps unites both conceptions. Later the idea of something vague, weak, and transient begins to supplant the concept of darkness. In my undergraduate days dim, in our cant, stood for anything grey or dull. A witless or uninteresting man was voted dim. Dim in the sense of evanescent or ghostly occurs with magnificence in Siegfried Sassoon's sonnet 'On Passing the New Menin Gate'.

> Crudely renewed the Salient holds its own,
> Paid are its dim defenders by that pomp:
> Paid, with a pile of peace-complacent stone,
> The armies who endured that sullen swamp.

Browning finely alliterated it in his famous

> Still one must lead some life beyond,
> Have a bliss to die with, dim-descried.

Dim is but a meek, mild, midget of a word, but it has contributed to great utterance, of which I take these to be examples.

DISEMBOGUE

THIS massive word for outflow was used by Pope to describe the famous ditch by whose vanished banks I have spent much of my working life. I have heard that, though the foul Fleet Ditch, famed for a thousand stenches, has long been reduced to a decent drain, the taximen have inherited the term for a cab-stand hereabout and still talk of 'The Ditch'. Here are Pope's lines:

> This labour past, by Bridewell all descend,
> (As morning-pray'r and flagellation end)
> To where Fleet-ditch with disemboguing streams
> Rolls the large tribute of dead dogs to Thames,
> The King of Dykes! Than whom no sluice of mud
> With deeper sable blots the silver flood.

Disemboguing seems exactly right for so horrid a runnel. Southey, however, used it of fair streams and limpid waters. The verb originally meant to emerge from the mouth of a stream and was applied to ships getting to sea. But then it was transferred to the stream itself or to any eruptive object.

> Volcanoes bellow ere they disembogue,

was one of Young's Night Thoughts. Disembogue could be transitive too. The old Irish nurse's fearful menace of 'I'll tear the tripes out of you' (really uttered with no sort of unkindly or surgical intention) might have been spoken by her Tudor ancestress, 'I'll disembogue your innards'. But disembogue is best as Pope used it, especially for some Acheron of an industrial town, darkly oozing on its way. Manchester's Irwell surely disembogues.

DISGUSTING

In an account of the first Duke of Wellington's funeral, written by the present Duke and published in *History To-Day*, I met a striking observation on the meaning of the word disgusting. The writer was referring especially to the Lying-in-State in the Great Hall of Chelsea Hospital from November 13th to 17th, 1852. The crowds wishing to attend were enormous and, since the police arrangements were at first wholly inadequate, they were unruly as well. One man and two women were actually crushed to death. 'It is interesting to note,' remarked the present Duke in his article, 'that both Charles Greville and Lord Douro use the word "disgusting" of the funeral arrangements.' Then he added, 'They used it in the same sense as Jane Austen used it, meaning what we should call "antipathetic". Disgusting is one of the few words in the English language which time has strengthened instead of weakening.'

Disgust, by origin, means contrary to one's taste rather than revolting. When Greville wrote after this occasion that all public funerals are disgusting he meant that they were not to his liking and offended his sense of propriety. Now we should interpret his statement as meaning that he found public funerals actually nauseating. Disgust, as a noun, usually in the plural, once meant quarrel, affront, or snub.

The adjective disgustful seems to have vanished: a pity, since to call a book or a play that is full of bad taste disgustful is justly descriptive. So disgusting remains, usually intensified by an adverb such as utterly, to signify the odious and revolting. But a century ago one could claim to have found so-and-so's company or such and such a dish disgusting without implying that the person was completely unbearable and the victuals rancid or otherwise impossible to consume. None the less, returning to the Great Duke, we may well imagine that the morbidity and tumultuous conduct of the crowds at Chelsea were disgusting in our sense as well as distasteful to Greville and Lord Douro.

DISTASTE

NOT an impressive verb, perhaps, but it must be the peg for a note on Shakespeare's delight in the prefix dis-, which he often used where un- would be normal (e.g. dispiteous for unpitiful and disnatured for unnatural). Distasted means spoilt or put out of flavour and occurs in one of the least known among the loveliest of passages in Shakespeare. When Troilus and Cressida must part, Troilus cries,

> We two, that with so many thousand sighs
> Did buy each other, must poorly sell ourselves
> With the rude brevity and discharge of one.
> Injurious time now, with a robber's haste,
> Crams his rich thievery up, he knows not how:
> As many farewells as be stars in heaven,
> With distinct breath and consign'd kisses to them,
> He fumbles up into a loose adieu;
> And scants us with a single famisht kiss,
> Distasted with the salt of broken tears.

There, in the agony of war-time parting, is pictured for ever, with poignancy unmatchable, the short, snatched kiss of the railway-platform or the quay-side as the train goes out or the ship sails. If anybody is interested in Shakespeare's exquisite and no doubt unconscious use of alliteration, let him note the use of 's', letter of sighs, in the last five lines; the 's' is most delicately interlaced with the many 'l's, three initial 'f's, two 'd's, two 'k's, and the plentiful 't's of the last line. To me the last couplet is as moving as anything that Shakespeare ever wrote and always brings that physical shiver down the spine which A. E. Housman took to be the circumstance and proof of supreme poetry.

DOOF

THE Scots have a most satisfying variety of words for a blow: doof comes high up in the scale of violence, as is shown by this vigorous piece of 'Lallans' in a story by James Hogg, the Ettrick Shepherd. In a tale called *The Brownie of Bodsbeck* John Hoy, a herdsman, is examined by Claverhouse about some soldiers found killed.

'How did it appear to you that they had been slain? Were they cut with swords, or pierced with bullets?'
'I canna say, but they war sair hashed.'
'How do you mean when you say they were hashed?'
'Champit like; a'broozled and jurmummled, as it were.'
'Do you mean that they were cut, or cloven, or minced?'
'Na, na, – no that ava. But they had gotten some sair doofs. They had been terribly paikit and daddit wi' something.'
'I do not in the least conceive what you mean.'
'That's extr'ord'nar', man – can ye no understand folk's mother-tongue? I'll mak it plain to ye. Ye see, whan a thing comes on ye that gate, that's a dadd – sit still now. Then a paik, that's a swap or skelp like – when a thing comes on ye that way, that's a paik. But a doof's warst ava – it's –'
'Prithee hold; I now understand it all perfectly well.'

Of these skelp is perhaps the most frequently used today. I am reminded of a night-watchman on a rickety Scottish pier that had been much neglected. When it was suggested to him that a steamer coming in with a strong side-wind and a big sea running might knock it to pieces, he remarked reflectively, 'Ay, ane guid skelp and we're awa'.' Then he settled down, unperturbed, to await what skelps might awa' with him. Happily the pier is still there, no doubt reinforced by now. But had the accident occurred on a rough day, the patient watchman and his charge would surely have been daddit, paikit, doofed, champit, broozled and jurmummled.

DRINK, THE

IT is common knowledge that 'the dickens' (for the devil) is as old as Shakespeare. 'I cannot tell what the dickens his name is', says Mistress Page. It is less well known how much of our modern slang is as old as Dickens. The catch phrase of a generation ago, 'Yes, I don't think' is at least as ancient as the Weller family, and a correspondent has just reminded me that some of the Air Force slang of today was in use a century ago. An example of these phrases, born far-away and long ago and yet surviving, is to be found in the usage of 'the drink' for the sea or a wide river. This occurs in *Martin Chuzzlewit*, Chapter 23. The passage runs as follows:

> An instance of neglect which caused the 'Capting' of the *Esau Slodge* to wish he might be sifted fine as flour and whittled small as chips, that if they didn't come off that there fixing right smart too, he'd spill 'em in the drink, whereby the Capting metaphorically said he'd throw them in the river.

It is a striking reminder of the continuity of slang. For the 'Capting' of the *Esau Slodge* was, of course, an American: did he bring the phrase from England or did we bring it back from America?

DULSE AND CARRAGEEN

THERE was a music-hall song which announced,

> As soon as I touched my sea-weed
> I knew it was going to be fine!

And fine it is with the words for sea-weed. What could sound sweeter than dulse? This, however, is not Latin at all but comes from Erse and Gaelic roots and means an edible sea-weed of our western coasts. 'Dulse and sandhoppers,' boiled in milk, the sandhoppers being small shrimps, was a favourite dish of Kintyre, while the sterner men of the north-east crunched dulse and shells raw. As an Aberdonian I have a fancy for studying the history of my county in that anonymous piece of pastoral-comical, 'Johnny Gibb of Gushetneuk or the Parish of Pyketillim'. When the parties went to take the waters (sea and spa) at Macduff, with 'the hardy dookers' sea-bathing and shiversomely relishing a distant view of dim Caithness hills across the Firth, Maister Saun'ers said of dulse to Jock Will: 'They're a vera halesome thing ta'en with the water.' He then exhibited and consumed raw 'a bunch of short, crisp dulse powdered about the root-ends with clusters of tiny shells of the mussel species'. As he crunched this prickly mess, he remarked that 'shells hae a poo'erful effeck o' the stammack'. Well, that is one way of setting things in motion. My forebears were hardy men.

Dulse sounds good enough. But what of Carrageen? Yet, when I found that described as 'sea-weed blanc-mange' I felt some loss of appetite. But apparently it is a Hebridean delicacy as well as a salve against chills.

DUST

Is it, or is it not, an ugly little word? From German dunst, vapour. Therefore we get the earth's vapour or particles small enough to make a mist. Nothing much there to strike sense or sensibility. Yet listen to C. E. Montague:

> Besides this hold on affection a word may well have about it the glamorous prestige of high adventures in great company. Think of all that the plain word 'dust' calls to mind. 'Then shall the dust return to the earth as it was.' 'Dust hath closed Helen's eye.' 'All follow this and come to dust.' 'The way to dusty death.'

One could multiply the list by many scores of times. All epitaphic poetry is murmurous with dusty answers – and why has Meredith's

> Ah, what a dusty answer gets the soul
> When hot for certainties in this our life!

become almost a cliché unless because of magic in the epithet? Consider again,

> The troubles of our proud and angry dust.

Certainly Housman was wise to write dust instead of flesh. (Incidentally 'raising a dust about nothing' is not a modern phrase: it is as old as Sir Thomas Browne.)

Dust is an instance, surely, of a word beautified by its associations. Assigned to doom, occurring in sepulchral passages, voicing the poignancies of the withered hope and the fallen leaf, linked with the way of all flesh and the fading of the flower, dust, so often on the lips of the lords of language, has been impelled to raise itself to a higher power. That is really Montague's point. Dust is no piece of music in itself, but it so often joins the great funeral marches that it becomes not only hallowed, but gracious too. The company of ideas is often bountiful to words of mean aspect.

DWINDLE

WE have lost the verb 'dwine' of which dwindle is a derivative. It is a pity that the parent went. 'To pine and dwine away' is expressive: yet dwindle has charm. Who can forget Millamant's protest that, if she accepts the terms of Mirabel, she will 'dwindle to a wife'?

> Firm sands: the little dulling edge of foam
> That browns and dwindles as the wave goes home.

I like this as well as any of Rupert Brooke's many affections. Why prefer that relic of the clean swirl which looks like the remnants of a glass of stout? Only because it goes with firm sands and the air that makes you feel renewed, born again, re-embodied, re-created. Odd that the word recreation, which should signify the mightiest miracle of all, has dwindled to the company of asphalt school-yards, dart-boards, and table-tennis. A dwindle indeed!

The Scots retain dwine.

> What though the flesh be bruckle
>   An' fiends be slee,
> The joys o' the solid earth we'll pree or they dwine.
> We'll lauch at deith, an' man, an' the fiend, aw three,
>   Afore we dee.

Thus Robert Garioch dismissing 'ghaisties'. Pree is prove.

Kipling has 'Pine away – dwine away', in 'The Bee Boy's Song'.

I am reminded that another loss of a similar kind is that of 'dwem'. A correspondent quotes from Fanny Eden's letters (1840), 'She just dwemmed away'. This, with its hint of dimness and dreaminess, I found even more effective than dwine.

EAGER

To be eager is now to be keen; to call a man eager is hardly to impute a vice. Yet eager was originally sour: it is our form of aigre. Chaucer used it of sharp medicine. In Daniel George's rich scrapbook *Now and Then* I read of a 'Hackett, William, a fam'd Imposter', who later 'played the Hypocrite, counterfeited Sanctity, was taken by some deluded weak People to be the Messiah, and was later hanged at Tyburn for Blasphemy and Treason. In his childhood at Oundle he was so Cruel, Eager, and Insolent that he bit off his Schoolmaster's Nose and eat it before his Face, as he pretended to embrace him out of Love'.

At Oundle nowadays, where, I trust, the Lesser Cannibalism is no longer practised by the eager young at the expense of the ushers and their nebs, eat in this passage would be spelled ate. But one often finds eat as a past tense in the classics. Eager has come up in the world, as Master Hackett went steadily down from form-room to gibbet.

ECDYSIAST

ECDYSIS is accepted 'scientese', of the Hellenic type, meaning riddance, putting off or away. It is applied especially to the snake's sloughing of its skin or the bird's moulting of its feathers. It was used, in discussing 'Man's Place in Nature' by Huxley (Thomas Henry) and has probably been used by his grandsons, Julian and Aldous. It is the sort of word which the second of these does not easily resist and possibly what is now to be said about ecdysiast will attract him to it the more. The tale is told by H. L. Mencken (*The American Language*, Supplement 1). He writes that after inventing 'bootician', not for a cobbler or even for a fashionable vendor of glossy riding-boots, but for a high-toned bootlegger, he hatched – such was the strain – no further neologisms till 1940. Then a lady called Miss Georgia Sothern wrote to him thus from a Fifth Avenue address:

> I am writing this letter to you because I have read and admired your book on the American language and believe that semantics can be of some help to me.
>
> It happens that I am a practitioner of the fine art of strip-teasing. Strip-teasing is a formal and rhythmic disrobing of the body in public. In recent years there has been a great deal of uninformed criticism levelled against my profession.
>
> Most of it is without foundation and arises because of the unfortunate word *strip-teasing,* which creates the wrong connotations in the mind of the public.
>
> I feel sure that if you could coin a new and more palatable word to describe this art, the objections to it would vanish and I and my colleagues would have easier going. I hope that the science of semantics can find time to help the verbally under-privileged members of my profession. Thank you.

Let us here pause to comment upon the fine flow of English prose achieved by this artiste and the classic touches of 'semantics' and 'connotation'. Let us further stop to note the modish use of the word 'under-privileged'. It has in our time become one of those greasy evasions wherewith social reformers discuss the poor, apparently believing that to call the poor poor is to insult them.

Mr. Mencken, like a good American gentleman, always answers the letters of working-girls politely. So he replied as follows:

> I need not tell you that I sympathize with you in your afflic-tion, and wish that I could help you. Unfortunately, no really persuasive new name suggests itself. It might be a good idea to relate strip-teasing in some way or other to the associated zoological phenomenon of molting. Thus the word moltician comes to mind, but it must be rejected because of its likeness to mortician.
>
> A resort to the scientific name for molting, which is ecdysis, produces both ecdysist and ecdysiast. There are suggestions in the names of some of the creatures which practise molting. The scientific name for the common crab is Callinectes hastastus, which produces callinectian. Again, there is a family of lizards called the Geckonidae, and their name produces gecko. Perhaps your advisers may be able to find other suggestions in this same general direction.

'Gecko' seems the perfect name for a new (and strip-teasing) Marx Brother, but naturally it did not satisfy Miss Sothern. She (or her press-agent) adopted 'ecdysiast' for those who strip to conquer and the word was wafted abroad, even into England. A Society of Ecdysiasts, Parade and Speciality Dancers, was formed and defended the practitioners of discreet uncovering against local bigotry and persecution by the police. One of their placard-slogans, used for demonstrations against the anti-moult wowsers and other forms of brutish authority, was 'They Got Me Covered and It Ain't Fair'.

So far Mr. Mencken had won laurels and roses all the way, but there were thorns ahead. The sharpest wound to Mr. Mencken's creative pride must have been that delivered by the Empress of all regular ecdysiasts, Miss Gypsy Rose Lee, who retorted sharply:

> 'Ecdysiast' he calls me! Why the man is an intellectual slob. He has been reading books. Dictionaries. We don't wear feathers and molt them off . . . What does he know about stripping?

And there we can leave the problems and pride of ecdysiasm, only wondering whether Miss Lee, who is, in addition, a respected authoress of detective stories, really meant to say 'slob' instead of 'snob'. Or has the ever-industrious and vigilant Mr. Mencken passed a misprint? Webster has 'slob, *n*. A clumsy, slovenly, or worthless person. *Vulgar*'. But could any slob be intellectual?

EMBRANGLEMENT

THE *O.E.D.* gives brangle as a form of wrangle. So embranglement should be, and sometimes is, a word for a fine tangle of argument and abuse. But, in the popular mind, the tangle can be material as well as mental. A correspondent tells me that it is a technical term of bell-ringers in certain areas. 'When a complicated piece of change-ringing is proceeding and one or another of the bells goes wrong, it is embranglement.' It is suggested that the jangle of the bells and the wrangle of the bellmen have both contributed to this usage. Country folk still use embranglement of any confusion or disaster. The same correspondent relates this of an incident in a Sussex wood. 'I was watching tree stumps being grubbed up with the aid of a traction engine. As sometimes happens on this sort of job the anchor holding the engine gave way and instead of the tree stump coming up, the engine lurched backward and rolled down a little bank, coming to rest at an angle of forty-five degrees or so with its fore-wheels cocked in the air. It looked rather a mess to me, but the engine-driver merely remarked that it was "a bloody fine embranglement".'

ENERGUMEN

To my astonishment I came across energumen in my morning paper and, though its general meaning was apparent, I had to consult the dictionary for the history and precise implication of this ugly but energetic word. It is a direct transliteration from the Greek. An energumen is not somebody ferociously working, but a person ferociously worked upon, chiefly by a devil or a frenzy. So an energumen is a demoniac enthusiast and raving devotee. The word, which was first employed in the beginning of the eighteenth century, may be rare, but the odious creature whom it depicts has been appallingly common in twentieth-century Europe.

EYELID, BATTING OF

HAVING satisfied Lord Wavell in the matter of brick-bats, as well as I could, I received a further (and most welcome) inquiry from Delhi, 'Why batting of eyelids?' Batting of this kind the dictionaries reasonably assert to be derived from the old falconer's term 'bat' and 'bate', which is found in Tudor writing. Bate then was chiefly a shortened form of abate and meant, most commonly, diminish. The hard-fisted master would bate a serving-man's reward. But there was another bate which meant flutter and here is our answer. *O.E.D.* quotes Latham's *Falconry* (1615): 'Batting, or to bat, is when a Hawke fluttereth with his wings either from the perch or the man's fist, striving, as it were, to fly away'. So the batted eyelid is a fluttered one. Bat in this case is the same as the bate known well to Shakespeare with his lore of field and fowler. Says Petruchio, after having starved his Shrew,

> Thus have I politicly begun my reign,
> And 'tis my hope to end successfully,
> My falcon now is sharp, and passing empty;

And, till she stoop, she must not be full-gorged,
For then she never looks upon her lure.
Another way I have to man my haggard,
To make her come, and know her keeper's call,
That is, to watch her, as we watch these kites
That bate, and beat, and will not be obedient.

Bating of breath is the other kind of bating and means diminishing. Now a cliché, the phrase is traced back by *O.E.D.* only as far as George Eliot.

To his dying day he bated his breath a little when he told the story.

But I fancy it must be older than that. Batting of eyelids the great dictionary traces to American usage of the 1880's. Once more it is America that has kept and returned to us an old and picturesque word taken, in this case, from the Tudor Sportsman's lexicon.

FALBALA

SOMEBODY once asked me whether a furbelow is called a furbelow because it has (or had) fur below. No. It is a light flounce and merely a corruption of falbala, and falbalas used to abound in eighteenth-century wardrobes. Cinderella, equipped for the ball, should have dazzled Prince Charming with falbalas as well as with her face and foot. Austin Dobson, so precise about this period, did not forget falbalas when he wrote 'Lines on a Fan' (painted by Vanloo) that had belonged to the Marquise de Pompadour:

See how they rise at the sight,
    Thronging the *Œil de Bœuf* through;
Courtiers as butterflies bright,
    Beauties that Fragonard drew,

> *Talon-rouge*, falbala, queue,
>   Cardinal, Duke, – to a man,
> Eager to sigh or to sue, –
>   This was the Pompadour's fan!

Hence, then, our furbelows.

FASCINATE

MOST words descend in value: fascinate has actually climbed
in reputation. It now refers mainly to attractive and radiantly
enchanting things. To call a woman fascinating would be wholly
complimentary. But once it would have been an accusation of
witchcraft and even a stake-and-faggot matter. Fascinate
originally meant to submit to the evil eye and exact writers,
like W. H. Hudson, would still so apply it. He used it, for
example, of the uncanny spell exercised on other animals and
on small birds by the stoat and weasel. Both of these can paralyse
the former, denying them power of flight, and leaving them
staggering and screaming in terror. The birds they allure to
come ever lower down the twigs, twittering in morbid ecstasy,
until they are within striking distance of the fierce, blood-lusty
fangs. In Hudson's *Hampshire Days* there is a wonderful picture
of this fascination in progress in a wood near Boldre, where he
watched a weasel chattering and spinning madly round the base
of a tree, while an audience of birds, 'chaffinches, wrens, robins,
dunnocks, ox-eyes, willow-wrens, and chiff-chaffs', fluttered
spell-bound ever closer to the crazy cunning of their foe. After
such fascination (Hudson calls it 'the good, old word') one
might be inclined to avoid it in social compliment, but the ancient
connection with the evil eye has been entirely forgotten.

FETTLE AND THRUNG

FETTLE survives mainly in the south of England as a noun, but rarely outside the phrase 'fine fettle'. This means condition. To fettle, more common in the north, is to make ready or to mend. A correspondent sends me the following: 'Cleg and fettle were verbs used in Northumberland meaning "to mend". I have never succeeded in finding any difference in meaning between the two words, but there is a difference. A Durham miner whom I questioned could do no better than "There's some things you clegs, and some you fettles". In Lancashire the engineering finishing-shops are called "fettling-shops", but "to fettle" seems never to mean "to finish" but rather "to repair".' He also sends me thrung, dialect past participle, equivalent to thronged, meaning packed, cluttered up. Thus a cobbler's shop might be thrung with shoes waiting to be fettled.

FIEND

A FIEND was originally any hated one, any enemy, any opposite to friend. (From old English, feon, to hate.) But, when enemy became a general term of common use, the fiend was particularized as the enemy of the soul, the Hated One of all good Christians, the Devil. Though Shakespeare and Milton used it freely and powerfully of things Satanic, it is an odd fact, as Henry Bradley pointed out in *The Making of English*, that there is no Fiend mentioned in the Bible or the Prayer-Book. Yet Bunyan used it of his Apollyon.

Shakespeare's texts, from *Titus Andronicus* onwards, screech of fiends, in fearsome plenty, often with the adjective foul or with the suffix 'of hell'. The implication was still that a fiendish fellow is a man Satanically possessed: the adjective fiendish, which has now, like devilish, been weakened to mean little more than nasty (e.g. 'fiendish weather we're having') is not in Shake-speare at all. It was an odd fancy of Blake's that he put in 'Infant Sorrow',

> My mother groan'd, my father wept,
> Into the dangerous world I leapt;
> Helpless, naked, piping loud
> Like a fiend hid in a cloud.

If fiend has been degraded in the current employment both of the noun and of the adjective fiendish, the Scots have played down this form of devil even further. Their word 'fient' now means little more than scarcely. 'Fient a chiel was there' suggests scarcely anybody present. The English might also say 'Devil a man to be seen'. But they would not say 'Fiend a fellow about'. The Scots, turning fiend to fient, would do so. They have reduced the foul fiend Flibbertigibbet, 'who squints the eye and makes the hare-lip, mildews the white wheat and hurts the poor creatures of the earth' – a Fiend indeed – to be the faint shadow of a mild expletive. What a fall for Lucifer! Mention of the Fiend and his devilish tricks brings to mind a superb remark made to me by a London bus-conductor. We were going along Oxford Street on a Saturday night and passed an enthusiastic young man who was walking along in the road brandishing a banner announcing the love of Jesus. He raucously called us all to salvation through a megaphone. The conductor looked with tolerant amusement at this emissary of heaven and said, 'He does it for devilment'.

FILEMOT AND MURREY

You can find the former with a Tudoresque variety of spellings. Filemot, philamot, philomot, phyllamort, feulamot show their orange-tawny hues down the centuries. For this is feuille morte, the sear, the yellow leaf, sometimes used as a noun, sometimes as an adjective for the ochred woods of autumn. It was in connection with ochre that I came across it recently in a poem by Mr. Andrew Young. This singer has been bemedalled for his good verses by the Royal Society of Literature and rightly so. Belonging to no clique and never pushing, he remains 'known to his own', in the old honorific phrase, but insufficiently quoted and seized by the anthologist. His particular genius is for the description of Britain's wintry scenes: he walks with a flashing vision among the vaporous hills and rain-swept fields, a natural laureate of the children of the mist. His Muse is as simple as Wordsworth's. He is a master of the monosyllable and as brief as lucid in his writing.

Of autumn he writes,

> The leaves hang on the boughs
> Filemot, ochreous
> Or fall, and strangely greet
> Green blades of winter wheat:
> The long buds of the beech
> Point where they cannot reach.

Browning talked in 'Sordello' of changing 'a murrey-coloured' robe for 'philamote' (surely the worst of the spellings). Murrey is mulberry-coloured and is not often used nowadays, except by those who are being deliberately 'period'. But Thomas Hardy wrote of 'murrey-coloured brick'. That is odd, for brick is more often filemot. Medieval writing is deep-dyed in murrey. 'And where be my gownes of scarlet, sanguyn, murreye, and blewes sadde and lighte?' The usage of sad for dark bears a trifle hardly on Oxford, which surely had not yet to weep over lost causes when Hoccleve wrote this in 1412. Dickens has something to say about mulberry as the vulgarian's choice. 'If ever there was a wolf in a mulberry suit, that 'ere Job Trotter's him.' I cannot remember him using murrey. It is queer that the shorter word should pass, while the longer lives on. Usually it is brevity that survives.

FINNIMBRUNS

READERS of *The Compleat Angler* will encounter Finnimbruns, but I am not aware that they will meet this finery anywhere else. *O.E.D.* cites no other example. Finnimbruns were the trinkets and fal-lals likely to be bought at old-time fairs. They were the stock-in-trade of Autolycus, 'riband, glass, pomander, brooch, table-book, ballad, knife, tape, glove, shoe-tie, bracelet, horn-ring', and

> Gloves as sweet as damask-roses,
> Masks for faces and for noses;
> Bugle-bracelet, necklace-amber,
> Perfume for a lady's chamber;
> Golden quoifs and stomachers
> For my lads to give their dears;
> Pins and poking-sticks of steel,
> What maids lack from head to heel.

Autolycus had a fair-sized cargo of finnimbruns and, though he talks of his pack and is usually staged with no more than that amount of small baggage, he really should arrive with a go-cart if he is to include

> lawn as white as driven snow

Quoif and stomachers (caps and 'ornamental coverings for the breast and upper abdomen'), if carried in profitable quantity, would alone occupy considerable space in any pack of finnimbruns.

How did this word happen? Plainly it began with finery; but of what are the 'imbruns' a corruption? The dictionary cites, as a parallel to this word, the coninbrum which a conundrum occasionally became; the origin of conundrum is itself a conundrum; it is probably a mixture of some Latin words. Imbrue meant to dye or stain before it was specially applied to blood (e.g. Ancient Pistol's 'shall we imbrue?') So finnimbruns might possibly be a slurred form of fine imbruings, i.e. of fine coloured stuffs and bright gew-gaws.

FLABBERGAST

The root 'flab' means puff: a flabellum or flabel is a fan and flaberkin is an Elizabethan adjective for puffy. Falstaff and Sir Toby could have been described as owners of flaberkin faces. Hence came the terms flabergudgions and flabergullions, for puffy, wheezy louts. So I take it that when a man has been flabbergasted he has had his breath taken from him, has been reduced to flabbing, and then has been struck aghast. In Scotland flabbergast has been used to mean boast or show off; I think it is far better employed to suggest overwhelming with surprise or dismay. I do not easily visualize a saucy coxcomb flabbergasting happily about the place, but I could happily see him flabbergasted by some just humiliation.

FLAYSOME

'Fair flaysome' was part of Joseph's vocabulary of denunciation in *Wuthering Heights*. I suppose flog-worthy would be an adequate translation, but flaysome is certainly the briefer and better word. The 'some' termination in adjectives is used with several senses: a mettlesome horse is one full of mettle, but a fearsome person is one causing fear, not one afraid. So, too, a gruesome figure is one causing shudders, not a shuddering person.

Why have the English kept the excellent adjective gruesome while abandoning grue as a verb? It remains alive and vivid in Scotland. 'The flesh is said to grue when a chilly sensation passes over the surface of the body, accompanied by the rising of the skin' (Jamieson). 'It gars me grue' must have often been the sentiment of a flaysome lad when caught and up for punishment. Recent discussions on the most efficacious punishment of young thugs might have been improved by the use of the simple old word flaysome.

FLUMMOX

OUR English words for overthrown, and especially for confounded and confused, both of the dialect and of the dictionary kind, are rich and numerous. We are mithered and moidered, niddered and nithered, according to locality (mithered, I am told, is Nottinghamese, and may mean cold) and so forth and so on. Flummox is of general and long-standing usage. The dictionaries attribute it to English dialect, but Mr. Weller thought otherwise. 'If your governor don't prove a alleybi, he'll be what the Italians call reg'larly flummoxed.' 'Ingenious Italy' again! Whence Mr. Weller derived this derivation I cannot imagine. To say that Fascism was finally flummoxed seems inadequate: but the word is good for general perplexity and wit's end agitation.

FORLORN

RARELY is so much meaning carried in the sound of two syllables as in the case of forlorn.

> Forlorn, the very word is like a bell
> To toll me back from thee –

Keats summed it up. The deep clang of the two 'ors', with the liquid to introduce the second syllable, makes the true music of desolation. Shakespeare is sparing with forlorn, but, when he does employ it, the sense of solitude and destitution is absolute, as in 'Forlorn and naked hermitage' or 'rogues forlorn, in short and musty straw'.

Beddoes, indulging 'the mighty thought of an old world', wrote:

> My waking is a Titan's dream
> Where a strange sun, long set, doth beam;
> Through the fern wilderness forlorn
> Glisten the giant hart's great horn
> And serpents vast with helméd brow.

Fern is here used in its antique form as an adjective signifying 'far away and long ago'. 'Fern wilderness forlorn' is a wonderful phrase for the kind of England that is symbolized in Avalon and Egdon Heath and Stonehenge, the world of Lear and his Fool and others cast out and couched in musty straw.

There is a strong pathos in the prefix 'for' when used to signify excess. Forlorn is the past participle passive of forlese, to lose. Forlese is more than lese: so forlorn is more than lorn, as forspent is more than spent and forswunk more than swinked or swunk, i.e. tired out. None the less, alliteratively used with lone, the brief lorn can be powerful too, as that 'lone, lorn creature' Mrs. Gummidge knew. Forlorn has such poignance in its word-music as almost to make poetry whenever it appears. So, too, has forsaken.

FRAMPLE AND FRANION

Why did frample or frampold for peevish or sour disappear? It is a vivid, effective word. Tudor and Jacobean drama has a number of frample jades. Mrs. Quickly said to Falstaff of Mrs. Ford, 'Alas, the sweet woman lives an ill life with him (Ford). He's a very jealousy man and she leads a very frampold life with him, good heart'. Here frampold seems to mean soured rather than sour. As a rule it suggests an actively pettish person and might be applied (and perhaps somewhere is so applied) to its dictionary neighbour, franion, a favourite of George Peele, the author of *The Old Wives' Tale*.

Franions were usually licentious creatures, male or female, but Peele also used the word for a wandering or idle person. His character Frolic, who is lost in a wood with Antic and Fantastic in the comedy mentioned above, claims to be 'frolic franion' and another character talks of 'the frolic'st franion among you', but elsewhere franions are not so innocently jocund and can be frample.

FRIBBLE

To fribble is to act feebly, to be frivolous in a petty, fiddling way. The verb is also used as a noun, a fribble being a trifler. Its close rhyme with dribble suggests to me a dotard far-gone in years and folly. Mr. Justice Shallow was the fribble at his most likeable. Captain Charles Morris, who wrote some genial, toss-pot rhymes in the eighteenth century, observes:

> I find too when I stint my glass
> And sit with sober air,
> I'm prosed by some dull, reasoning ass
> Who treads the path of care;
> Or, harder tax'd, I'm forced to bear
> Some coxcomb's fribbling strain,
> And that I think's a reason fair
> To fill my glass again.

To be prosed, as a passive verb, is good and should appeal to all who have been much pent in conventicles and lecture-rooms.

FRISGIG

THIS, for a silly young woman, is not an orthodox dictionary word, but well it might be, for it is an excellent example of the vividness of Lancashire dialect. It so nicely telescopes the friskiness and giggles of a lively, vapid miss that it really ought to be taken into common English usage. It reminds me of the Elizabethan giglot, which began by meaning a wanton and then, because of its closeness in sound to giggle, went on to suggest a party both more innocent and more infuriating, the tittering, romping wench. Giglot, as well as frisgig, merits renewal, especially in its later sense. For wantons we had, and have, so many words. Ben Jonson alone will yield a column or so, of which callet is the chilliest and fricatrice the most candid. There are fewer terms for the titterers. So what Lancashire thought on this subject yesterday, England might well think again tomorrow.

FRITINANCY

I OWE to a volume called *D.O.U.W.* (*Dictionary of Unusual Words*) a quotation from Eric Linklater's *Poet's Pub*,

> 'The most significant noise of earth is the singing of birds,' said the professor with determination.
> 'Fritinancy,' declared the young man beside the fire.
> 'What's that?' said the professor.
> 'I said fritinancy, which is the whimper of gnats and the buzzing of flies.'
> 'You're talking nonsense.'

Sir Thomas Browne has fritinience for twittering. The Linklater version of the word is even happier. Hamlet's 'Buzz, buzz' suggests that he too might have liked the term. His Osric was obviously a fritinancy boy and there is a plentiful fritinience in Rosencrantz and Guildenstern. The letters 'fri' appear to suit the mood and practice of tedious levity. For example, who more naturally prone to fritinancy than some old frizzed fribble, out on a frisk and meeting a fringillaceous fricatrice who happens to be free and soon gets fried.

(Fringillaceous means finch-like, fried is modern for tipsy, and fricatrice is Jonson's frank label for a 'broad').

He frets her with the frills and frippery of small talk and fritters his time away with the frivolous company of his sweet fritillary (butterfly). To which it may be replied that a friendly but frigid friar, of morals not easy friable, would, with the same initial letters, set a very different example. But, on the whole, the 'fri's' are light company. They may, at their worst, be lewd as well: in their most innocent and not least tiresome form, they are sure to be fritinant.

FROLIC

FROLIC is almost always a noun or a verb to us, as it was to Thomas Woodcock who wrote of academic life and its oddities in the later seventeenth century.

> Of Dr. Thomas Goodwin, when ffelow of Catharine Hall. – He was somewhat whimsycall, in a frolick pist once in old Mr. Lothian's pocket (this I suppose was before his trouble of conscience and conversion made him serious). . . . He prayed with his hatt on and sitting. Undoubtedly a man of whim.

It is perhaps as well that the donnish sense of a frolic has since altered. But it is a pity that the same century's use of frolic as an adjective has virtually disappeared. Milton's 'frolic wind that breathes the spring' is, of course, familiar. Herrick found wine to be both 'frolick' and 'frantick'. 'Come shake the frolic cocktail on the ice' would ring well today. There are occasions, no doubt, when frantic would be more accurately applied to that form of refreshment.

FRORE

THE Miltonic past participle of freeze hardly survives, though it was an occasional usage of most poets up till 1900. Indeed, the rather ugly and Latinate 'gelid' has had more life in our poetry. Frore has the right crisp sound for a nipping and eager air and brings to mind a day of black frost when the miry fields are turned to metal underfoot. Churchill made 'Frore January, leader of the year'. Swinburne used it well:

> Full-charged with old-world wonders,
> From dark Tintagel thunders
> A note that smites and sunders
> The hard, frore fields of air.

Although the poem is about autumn, the last line has as much of essential winter in it as any Meredithian line about 'a wind with fangs'. The fliers were later to discover the whole and horrible truth about 'hard, frore fields of air'.

Sir John Squire in his poem on 'Rivers' proclaimed that the aged Brahmapootra, beyond the white Himalayas,

> Passes many a lamassery
> On rocks forlorn and frore.

Douglas Young, the Scottish Nationalist champion and excellent scholar of Hellenic, Gaelic, and other tongues, comments thus, among his many pleasing verses, upon Edinburgh's Calton Hill,

> A fine fantasy of the Whig literati
> To build a modern Athens in our frore islands,
> Those elegant oligarchs of the Regency period,
> Philhellenic nabobs and the Scots nobility.

FRUITION AND INCHOATE

FRUITION, rightly used, is a delightful word. But how often is it so employed? Even the most august authors may be daily discovered confusing it with fruit and maturity. Leader-writers, even in *The Times*, hold forth about plans 'coming to fruition'. The word, in fact, has nothing to do with fruit, but is derived from the Latin 'fruor', I enjoy, and means enjoyment. The meaning of ripeness, says the *O.E.D.* firmly, 'is not countenanced by dictionaries in this country, nor by Webster'. Fruition was rightly and exquisitely used by Marlowe.

> That perfect bliss and sole felicity,
> The sweet fruition of an earthly crown.

Charles Lamb in his rhymed 'Farewell to Tobacco' moaned, correctly as well as pathetically, that he had lost his seat among the 'blest Tobacco Boys'.

> Where, though I, by sour physician,
> Am debarr'd the full fruition
> Of thy favours, I may catch
> Some collateral sweets, and snatch
> Sidelong odours, that give life
> Like glances from a neighbour's wife;

We owe it to Marlowe and to Lamb to save fruition from the hackneyed misuse to which modern ignorance and carelessness have brought it.

Inchoate provides an exact parallel of verbal confusion and abuse of meaning. In this case its trouble is caused by a careless confusion with 'chaos'. The altered position of the vowels does not deter people from this muddle and politicians will announce that 'The Government's plans have now become utterly inchoate' which is to say that a boy has become a baby. 'Inchoate' is a good, resounding Latin word meaning beginning or just begun and was properly used by the judicious Hooker when he contrasted the inchoation of spiritual grace with its consummation.

FUBSY

'FAT and fubsy Fellows of Colleges' hardly exist nowadays. Nor does fubsy, which used to mean squat and stout. The modern don is usually a lean young man. Instead of brimming with port and erudition, he avoids the former and conceals the latter, walking the quadrangle with a sad stoop, as it were a perambulant question-mark, dubiety on stilts. Our lean years have not made Oxford or Cambridge richer in 'fubs', which is the noun for fubsy folk – and a good noun too. The verb 'fub' means, or meant, cheat, being a corruption of fob. In the north of England pubble is a dialect word for fubsy animals. 'At Michaelmas a pubble goose – at Kersmas, standin' pie.' Sir Thomas More used fobby for fubsy. 'Glotony maketh the body fat and fobby.' But fubsy is the obvious term here. It almost lards the page as one writes it, as sweating Falstaff larded the earth below him. But Falstaff, though a fubber-off of landladies, was not fubsy himself. He outranged the term altogether. Fubsy is for small, plump men, not for adiposity's masterpiece.

FUSCOUS

PURE Latin, except for the intruding 'o', meaning dark and sombre. It is strange that so expressive a word should have been limited mainly to the technical lingo of Natural History. Weather and hill-scenery in rain often strike me as fuscous, but they are never called so. I was reminded of fuscosity by discovering it in a very queer passage written by Alfred Tennyson at the age of fourteen. The precocious boy found relief from the glooms and storms of his father's Rectory by writing a play in verse called *The Devil and the Lady*. The character Magus on finding the Devil disguised as a woman cries,

> How now, my Hellish Minister, dark child
> Of Bottomless Hades: what rude waggery,
> What jejune, undigested joke is this,

To quilt thy fuscous haunches with the flounced
Frilled, finical delicacy of female dress?
Hast thou dared to girdle thy brown sides
And prop thy monstrous vertebrae with stays?
Speak out, thou petticoated solecism,
Thou hairy trifler.

There's vocabulary for you! The deeply and widely read boy
had the trick of it early. Fuscous haunches powerfully suggest
decaying venison to me. But who, if asked to name the author of,

And prop thy monstrous vertebrae with stays

would have said Tennyson?

GALAXY

A GALAXY is Greek for a spill of milk, and the Milky Way, as
Chaucer pointed out, is indeed a galaxy. But galaxies soon became
compact of human radiance and 'star' company. While reading
with pleasure the Cheltenham Guide of 1826, a most eloquent
conductor to the Fourth Georgian pleasures of that spa, I found
the Assembly Rooms to be galactic indeed.

> The ball-room, with scarcely the intermission of a month
> throughout the year, presents, on the evenings allotted to
> the assemblies, a scene of the most refined amusement and
> a delight of which every heart must be susceptible in con-
> templating the galaxy of beauty, shedding its soft and
> bewildering radiance over all.

Admission to the refined amusement of a Cheltonian galaxy
(1826) was not easily come by. Tests of fitness included scrutiny
of career, wardrobe, and footwear. You had to get past the
Master of the Ceremonies, who was a considerable dictator of
the decencies. For instance, 'no clerk, hired or otherwise in this
town or neighbourhood; no person concerned in retail trade;
no theatrical or other public performer' could be admitted.

There was a further rigorous ban on gentlemen in boots or half-boots except officers in uniform. And the sporting of 'undress trousers or coloured pantaloons' absolutely ruled out the would-be galactician.

The Guide makes it perfectly plain that outsiders would stay outside. 'The style and well-regulated order of society in Cheltenham is not its slightest recommendation: in so numerous a concourse of visitors it is the singular good fortune and justly proud boast of our town that among its patrons are included the first personages in the country, in station, affluence, and respectability, while no unprivileged footstep is suffered to intrude upon the circle of their pleasures.'

This galaxy in the most polite end of Gloucestershire seems, in short, to have had something in common with a fortress. It was certainly no place for those unprivileged in purse and status or rudely gay in their choice of pantaloons.

GALINGALE AND GALLIMAUFRY

GOING back to boyhood's favourites, some of the more golden reaches of Tennysonian iambic, I ran into galingale. For Tennyson it decorated the land of the Lotos-eaters.

> Border'd with palm and many a winding vale,
> And meadow, set with slender galingale.

The galingale, which to us may suggest some 'period' boskage among which a lady in a farthingale listened to a nightingale, is an Eastern aromatic root. The Elizabethan men, so avid of all spices, used it carnally for cooking, but Tennyson, more loftily, for atmosphere. Remaking its acquaintance led to some dictionary-loitering in which I was reminded of the jovial and fine-sounding mixture of words beginning with 'gal'. Here is a question for a General Knowledge Paper. Distinguish between, Galingale, Galipot, Galligaskin, Gallimaufry, and Gallowglass. Also between Galliard and Galliass.

One answer, at least, must be given to these previous queries.

A good-sounding medley or hodge-podge is a gallimaufry and one that came easily to the roaring play-boys and pamphleteers of Tudor London. Nashe, commenting on the stage of his time ('Our players are not as the players beyond sea, a sort of squirting bawdy comedians') goes on to complain that the ancient Romans always over-praised and over-wrote their native talent, 'thinking scorn to any but domestic examples of their own home-bred actors, scholars, and champions: and them they would extol to the third and fourth generation: cobblers, tinkers, fencers, none escaped them, but they mingled their all in one gallimaufry of glory'. This last attractively alliterative phrase itself sums up the temper and achievements of Nashe's aspiring, brilliant, and cantankerous world, a gallimaufry of galliards (men of spirit and fashion). Incidentally, was ever a tedious stream of third-rate smut so brilliantly punished in a phrase as by 'a sort of squirting, bawdy comedians'? The origin of the word gallimaufry is unknown.

GALLOW

Is gallow, to frighten, derived from the terror associated with the gallows? The dictionary looks back to an old English word meaning alarm, which created the verb to gally for to scare. ('Now dialect and in the whale fishery.') I cannot see why this gally should have fathered the gallow used by Kent in the Storm Scene in *King Lear*.

> The wrathful skies
> Gallow the very wanderers of the dark
> And make them keep their caves.

Why should the shorter gally make the longer gallows? I suspect that the fear inspired by the gibbet and its burden of flesh – a fairly common spectacle in Tudor times – was the source of gallow as a transitive verb. Scare-crow has been gally-crow in its time and there again the fantastic and fearsome figure in the field might plainly be derived from the gibbeted corpse.

The hangman's gallows began as 'a gallow', but the plural prevailed. Was the word ever better used with sinister suggestion than in Gonzalo's remark concerning the Boatswain in *The Tempest*, 'His complexion is perfect gallows!' That suits so well the waxy pallor of those gallow-birds who stand in the Chamber of Horrors at Madame Tussaud's.

Then the double plural gallowses came into the vernacular. Said the humane First Gaoler in *Cymbeline* 'O there were desolation of gaolers and gallowses! I speak against my present profit.' From these gallowses, the merciless suspenders of a corpse, came descent to the blameless utility of the haberdashers' suspenders and braces. Gallus or galluses is, I suppose, dismissible as dialect. But it is still commonly used in certain parts of the country to signify the safeguard of the trousered man.

GECK, GIRN, AND GOWL

THE fate of James Hogg's 'Bonnie Kilmeny' does not greatly stir me. But the Ettrick Shepherd had the vocabulary of his time and place and it is a good one. The singer of Birniebouzle and Balmaquhapple was certain to have a lingo with the Border wind in it and the smell of neeps after rain. (Surely that exquisite aroma is essential Scotland: it has the sharp tang of so many Scottish things, of whisky, especially, and smoked fish, of pine-woods and peat.)

Hogg in the aforesaid 'Bonnie Kilmeny' has one passage containing the three words geck, girn, and gowl, which make a sombre and a striking trinity.

> He gowled at the carle and chased him away
>   To feed with the deer on the mountain gray.
> He gowled at the carle and he gecked at Heaven.

Previously the carle had 'girned amain'.

If a carle (or churl) girned amain at me, I should certainly deem it fair to geck and gowl, as well as girn, back at him. Taking them in order, geck, either as a verb for 'to mock' or as a noun for a person mocked, is by no means Scottish only. Cries Malvolio,

> Why have you suffered me to be imprisoned,
> Kept in a dark house, visited by the priest,
> And made the most notorious geck and gull
> That e'er invention played on?

The phrase 'geck and scorn' also appears in *Cymbeline*. Girn is supposed to be a mistaken form of grin. It means to show the teeth at, snarl, and generally grizzle and rail. Gowl is more vociferous and is a picturesque form of howl. One might put it this way: if you unfairly geck a fellow-creature, he first girns at you and then, if nothing happens, gowls.

GINGERLY AND JAUNTY

GINGERLY has nothing to do with ginger. The latter word I found mysteriously linked with Queen Guinevere in a book called *Phrases and Names* by Trench Johnson. The idea was that the royal lady had red hair and so Guinevere was really a synonym for Carrots or for ginger-head. This is surely nonsense. Other authorities link Guinevere with the Celtic gwen meaning white. In that case she is in the Gwendolen class. Eric Partridge suggests White Wave as the meaning of the name. In any case I could never think of Miss Ginger Rogers as a Guinevere. Ginger is 'the rhyzome of the tropical plant Zingiber Officinale'. Tropical plant is more suitable than White Wave for young ladies called Ginger.

Returning to gingerly, we can claim that the word, although more quaint than beautiful, has a lordly origin. Its parent appears to be the old French *gentior*, a comparative of *gent*, nice. We think now of walking gingerly or handling things in a gingerly way, i.e. cautiously, but people could look gingerly too in Tudor or Stuart times. In a play of Webster's it is said of a lady: 'Oh, she looks so sugredly, so simperingly, so gingerly, so amorously ... she's such an intycing she-witch.' That fierce Puritan Stubbes, sworn foe of all things nice or naughty, denounced 'the dancing minions that minse it ful gingerly'. A maid 'looking gingerly' seems to have been what is vulgarly known as 'hot stuff', and of course a confusion between gingerly and ginger (*gentior* and Zingiber) soon became inevitable. It was easy to suppose that one picked a thing up gingerly because it was hot.

Jaunty also owed its origin to the French gent or gentil and meant well-bred, poised, easy of manner. Then the easiness became too easy and was associated with carelessness and impudence. By the beginning of the nineteenth century a slattern could be jaunty, which would have seemed absurd in the seventeenth and eighteenth when fashion was described as 'ganty' or 'jauntee'.

> A bag-wig of a jauntee air
> Tricked up with all a barber's care.

But a jaunty manner today means a pert insolence rather than a modest grace.

Jaunt, as a trip, which seems to have an independent origin and was sometimes spelt Jaunce, went the other way and climbed. It began as a troublesome journey and became a light or gay one, made in pursuit of pleasure. Twice Juliet's Nurse speaks of a jaunt as sore labour:

> Fie, how my bones ache! What a jaunt have I had she cries
> in Capulet's garden;

and again:

> Beshrew your heart for sending me about
> To catch my death with jaunting up and down.

How many know that 'to catch your death' is Shakespearean English? Here it seems to refer to the head-ache and bone-ache caused by exertion and not to the catarrh of a common cold.

GLEED AND SMEECH

A WORCESTERSHIRE man has asked me whether a 'gleedy fire', for one that burns low, to hot, red embers, is known outside the Midlands. That I cannot answer, but gleed is Chaucerian English for a glowing coal and burns brightly in our language throughout the seventeenth century. There are metaphorical gleeds in Bunyan, 'sweet and warm gleeds of that promise'.

Gleed as an adjective reminds one of the Scottish 'agley'. It means crooked, especially of the eyes. That is mainly a Scottish use; north of the Tweed, gait as well as aspect could be gleed. I like gleed better as a live coal than as a squinting man. For ancient forms of crookedness there is kim-kam. I can more easily think of gleeds in the hearth than of a gleed fellow as a twister. This reminds me that in England's Middle and West a gleedy fire, having lost its gleam, might turn smeechy. Smeech or smech for smoke is an abiding word and I have heard of folk being warned to see that an oil lamp does not suddenly start smeeching.

GOOSE

THE common theatrical phrase 'Get the Bird' must come, I suppose, from the noise of hissing; and an angry goose hisses. There is thus the implication, consoling for the victim of 'a bird', that the audience are geese not to appreciate his points. Nowadays one hears it said that 'so and so got a screaming bird'. But this kind of reception is wrongly so named. It was once a hiss; it is now, as a rule, not a scream but a melancholy moan.

At any rate to goose was Victorian English for hiss in the showman's world. When poor Jupe, in *Hard Times*, was doing feebly in Sleary's Circus-ring, Mr. E. W. B. Childers, 'so justly famous for his daring vaulting act as the Wild Huntsman of the North American Prairies', said of the poor wretch, 'He was goosed last night, he was goosed the night before, he was goosed today. He has lately got into the way of being always goosed. And he can't stand it.'

Mr. Gradgrind inquired about this Goosing, 'forcing the word out of himself with great solemnity and reluctance'. Mr. Childers replied that poor Jupe's limbs were turning stiff, but that he had still had points as a Cackler, i.e. talker. Jupe had been 'missing his tips' and loose in his ponging (short in his leaps and bad in his tumbling). Hence the goose-hiss and the bitter chagrin of Jupe. 'It cut that man deeper', concluded E. W. B. Childers, 'to know that his daughter knew of his being goosed than to go through with it.'

I never hear this verb of menace used today. But as a first-nighter I hear, on dismal occasions, the groan from aloft which has taken its place. It resembles no utterance of any bird, save possibly the last of the owl's four syllables. But 'get the bird' seems to be well fixed now as a description of this misery.

GRIPPLE AND SNUDGE

GRIPPLE, as an adjective for mean or stingy, is good. Spencer's use of it ('Gripple covetyse') lived, rather scarcely, until William Watson. I came across it in a song by Thomas Thompson in his play *The English Rogue* (1688):

> If we love, 'tis enough,
> Hang political stuff!

That is the theme and it is sustained with a lofty derision of the arts and with ample praise of the epicurean.

> Come let us frolic, and call for our tipple,
> Our pockets we'll empty and our veins we will fill,
> For sack we'll not lack, nor will we be gripple,
> But carouse in despite of the two-toppèd hill.

Chorus:
> Parnassus shall pass us,
> Nor will we inquire
> For the font of the Muses;
> 'Tis sack we desire.

The two-toppèd hill is Parnassus. Thompson was as much devoted to sack as Falstaff himself. He would banish the Rhenish and the English Metheglin (Mead) in favour of 'brave Spanish liquor'. He says nothing of champagne which was now beginning to bubble up in English life and letters. Etherege was singing its merits at just that time. He observed that sparkling champagne

> Quickly recovers
> Poor languishing lovers.

Etherege, like most of his contemporary playboys and singers, was no friend of the gripple virtues.

The Scots form of gripple is nippit, which is also good. Hugh Haliburton, of *Horace in Homespun*, sings of his nippit neighbours in the Ochill farms.

An alternation to gripple is snudge. It is either a noun, meaning miser, or a verb, meaning to hoard or grudge. Nashe has a fine passage for word-fanciers in his 'Lenten Stuffe'. In it we meet snudgery. Here is the piece:

> Those gray-beard huddle-duddles and crusty cum-twangs were strooke with such stinging remorse of their miserable euclionisme and snudgery that hee was not yet cold in his grave but they challenged him to be borne amongst them.

This is great verbal battery, no doubt. But did even his immediate readers understand it all – without research and consultation?

Euclionism is another word for stinginess based on the character of Euclio, a miser in a comedy of Plautus. Huddle-duddles and cum-twangs are presumably various forms of nasty old men. Nashe was never snudge with such inventions.

GRUNTLE

DISGRUNTLE, meaning to disgust, to set a-moaning and a-groaning, is no particular friend of mine. But it is older than most people think and has dictionary status. It is sometimes mentioned as one of the words which is a negative without a positive. As a matter of fact gruntle is known as a verb signifying continuous grunting or lamentation. Undoubtedly, however, 'disgruntled' has thriven on its own suitability of sound: it does very well suggest a disgusted person who is emitting something between a sustained grunt and an angry grumble.

Gruntle, sometimes spelled gruntile, is in Scots a snout, so that disgruntled might mean one whose nose has been put out of joint. I came across gruntle in its snout-sense in a striking little poem by Albert Mackie. The subject is the Mole-catcher and his row of victims. Mackie describes the 'Mowdie-man' striding by like the Angel of Death.

> Alang his pad (path) the mowdie-worps
> Like sma' Assyrians lie.

What, after all, Mackie asks, are these poor, withered hosts?

> Sma' black tramorts wi' gruntles grey,
> Sma' weak weemin's han's,
> Sma' bead-eeen that wid touch 'ilk hert,
> Binnae the mowdie-man's.

Tramorts are corpses; binnae, but not or except.

To anyone who has ever been driven to trapping moles in order to save a lawn, the picture is strangely disturbing. How one remembers those 'gruntles grey' and the little feminine hands!

Returning to disgruntled, I would express a preference for 'disjaskit'. This is more common in Scotland than in England and it is applied, as tumble-down, to a house as well as to the hopes and tempers of men and women.

GUMPTION

Do not tell me that Finance and Industry have no poetry. Consider this from a financial prospectus concerning 5 per cent Pref. Cum., etc. Were I an investor in the Company concerned, I would be an owner and vendor of 'Masticon, Gumption, and

Multicore Solder'. 'Almost singing themselves they run.' Immediately and songfully I see the Company's chairman as

A Masticon, Gumption, and Multicore Solderman,
Member of Parliament, J.P. and Alderman.

What exactly is gumption, when it is not shrewdness, commonsense and the presence of gorm? Presumably there must be a quality of gorm, if stupid people can be gormless. (Vernon Bartlett wrote to me from some blue void in far-off seas to remind me that the Russian for stupid sounds like 'gloopy', which would be a perfect word, half loopy, half goofy, for our own lackers of gorm, nous, and gumption.) But let us return to Gumption, in this case (see Prospectus) a Smooth Paste Cleanser. But it is also (see Dictionary) the art of preparing colours. It is odd that a nation, not wildly aesthetic in taste, should have taken from the paint-box its synonym for sturdy common sense and for absence of 'gloopiness'.

HABERDASHER

THE origin of this handsome Elizabethan fellow is obscure. He was at first a hatter and only later on became the general draper, the dealer in laces and ribbons and petty clothing of all kind. Autolycus, a strolling-haberdasher to us, was not such to Shakespeare, who mentions the word but once, when he alludes (*Henry VIII*, V. 3) to a haberdasher's wife in a crowd with a 'Pinkt porringer on her head'. The Tudor gallant would pay high for his lady's haberdashery, forty shillings or more, an enormous sum in those days. But for that he expected an exclusive model, 'the impression extant but that morning', as Dekker puts it in an amusing passage in *The Gull's Horne-Booke*. He is explaining the art of behaving badly in a theatre and has pointed out that the most offensive thing to do is to leave your seat (at the side of the stage) as noisily as possible during the play and 'draw what troop you can from the stage after you'. If you do not move then 'my counsel is that you turn plain ape. Take up a rush, and tickle the earnest ears of your fellow gallants, to make other fools fall a-laughing; mew at passionate speeches; blare at merry; find fault with the music; whew at the children's action; whistle at the songs; and, above all, curse the sharers, that whereas the same day you had bestowed forty shillings on an embroidered felt and feather, Scotch fashion, for your mistress in the court, or your punk in the city, within two hours after you encounter with the very same block on the stage, when the haberdasher swore to you the impression was extant but that morning'. (The sharers would now be called 'the management.')

The hatter, no longer monopolizing the great name of haberdasher, still uses block, felt, and feather and even, for sporting modes, 'Scotch fashion' as well as French.

HALIBUT

A BUT or butt is a flat fish and a halibut is a holy example of the species. (I am reminded of the Butt and Oyster Inn at Pin Mill on the Ipswich River.) I have always liked the sound of a halibut (leaving flavour aside for the moment). The name is well up to the size of this largest of our flounders. Cowper even broke into verse in praise of halibut, after feasting well thereon during an April day of 1784. He praised the tenacity which carried the halibut from its 'minikin and embryo state' to outlive tempests,

> grazing at large in meadows submarine.

The poet proceeded to wish good luck to all pursuers of the halibut 'in the billowy gulph' and ended with a piece of astonishing conceit,

> Thy lot thy brethren of the slimy fin
> Would envy, could they know that thou wast doom'd
> To feed a bard and to be prais'd in verse.

The notion of fish pining to become the raw material of indifferent, or even of the best, poetry and to serve as the sustenance of human authorship is one which is beyond comment.

Oddly enough this rhyme of Cowper's evoked from Saintsbury not a curse on his bad verses but an outburst on his bad taste. To me halibut seems, after turbot, one of the better flatfish and a grilled halibut steak would appeal to me much as it once did to Cowper. But hark to the melody of Saintsbury baying against halibut!

> Cowper's subjects were occasionally inadequate; he was right to be fond of fish, but a poet who can celebrate halibut must lack some of that discrimination which should be a characteristic of the poetical character. In the eighteenth century dwellers inland had to take what they could get in the way of what the French delightfully call *marée* – a term which surrounds the actual fish with the sound and the sight and the smell of the sea. But when there are not only salmon and trout, turbot and brill, John Dory and mullet, but whiting and whitebait and sole and herring and flounders and sprats – nay even plaice and bass and skate and gurnet and other worthy if second-rate fish – to eat and to celebrate in verse a thing which is at best a cooked cotton counterpane is shocking.

Well, Saintsbury can have his brill, a fish that once became endemic in the restaurant cars of British railway trains and was served tepid with a dash of pink glue to emphasize its insipidity. Halibut, my halibut, must you be less than the whiting, the skate, and the brill? Saintsbury could not even leave halibut to sink under his own broadside. He had to bring up other violence.

> It is comforting to remember that Peacock, who seldom goes wrong on such points, has solemnly, through the competent and canonical mouth of Dr. Opimian in *Gryll Grange*, excommunicated this abominable Brobdingnagian dab.

But both Peacock and Saintsbury lived in an age of civilized feeding. We who have queued for a half-thawed slab of Icelandic cod have touched the lowest depths of fishmongery. To us a halibut is a noble article and also, I suggest, a fine, imposing title for the hallowed giant of all the demersal species.

HEBETUDE

HEBETUDE, both meaning by classical derivation and suggesting with its sound a dull heaviness and crass stupidity, is now rare. It was used by A. E. Housman in his dismissal of inferior Latinists and Housman was never the kind of scholar to display nervous hesitation in the criticism of his fellow-classics. He brought 'hebetude' crashing down upon their skulls as though it were a lexicon itself. I regret its rarity, for it has a fine, ponderous expressiveness. Another classical rarity, concinnity, might well be restored to common use along with hebetude. It happens to be almost its opposite in meaning, since it signifies the skilful harmonizing of parts in thought and speech and so implies elegance of style. The first Lord Birkenhead, himself a relentless hammer of all hebetude, employed concinnity as a word and often displayed that quality in his quick forging of a sharp and shining phrase.

HEN

NOT long ago I wrote an article on the then (and perhaps still) prevalent and friendly habit of calling unknown people 'ducks', and of saying 'love' at first sight, e.g. 'Hold tight, love' or 'Here's your change, ducks', as shouted by the London bus-conductress to her passengers, male or female. I suggested that the men might at least be 'drakey, dear' instead of being lumped with the ducks. It was then pointed out to me, by a correspondent in Glasgow, that on the public transport vehicles of that city I would find myself addressed as Hen. Is this yet another reference to human beings as the poultry of the Welfare State? Or is it a corruption and abbreviation of hinny, which is itself a corruption of honey? Have the hinnies of the Northern English counties crossed the border and become the hens of Glasgow?

The equalitarian practices of our time have made a queer muddle of our forms of greeting. A barrow-boy may greet my wife with a 'Nahce bananas, lidy!' which is almost reverent, or he may cry 'Nahce bananas, ducks!' which is not. Me he will probably call 'Guv' and to be a Governor is to be an Excellency; this is high compliment indeed. Recently I was called Governor, when my fare was demanded, and Mate, when it was paid. The good lady who kept my 'local' fifteen years ago used to greet her selected customers of the Saloon Bar with 'Good evening, Squire'. To be in the squirearchy does not, in fact, imply such high social station as a Governorship, but Governor did fall a trifle when it was the fashion for schoolboys to call their fathers by this name, a habit which *O.E.D.* marks as beginning in 1827.

Another form which the barrow-boy may use to me is 'cock'. Well, that is better than the 'hen' which I am promised in Glasgow.

Darling, as used between those who hardly know each other and almost certainly dislike each other, is used in England mainly by Bohemians and 'theatrical parties'. But I am told of a 'daily help' who, on leaving her employer, always says, 'Ta-ta, madam, darling'. Perhaps my bus-conductress will soon be greeting me with a 'Hold tight, Squire Ducks'. Or 'Hold Very Tight'. Why, I wonder, do the London Transport workers love to be so emphatic? I would have thought that 'Hold Tight' was a sufficient warning of a jerky start to come, but the usual form is 'Hold Very Tight There'. As it is the habit to slur the first word and stress what follows, I am continually hearing 'Very tight, there' shouted at passengers who seem to be perfectly sober.

HEYDEGUISE

MOST of our dances are aliens. A fine romantic rout they are, bergamask and lavolta, rigadoon and saraband, to mention but a few. But our native frisks can look imposing too. What of heydeguise, or heydeguy, spelt alternatively with hay for hey, reminding us of Marlowe's antic hay?

> By wells and rills in meadows green
>   We nightly dance our heydeguise
> And to our fairy king and queen
>   We chant our moonlight harmonies.

This comes from an anonymous seventeenth-century dithyramb on 'Robin Goodfellow', which also contains the nice verb 'to whirry', a compound of whirl and hurry.

> More swift than wind away I go
>   O'er hedge and lands,
>   Through pools and ponds
> I whirry, laughing 'Ho, ho, ho'.

Heydeguisers probably whirried a good deal in the practice of their ho-de-ho sport. Drayton, too, knew the antic.

> While some the ring of bells and some the bagpipe ply,
> Dance many a merry round and many a heydeguy.

Folk dances are plainly one of the most strenuous forms of exercise and those who have endured 'a running set' are athletes indeed. Drayton's allusion to 'many a heydeguy' suggests that a singleton of this kind might have been easy going, but Puck or Robin Goodfellow on the 'whirry' would not have been satisfied with anything merely gentle or static.

HIGH-MINDED

IN contrast with the many words that have lost prestige, high-minded is one that has climbed the ladder of estimation. To the translators of the Bible a high mind was much the same as a stiff neck: it went with vanity, pride, and sinful ambition. The high-minded man was to the translators of the Authorized Version what Shakespeare would have called orgulous. ('The princes orgulous, their high blood chafed.') Coverdale had 'Lord, I am not high-minded, I have no proude lokes.' A correspondent has reminded me of the form of Prayer with Thanksgiving in the old Prayer Book. 'Almighty God . . . Who didst in a most extra-ordinary and wonderful manner disappoint and overthrow the wicked designs of those traitorous, heady, and high-minded men . . .' Nowadays we are more respectful to ideas of height whether in temper, spirit, or mind. High-minded, though it may to some convey a notion of priggishness, is, in general, praise unqualified. We shall never now say of Adolf Hitler in our history books that he was a high-minded man. Yet, in the English of the sixteenth century, he was just that.

HIRPLE AND HOAST

HIRPLE, to limp, is a vivid word for slow and painful motion, known in the North of England. It is common in Scots and occurs in Burns's ballad 'What can a Young Lassie do wi' an auld man?' Little indeed, if it be true that:

> He's always compleenin' frae mornin' to e'ening,
> He hoasts and he hirples the weary day lang;
> Hey's doylt and he's dozin', his bluid it is frozen,
> O dreary's the night wi' a crazy auld man!

(Doylt means scant-witted.) Hoast, for cough, is a vivid piece of Scots. Perhaps the English 'hawk' is more accurate for the early-morning activities of the cigarette-smoker; hoasting I fancy to be a less aggressive business, an anxious, wheezy, strained affair. It reminds me of Max Miller, that unbiddable Cockney comedian of the bright and roving eye, as he taps his chest and says, 'Tight, lady. Just there. Tight.' I cannot spell the Cockney Tight. It is neither tate nor toit. But it has the whole of February's bronchial horror in it when Max Miller hoasts it out.

The two verbs for limp and cough are also associated by Burns in the 'Epistle to James Smith':

> The magic wand then let us wield;
> For, ance that five-an-forty's speel'd,
> See crazy, weary, joyless Eild,
>   Wi' wrinkled face,
> Comes hoastin', hirplin', ow're the field
>   Wi' creepin' pace.

Eild, the Southron need hardly be told, is old age. The 'magic wand' is pleasure which makes the hours dance.

Returning to Hirple, I am reminded that it can have a sombre beauty as well as sounding its note of awkwardness and pain. It occurs beautifully in Burns's lines 'On the Birth of a Posthumous Child':

> November hirples o'er the lea,
>   Chill on thy lovely form:
> And gane, alas, the sheltering tree
>   Should shield thee frae the storm.

'Hirples o'er the lea' renders a perfect image of the dull droop of a November day. We can see and feel the mist slowly clambering along the side of the brae, wreathing the purple of the stripped and leafless copse, and loitering in smoky patches on the fields once green but now famished into greyness or umbered with the visitation of the plough.

HOCUS POCUS AND INCUBUS

THOMAS BURKE in *The Streets of London* quotes thus from an old story of Bartholomew Fair:

> Here a knave in a Fool's Coat, with a trumpet sounding, or a drum beating, invites you to see his puppets; there a Rogue like a Wild Woodman, or in an antic shape like an Incubus, desires your company to view his motion; on the other side Hocus Pocus, with three yards of tape or ribbon in his hand, showing his art of leger-de-main to the admiration and astonishment of a company of cockroaches.

Both Hocus Pocus and Incubus began as persons and became things. On the Tudor fairground Hocus Pocus was the conjuror, so named because that was the kind of bogus charm that he muttered. Now the word refers only to the trickery. In the same way an Incubus is now only a burden; but he was once a fiend, especially a rapacious fiend likely to descend on sleeping beauties. He thus came to be the symbol of a nightmare, as Master Hocus Pocus became the symbol of illusion and deceit.

So Milton knew him. Belial, in his opinion, was not only 'the dissolutest spirit that fell' and 'sensuallest', but also 'after Asmodai the fleshliest Incubus'. Poor Incubus! After being fouler than a Black Fiend, it has become the small brother of a White Elephant.

HORBGORBLE AND HORNSWOGGLE

THIS from a correspondent now in America, but once well acquainted with the ways and words of Caithness. I shall in a moment proceed to the mysterious Hornswoggle and I shall at least suspect that my friend's memories of horbgorbling were stirred by the sight or sound of hornswoggling in U.S.A. The latter appears to be quite commonly used, since just before writing this I heard it in the text of a musical comedy called *Wonderful Town*.

P. G. Wodehouse brought hornswoggle, for cheat, back from America and released it for service in the Drones Club of London. When it came to collecting a purse of gold what man could touch, not to mention hornswoggle, Oofy Prosser, that ace of Untouchables and prince of Non-Parters? Hornswoggling, I gather, began in American politics more than a century ago. It was an equivalent to honeyfogling and arrived in the same year, 1829. This I learn from the boundless researches of H. L. Mencken, who adds a striking tribute to hornswogglery from a 'presumably reverend writer in *The Church Standard* of Sydney, Australia, November 27th, 1936'. This gentleman confessed himself 'breathless with admiration' in the presence of such a word.

Horbgorble, I am told, means to putter about in a feckless, ineffective way. The correspondent who gave it me recollected the trials of a Caithness man for an alleged sexual assault upon a servant girl. Both the young man and the young woman involved – the accusation came from the employer of the latter – were puzzled by the legal terminology. All was understood in Court, however, when the lass explained that the fellow was just horbgorbling and no worse: the word, and the plea, were accepted and the case was dismissed.

Horbgorbling is only a stage on the road to ruin and to that which Robert Burns called houghmagandie. Of the 'Holy Fair' he wrote:

> There's some are fou o' love divine
> And some are fou o' brandy,
> And monie jobs that day begin
> May end in houghmagandie
> Some ither day.

Horbgorbling came first on such occasions, and there was probably also some hornswoggling about honourable intentions.

HORRID

THE decline of horrid is lamentable. It should carry the idea of something bristling and frightful with a spiky menace and not merely be a mild term for nastiness. Vergil's 'Bella, horrida bella' sets spears and swords flashing in the air and does not refer only to the discomforts and incivilities of war. Milton is always exactly classical in his employment of such words. The Elder Brother in 'Comus', in the famous speech on Chastity, says that the owner of that virtue can traverse without harm 'Infamous hills' (i.e. unknown country) and pass

> where very Desolation dwells
> By grots and caverns shagged with horrid shades

unmenaced by goblin or 'swart faery of the mire'. Shakespeare, writing earlier than Milton, is none the less often closer to us in his usage. So it happens with horrid, which he applies vigorously to ghosts, night, thunder, speech, and hent. Hent, by the way, means to seize, or, as a noun, a seizing or design.

Horrible has suffered equal decline. When Cowper, musing on 'The Solitude of Alexander Selkirk', remarked

> Better dwell in the midst of alarms
> Than reign in this horrible place,

he meant something far more frightening than his adjective now implies. The same thing has happened in his next verse, which is made wellnigh ridiculous by the change of meaning in 'shocking'.

> The beasts that roam over the plain
> My form with indifference see;
> They are so unacquainted with man,
> Their tameness is shocking to me.

While on the subject of epithets in mutilation or decay, let me quote this recent advertisement of a popular musical play: 'Terrific cast of 50.' That was meant to attract, not deter. Poor terrific!

HOYT

Miss Rose Macaulay in her delightful anthology *The Minor Pleasures of Life* includes, under the caption 'Huntin',' an excerpt from an anonymous poem of 1675 called 'The Chase'. This describes Dian's young and virginal nymphs a-chasing the stag:

A light-foot Host, green-kirtl'd all they came
And leapt, and rollickt, as some mountain Streame
Sings cold and ruffling thro' the Forrest Glades;
So ran, so sang, so hoyted the Moone's Maids.
Light as young Levretts skip their buskin'd feet,
Spurning th' enamell'd Sward as they did fleet.
The Wind that buss'd their cheekes was all the Kiss
Was suffer'd by the Girles of *Artemis*,
Whose traffique was in Woods, whom the winged Boy
Leaguer'd in vain, whom Man would ne're injoy,
Whose Bed greene Moss beneath the forrest Tree,
Whose jolly Pleasure all in Liberty,
To sport with fellow Maids in maiden cheere,
To swim the Brook, and hollo after Deer.
Thus, the winds wantoning their flying Curles,
So rac'd, so chas'd, those most Delightfull Girles.

The last couplet is indeed a gem.

Hoyt or hoit is to act the romp or hoyden. Winsome and spirited maids go hoyting across the English stage of the seventeenth century. Hoity-toity is an expansion of the same word and originally was applied to frolicsome women. D'Urfey in his *Pills to Purge Melancholy* wrote of a 'Hoity Toity Frowzy Browzy Covent-Garden Harridan' (Harridan meant originally a broken-down horse). The meaning of hoity-toity was altered to become an expression of petulance and surprised disgust, in which function it remains common. The verb to hoit has almost disappeared; it is a pity, for it went well with the racing and chasing of 'Delightfull Girles'.

HURDY-GURDY

It is odd to think that the hurdy-gurdy began as a lute-like instrument, whose strings were sounded by the revolution of a rosined wheel. To me the noisy-sounding double-barrelled name seems exactly right for the raucous, jovial barrel-organ which is now so rarely a disturber of the peace or a stimulant of free-and-easy dancing in the street. Towards the close of the last century the House of Commons considered hurdy-gurdies gravely, setting them time limits for their services, morning and evening. The night was to be kept inviolate from the sacred music of Calverley's

> Grinder who serenely grindest
>   At my door the Hundredth Psalm,
> Till thou ultimately findest
>   Pence in thy unwashen palm.

J. K. Stephen sprang to the defence of the grinder against this oppressive measure.

> When the dawn with rosy finger
>   Dissipates the eastern gloom,
> You and your machine must linger
>   Silent in your silent room.

The hurdy-gurdy achieved the honour of salutation by two of England's past masters of light verse. But neither of them gave it that good name.

IMBROUN

This word may look strange, but it is only Miltonic for embrown. 'In the Garden of Eden'

>   the crisped Brooks,
> Rowling on Orient Pearl and sands of Gold,
> With mazie error under pendant shades

Ran Nectar, visiting each plant, and fed
Flours worthy of Paradise, which not nice Art
In Beds and curious Knots, but Nature boon
Powrd forth profuse on Hill and Dale and Plaine,
Both where the morning Sun first warmly smote
The open field, and where the unpierc't shade
Imbround the noontide Bowrs: Thus was this place,
A happy rural seat of various view.

Pope has the same verb in a passage which surprisingly and
charmingly forecasts the breaking-up of parkland at the Nobleman's Seat for the needs of modern war.

Another age shall see the golden Ear
Embrown the Slope, and nod on the Parterre,
Deep Harvests bury all his pride has plann'd,
And laughing Ceres re-assume the land.

The second couplet shows Pope out of his urban element, as an
Augustan poet, but none the less in form.

Imbroun, Embroun, why mention so plain a word? It is worth
realizing, surely, how much value can be added to a simple noun
or adjective by making it a verb with a prefix. Shakespeare was
continually at it, incorpsing a rider with his horse or distasting
farewell kisses with the salt of broken tears. Or, rising higher,
one meets and revives such stately beauties as incarnadine, im-
paradise, unparagon.

Brown is an adjective of humble service and, though not mean,
makes no particular appeal to the ear. (Londoners making it
Brahn, Bre-own, and almost Bryan, play hell with it, as I am
frequently made aware.) To put im- or em- in front of it does
considerably add to its stature and dignity and creates a verb
worthy of harvest and of autumn. That is sufficient compliment.

IMPOSTHUME AND PLOOK

Do you want Lamb at his most whimsy-whamsical? Then try this from *Amicus Redivivus:*

> Had he been drowned in Cam there could have been some consonancy in it: but what willows had ye to wave over his moist sepulture? – or, having no name, beside that unmeaning assumption of eternal novity, did ye think to get one by the noble prize, and henceforth be termed Stream Dyerian?

> > And could such specious virtue find a grave
> > Beneath the imposthumed bubble of a wave?

This follows 'pails of gelid and kettles of the boiling element' for hot and cold water. Elia in this mood can be very tiresome. He anticipated the George Augustus Sala species of journalese. But I like his quotation for its 'imposthumed bubble'. The lines we owe to the Cavalier, John Cleveland: they occur in his contribution to the volume of elegies on the drowned Edward King, the book in which Milton's 'Lycidas' first appeared. Cleveland's words were slightly, but not substantially, different from Lamb's version. 'Imposthumed bubble' is his.

If you suffer from anything so painful and humiliating as a boil, why not, by way of compensation, dignify the odious lump with the fine old English title of imposthume? Imposthume started life, apparently, as aposthume, which is Greek for an abscess. Somehow it became emposthume in English and so imposthume, an imposing name for a mean affliction. Cleveland's 'imposthumed bubble' is really a most graphic term for the seething of a wave-top. Shakespeare's Thersites, when he wished to reel off the commoner plagues of miserable man, listed

> the rotten diseases of the south, the guts griping, catarrhs, loads o' gravel i' the back, lethargies, cold palsies, raw eyes, dirt-rotten livers, wheezing lungs, bladders full of

imposthume, sciaticas, limekilns i' th' palms, incurable bone-ache, and the rivelled fee-simple of the tetter.

Hamlet, less clinically, describes war about little or nothing as 'the imposthume of much wealth and peace'. 'Imposthumed Braines' occurs in Dekker for poisoned minds.

Tetter, a general (and horrible) term for skin-disease, appears formidably in Hamlet's father's diagnosis of his own fatal affliction:

> A most instant tetter bark'd about
> Most lazar-like, with vile and loathsome crust,
> All my smooth body.

Shakespeare's interest in disease naturally increased with his friendship for Dr. John Hall, who settled in Stratford about 1600 and later married the poet's elder daughter, Susanna.

To the vocabulary of imposthumes the Scots add Plook for a nasty pimple or boil. It seems to say everything of a physical blemish and of its capacity to create a sense of shame. The imposthume known to the Elizabethans sounds more dignified, and also more formidable. Smollett's Doctor L., who came to Bath 'to ply for custom' and talked with such profundity as to madden Mr. Bramble (no difficult achievement), submitted a wart on his nose to the not very tender handling of young Mr. Melford. Caustic was applied later but the wart 'spread in such a manner as to produce a considerable inflammation, attended with an enormous swelling: so that, when he next appeared, his whole face was overshadowed by this tremendous nozzle'. Nozzle or plook? Neither sounds as impressive, and perhaps neither may be as painful, as a carbuncle or imposthume; but they have a mean squalor of their own.

INEBRIATE

THERE is a certain solid splendour about inebriation. A Home for Inebriates sounds almost respectable. Amid the squalid modern terms for exaltation by the grape or the grain, the blottos, stinkos, plastereds and so on, the inebriate stands like a gentleman with vine-leaves in his hair. Let the stinkos stagger and the blottos lurch. Inebriation has the dignified tread of one who knows that he must, despite all cause and inclination to sway, put up a seemly show of unwavering progress. As for the uninebriating cup of tea, most people attribute the notion of its sober virtue to William Cowper.

> And while the bubbling and loud hissing urn
> Throws up a steamy column and the cups,
> That cheer but not inebriate, wait on each,
> So let us welcome peaceful evening in!

But Cowper was borrowing. The idealist philosopher George Berkeley, so crudely refuted by Dr. Johnson in the matter of objective reality, had already applied the phrase to tar-water, whose virtues he strongly proclaimed. He described this fluid as being 'of a nature so mild and benign and proportioned to the human constitution as to warm without heating, to cheer but not inebriate'.

Disraeli's description of Gladstone as 'a sophistical rhetorician, inebriated with his own verbosity' is, incidentally, a pretty piece of involved alliteration. Note the pattern of the 's's, 'r's, and 'b's. The weight of inebriated, matching verbosity, is necessary to the sentence. 'Drunk with his own garrulity' would never have been remembered as a direct hit upon the political wind-bag, which Disraeli, justly or unjustly, associated with his rival.

A charming reference to uninebriation occurs in a poem on Milk by 'Gentleman Jerningham' – and how genteel that eighteenth-century dramatist and minor poet could be! He felt deeply on the subject of Wet Nursing and those who

> To venal hands the smiling babe consign
> While Hymen starts and Nature drops a tear.

How much more praiseworthy are the nursing mothers.

> For you, ye plighted fair, when Hymen crowns
>   With tender offspring your unshaken love,
> Behold them not with Rigour's chilling frowns,
>   Nor from your sight unfeelingly remove.

> Unsway'd by Fashion's dull unseemly jest,
>   Still to the bosom let your infant cling,
> There banquet oft, an ever-welcome guest,
>   Unblam'd inebriate at that healthful spring.

What better praise of that gremial Shrine, as Jerningham so movingly described it, 'where Nature with presaging aim . . . The snowy nectar pours, delightful streams!'?

INFLUENCE

A SAD decay has overtaken this once magical word. It was originally associated with the effluent power of the stars as it entered into man. In Milton's Nativity Hymn,

> The Stars with deep amaze
> Stand fixt with stedfast gaze
>   Bending one way their precious influence.

The Bible Translators had already made question, 'Canst thou bind the sweet influences of the Pleiades or loose the bands of Orion?' So, moving across from the sublime to the sinister, we find Edmund in *King Lear* denouncing the foppery of the world which excuses its vices by the stars and claims that men are 'drunkards, liars, and adulterers by an enforced obedience of planetary influence'.

Next comes the idea of a magic spell, or inspiration, and we hear from Milton of

> Ladies whose bright eyes
> Rain influence.

Crashaw too writes of a brisk cherub who sips 'sweet influence' from a lady's eyes and 'so adds sweetness to his sweetest lips'. The modern sense of the word as a social force or corrupting pressure is oddly anticipated in Milton:

> So spake the false Arch-Angel and infus'd
> Bad influence into the Unwarie brest
> Of his Associate.

Thus was the way prepared for the present meaning of importance or effect. Influence has become examination English. Are we not always inviting (or invited) to trace the influence of this or that? Certainly the magic has departed and bottom depth was touched when Influenza, itself first meaning an infusion of astral power, was exclusively devoted to 'a febrile, zymotic disorder, whose symptoms and sequelae are rapid prostration and severe catarrh'. We most of us know all about that, without recourse to such words as sequelae.

So influence comes streaming down our centuries of poetry, gradually losing its sense of starry or divine afflatus, dwindling into an ugly form of social pressure, and even sneezing itself into the humiliations of a streaming cold. Perhaps the most recent kind of stars are now in their own way vehicles of influence. It is by the image of the cinema's beauties that millions now appear to be

> Foster'd, illumined, cherished, kept alive,

to use Valentine's words about the effect of Silvia's influence on him.

JO

WHEN asked what the Jo meant in 'John Anderson, my jo', I could only reply rather vaguely, 'Friend'. This indeed it frequently did mean, but the word began as an abbreviation of Joy. So it was properly used in 'The Gude and Godlie Ballatis',

> In dulci jubilo, now let us sing with mirth and jo.

Later the Jo that was also a Joy became mainly personal in Scottish application, but the usage does not seem to have travelled far south. Allan Ramsay sang of his 'Jo Janet'. Scottish song continues to use jo in the sense of dear companion or lover. Violet Jacob, singer of Angus and the Mearns, spells it Joe.

> My grannie spent a merry youth,
> She never wanted for a Joe.

The word appears also in the rhymes of baby-talk and there, I think, most happily. Jo for a laughing child seems apter than for an adult and frosty-powed Anderson.

JUJUBE

ASKED to comment on jujube, I reply that it is my least favourite sweet (liquorice excepted) and that it is not unfairly labelled with such a hideous name. (Sweetened and thickened into a Fruit Pastille the jujubish article can be soothing, but in its smooth, half-transparent form it is no better than a cough drop.) The name suggests African jungles to me: so I was astonished to discover that the jujube is an Ancient Greek, being a corruption of zizyphon, 'an edible berry like drupe', the latter being 'a pulpy fruit with a nutty kernel'. Hence a gelatinous sweet of somewhat the same shape became a zizyphon and later a jujube. *O.E.D.* mentions 'The Lotos Eaters, whose favourite fruit still grows under the name of the jujube on the same coast'.

Tennyson, lyricist of Lotos-eating, appears to have missed something here. He might have written,

> The Jujube blooms below the barren peak:
> The Jujube blows by every winding creek:
> All day the wind breathes low with mellow tone;
> Through every hollow cave and alley lone,
> Round and round the spicy down the yellow jujube-dust is
> blown.

He could also have ended with

> Oh rest, ye brother mariners, we will not wander more
> But jubilate for ever on this Jujubaceous shore.

But he remained loyal to Lotos.

The names of sweets are sometimes oddly gloomy. Lozenge, for example, the jujube's cousin, originally meant a tombstone, being a slab of the burial kind. It then became a rhomb or a diamond-shape. Next it was something of that form small enough to be dissolved in the mouth. Now we have abundance of throat-lozenges which seek to save us from coughing our way into the ancient lozenge that was lapidary and sepulchral.

KIM-KAM

THE admirable gossip John Aubrey, while recording his own affairs or 'accidents', as he justly said of a disturbed life, had a bad time in 1664. He went to France, reached Orleans, was prostrated by 'a terrible fit of the spleen and piles', returned home, fell off his horse, suffered, in a very uncomfortable corner, 'damage, which was like to have been fatall'. But he recovered sufficiently to go a-wooing, for he observes 'made my first addresse (in an ill houre) to Joane Sumner'. He next has to admit,

> This yeare all my businesses and affaires ran kim-kam.
> Nothing took effect, as if I had been under an ill tongue.
> Treacheries and enmeties in abundance against me.

The psychologist would here diagnose Conspiracy Mania.

Next we read 'Arrested in Chancery Lane, at Mrs. Sumner's suite'. Kim-kam indeed! But better was to follow: 'Triall with her at Sarum. Victory and 600 *li.* dammage, though devilish opposition against me'. What it was all about he does not explain. There was some more legal trouble, but from 1670 onwards he enjoyed 'a happy delitescency', a nice word for freedom from writs. Possibly Mrs. Sumner had been cast off. Aubrey must have had a gay time on the whole, but his chronicle of 'accidents' is formidable. He started very kim-kam, asserting that he had an ague while in his mother's womb, was 'born like to die' and 'got no health' till 11 or 12. After that he had 'sicknesse of vomiting for 12 hours every fortnight'. His undergraduate life went kim-kam too. 'The smallpox at Oxon, and shortly after left that ingeniouse place: and for three years led a sad life in the country.'

Not a great deal, beyond his autobiography of 'ill houres', is known of Aubrey: nor is a great deal known of kim-kam, an expression taken to mean crookedly or in a contrary manner. It was mainly, but never very frequently, used in the seventeenth century. It appears to be much the same as Burns's 'agley'. The best-laid plans of ourselves and the mice go kim-kam south of the Border.

KITLING AND MOONLING

ALL the diminutives seem to gain attractiveness by the termination in 'ling'. Could anything fall more heavily on the fishmonger's slab than Cod? Codling is almost lively. Darlings, younglings, striplings and moonlings skip lightly into the mind. And a kitling, to me, seems more captivating and vivacious than even the friendliest kitten. Kitlings are not so common nowadays, but they frisked in Elizabethan drama and were a symbol of wantonness to Swift. Herrick was a kitlingite:

> Yet can thy humble roof maintain a choir
>   Of singing crickets by the fire,
> And the brisk mouse may feed herself with crumbs
>   Till that the green-eyed kitling comes.

He dealt likewise in younglings.

To Sir Desmond MacCarthy I owed a reminder of the Jonsonian moonling for a dreamy fool. One of Ben's women-characters rails at her husband as a moonling whom no wit of man can redeem from asininity. It seems a pity that so lovely a word as moon should have to be associated with idiocy. (In the matter of loveliness, I suppose the scanty use of the beautiful 'moonset' for the hour of the moon's vanishing is due to the scanty number who are about at that time to see it.) Moonling is a gentler word than moon-calf, which meant an abortion or monstrosity before it came to signify a simpleton. The moon has given its name to many a species: there are moon-ferns, moon-fishes, moon-flowers, moon-seed, and moon-wort. But only for men is the lunar prefix one of contempt. They can be moon-blind, moon-eyed, moon-faced, moonish, and moony. Shakespeare's Rosalind links moonish with apish, shallow, and fantastical and Shakespeare uses moon-calf with some frequency. But for once Jonson has the better of him. Moonling offers the most vivid notion of a nice weak-minded creature, a Mr. Skimpole, who was almost a human kitling.

KITTLE

KITTLE means tickle, possibly by confusion of the two sounds, both of which are based on the light noise of the action itself. So one kittled the strings of a violin. Curiously both verbs are used in the same way as adjectives, meaning difficult or risky. We all know that women are 'kittle cattle' and golfers, with any sense of language, know the terrors of greens that are kittle. Tickle, which now seems much more delicate than ticklish because the latter has been so much used of purely physical reactions, occurs in Sir Walter Raleigh's great poem 'The Lie'.

> Tell wit how much it wrangles
>   In tickle points of nyceness,
> Tell wisedome she entangles
>   Her selfe in over wiseness,
> And when they doe reply
>   Straight give them both the lie.

It was good legal English of the Elizabethans to 'stand upon a tickle point'.

LEMONADE

WHILE no great devotee of lemonade as a beverage I cannot deny the beauty of its look and sound upon a printed page. I think of it when I read that the Crystal Palace is to rise from its ruins and its ashes and once more to be a pleasure-ground and possibly a centre of sporting instruction. For to C. S. Calverley this was a Victorian picnic haunt where

> maidens crunch
> The sounding celery-stick or ram
> The knife into the blushing ham.

Above all, it was the home of soft drinks and the tender passion.

> Such are the sylvan scenes that thrill
> This heart! The lawns, the happy shade,
> Where matrons, whom the sunbeams grill,
> Stir with slow spoon their lemonade:
> And maidens flirt (no extra charge)
> In comfort at the fountain's marge!

John Betjeman, too, in 'Archaelogical Picnic' cries

> Drink, Mary, drink your fizzy lemonade.

He bids the elders make their ecclesiastical and architectural research among

> Sweet smell of cerements and cold wet stones,
> Hassock and cassock, paraffin and pew.

But for the children let there be relief from scholarship and a slaking of thirst.

> For you, where meadow-grass is evidence,
> With flattened pattern, of our picnic made,
> One bottle more of fizzy lemonade!

The word chimes: the poet might be referring to a noble vintage for consumption with a serenade.

How different is ginger beer! One cannot feel lyrical on hearing of such 'pop'. Accurately Betjeman has likened it to the foam of the seas on a Cornish shore.

> But all that August those terrific waves
> Thundered defeat along the rocky coast
> And ginger-beery surf hissed 'Christabel'.

Such surf is frothy to the eye in the way of bottled 'minerals' and it does hiss, as Betjeman suggests. But, by a test of noise and looks, lemonade is my choice. Ginger-beer I set aside with Tizer and Cydrax. Lemonade can be effervescent or serene in any verbal company.

LIBERAL

LIBERAL has always seemed to me an adjective most fascinating in the variety of its uses. I was at one time much allured by the announcement of 'Liberal Table' in the old advertisements of boarding-houses. Two eggs for breakfast? Has this nice boast of plenty entirely vanished among war-time limitations on food in the larder and on space in the newspapers? Nowadays, in the Guest Houses which have taken the place of Boarding Houses, the customers seem to be keen isolationists: they are more attracted by separate tables than by liberal ones.

The use of liberal in Shakespeare alone would suffice for pages of comment and quotation. With him it could be applied equally to the rough peasant and the refined scholar. Prospero followed 'the liberal arts', i.e. those with no taint of technical or financial utility, the pursuits of a wealthy, leisured gentleman. (Dr. Johnson defined liberal as 'becoming a gentleman', the word being not yet applied to the Whigs whom he deemed no gentlemen at all.) Yet Shakespeare could equally speak of 'liberal shepherds', meaning peasants gross of speech. It is noteworthy that the master-dramatist could stop in the middle of a most poignant passage, Queen Gertrude's description of Ophelia's watery end, to drag in a bawdy jest upon the name given by those English 'liberals' in their taverns and steadings to a certain kind of flower, the long purple. Anything less dramatically apposite than this introduction at such a moment (and in Denmark!) of a smutty joke beloved of English hinds and drovers could hardly be imagined. Yet what a lovely speech remains!

Liberal, therefore, means free of mind, free of speech, and free of purse. A man could be 'profane and liberal' just as much as he could be liberal and charitable.

> Kent, in the Commentaries Caesar writ,
> Is term'd the civil'st place of all this isle:
> Sweet is the country, beauteous, full of riches,
> The people liberal, valiant, active, wealthy.

This topographical observation, probably by Shakespeare, was a piece of special pleading made to Jack Cade, playing on Kentish pride. Liberal, to the translators of the Bible, meant generous and was contrasted in Isaiah with churlish. The churl devises wicked devices to destroy the poor, but 'the liberal deviseth liberal things and by liberal things shall he stand'. This shows the width of meaning possessed by liberal in Elizabethan and Jacobean times, for it also meant licentious and was commonly applied to seducers.

Liberal, as a political term, came to us early in the nineteenth century. In 1859 John Bright said 'I am for Peace, Retrenchment, and Reform, the watchword of the great Liberal Party thirty years ago'. The term was beginning to supplant the name of Whig in the eighteen-twenties, having arrived from Europe.

LITH

I HAVE always been accustomed to talk about the pig of an orange to describe one of its sections. I cannot explain why. A pig, short for piggin, can be a pot or vessel. Was pig a corruption of pick, since you pick the sections out? I was reminded of this by reading in James Bridie's autobiography called *One Way of Living*, about the lith of an orange. He was describing a soldier's improvised cocktail called a Tangerine Sling. The only available liquors were claret and rum. There were also tangerines and raisins. One tablespoonful of rum went to two of claret; the raisins were crushed into the rum and 'the juice of a single lith of orange' went into the claret. The recipe does not suggest the perfect apéritif. But 'it imparted a pleasant and enlivening sensation to the fingers and toes and made me wish to join the Flying Corps'. Lith is also a verb meaning to separate the joints one from another. Presumably one may lith a duck or a chicken and, less easily, a boiling fowl that has rashly been roasted. But are the legs and wings of poultry and game ever called liths? Boswell's father said of Cromwell, 'He gart kings ken they had a lith in their necks.'

LOCOFOCO AND FILIBUSTER

PEACOCK's Mr. Gryll gave this advice:

> Look across the Atlantic. A Sympathizer would seem to imply a certain degree of benevolent feeling. Nothing of the kind. It signifies a ready-made accomplice in any species of political villainy. A Know-Nothing would seem to imply a liberal self-diffidence – on the scriptural principle that the beginning of knowledge is to know that thou art ignorant. No such thing. It implies furious political dogmatism, enforced by bludgeons and revolvers. A Locofoco is the only intelligible term: a fellow that would set any place on fire to roast his own eggs. A Filibuster is a pirate under national colours; but I suppose the word in its origin implies something virtuous: perhaps a friend of humanity.

Locofocoism, for radicalism of an urgent kind and for the extreme wing of the American Democratic Party, turns up in *Martin Chuzzlewit*. The Locofoco was originally a species of fusee and was also a name for a kind of self-igniting cigar: presumably, you pressed a knob and the sparks flew outward. This useful (and formidable) article would naturally become a synonym for a self-kindling or explosive politician. Does the term persist in American politics? The Italian fuoco, hearth or fire, explains at least one end of this delightful word, about which there is a happy suggestion of steam and hot air.

Filibuster came by way of Holland and France and meant a freebooter, also a Dutch word for one who laid hands freely on booty. Then filibustering came to mean the practice of any kind of lawlessness. Locofoco may have gone, but filibuster remains and is now much associated with organized obstruction, especially in a legislative assembly. There is no truth in Mr. Gryll's suggestion that the word ever arose from virtuous company or had something to do with sentimental cosmopolitanism.

LONG

WHY do we long for things? Why did Cleopatra have 'immortal longings'? Can there be a derivation from, or at least a connection with, the old 'think long', which implied regret and desire as well as cogitation? I am reminded of that phrase as it occurs in the fifteenth-century Paston Letters. 'I think right long to hear tidings', Margery Paston wrote. 'Sir, I pray you, if you tarry long at London, that it will please you to send for me, for I think long since I lay in your arms.' There is an easy transition, by abbreviation, from 'thinking right long' to longing for a loved one.

I have been sent an Ulster poem (author Richard Rowley) in which thinking long occurs in the last line of each sad stanza. I quote one of them.

> A poor oul' doitered man
> That yammers and girns,
> A was quarely different onst
> Wi' wife and bairns.

> The house was full o' weans
> All straight and strong;
> It's desprit lonely now
> An' A'm thinking long . . .

The loneliness of the old could hardly be described with a simpler power and pathos.

Why do we use 'So long' for adieu or good-bye? Is it linked with the conditional 'so long', which has come to mean little more than 'if'?

> So long as men can breathe, or eyes can see,
> So long lives this, and this gives life to thee.

We can imagine how so long as, first meaning while, was changed into a conditional phrase. This slang 'so long' of ours — so long as life remains or fortune favours? — has a kind of sad poetry within it. It is less optimistic than cheerioh, less devout than adieu, less confident than au revoir, less melancholy than farewell, which, for all its good intentions, does ring a solemn bell. Unite long and farewell and what a width and depth of parting is implied.

> Farewell, a long farewell, to all my greatness!

Now it is 'good-bye to all that' or even 'so long to the lot of it'.

LUNGIS AND LUSK

WHAT an extraordinary origin has Lungis, the lanky lout, if the *O.E.D.* is correct in its attribution to Longinus, the supposed name of the tall centurion who pierced the side of Jesus with a spear. Lungis became the long and clumsy man, the lubberly creature. Cries the Citizen's Wife over Ralph the Apprentice in *The Knight of the Burning Pestle* after one of his romantically intended struggles,

Oh, husband, here's Ralph again! – Stay, Ralph, again, let me speak with thee. How dost thou, Ralph? art thou not shrewdly hurt? the foul great lungies laid unmercifully on thee: there's some sugar-candy for thee. Proceed; thou shalt have another bout with him.

It might occur, but does not, in the famous Rabelaisian list of oafs, knaves, and blockheads, which includes, among others,

> Prating gablers, lickorous gluttons, freckled bittors, mangie rascals, slie knaves, drowsie loiterers, slapsauce fellowes, slabberdegullion druggels, lubbardly lowts, cozening foxes, paultrie customers, sycophant varlets, drawlatch hoydons, flouting milksops, staring clowns, forlorn snakes, ninnie lobcocks, scurvie sneaksbies, fondling fops, base lowns, sawcie coxcombs, idle lusks, scoffing braggards, noddie meacocks, blockish grutnols, doddipol joltheads, jobbernol goosecaps, foolish loggerheads, slutch calflollies, grouthead gnatsnappers, lobdotterels, gaping changelings, codshead loobies, woodcock slangams, ninnyhammer flycatchers, and noddiepeak simpletons.

This is a glorious list, with which compare some modern Scottish specimens under the heading of 'Perjink and Others'. While missing lungis, it does include lusks, who are sloths. To lusk is to be idle, to be a lusk or luskish; the term has the right sound of a yawn, and is almost a collision of lie and bask. Another good old word for a loafing lout is gangrel. Lungis was linked with lusks and gangrels in Blunt's *Glossographia*, 1687. The Scottish gangrel is a tramp or wanderer: Violet Jacob sings of the gangrel loon who knows the Sidlaw Hills by heart as well as by eye. The English gangrel is a long loose-limbed, shuffling creature. In short, another lungis.

MAGAZINE

A MAGAZINE comes, by way of France, out of Araby. It has in its time meant any kind of store from a dairy (magazine of milk and butter, Defoe), to an arsenal. Charles Cotton, in a gay little song defying winter, described his resources for the campaign.

> There, under ground, a magazine
> Of sovran juice is cellar'd in:
> Liquor that will the siege maintain,
> Should Phoebus ne'er return again.

James Thomson inquired of the winds,

> Where are your stores, ye powerful beings, say,
> Where your aerial magazines reserved
> To swell the brooding terrors of the storm?

In the later eighteenth century the word added to its general utility by taking on its now common literary meaning. By 'Magazine of Taste' you might expect to find described one of the glossier and more expensive fashion-journals. But this imposing phrase was, in fact, the title of a dining-room utensil popular a century ago. This was a super-cruet, containing all possible condiments, 'zests' and sauces, and carried the proud, proprietary title of 'Dr. Kitchener's Magazine of Taste'. To remark 'May I trouble you, Sir Eustace, for the Magazine? did not imply a churlish desire to read at table, but only an interest in added savours.

MALTWORM

THIS is surely a very satisfactory term for a drinker. It suggests everything that a cocktail-bar is not and has not: dark panelling, armchairs of rubbed and faded leather, old prints, frowst, and the inevitable Major – a bore, but somehow forgivable because so apt to the spot – chuntering away by the fire. In short, 'the snug'. (Some of our public-house vocabulary is wrong, e.g.

saloon, but snug is proper.) The maltworm appears early in English song and revels, wriggling his way into the mid-sixteenth-century drinking catch 'Back and side go bare, go bare':

> And Tib, my wife, that as her life
>   Loveth well good ale to seek,
> Full oft drinks she till ye may see
>   The tears run down her cheek:
> Then doth she trowl to me the bowl
>   Even as a maltworm should,
> And saith, 'Sweetheart, I took my part
>   Of this jolly good ale and old'.
>   Back and side go bare, go bare, etc.

Maltworm to me is the just word for the slim, weedy little man discoverable in most snugs who entirely belies all the common attributes of alcoholism by remaining lean, pallid, and rather melancholy, but not sourly so. Shakespeare certainly saw the maltworm otherwise, namely as a fellow formidably hirsute and tinted from the vat. Cries Gadshill (in a speech good enough for Sir John himself):

> I am joined with no foot land-rakers, no long-staff sixpenny strikers, none of these mad, mustachio purple-hued maltworms, but with nobility and tranquillity.

The original maltworm was a weevil and, despite Shakespearean authority, I shall continue to think of the human maltworm as a small, pale, and pertinaceous drinker.

MANDRAGORA AND MITHRIDATES

SHAKESPEARE's mandragora is a drowsy syrup in its own right. The very syllables are a lullaby. It is the same article as the mandrake; the longer form of this plant represents its soothing qualities, while the shorter is usually associated with the shrieks it was alleged to give out when plucked. In Elizabethan poetry the mandrake is for ever raising its eerie voice; its screams and ululations go with moonlight and witchcraft and all things dark and sinister. To ward off the fatal effects of sinister foods and potions one could take a mithridate. This, of course, derived from the ancient King Mithridates of Pontus who, like our own James I, went in great and constant dread of assassins. But, whereas James wore padded clothes as his defence against a stiletto, Mithridates took a poison-course and so pickled his inside that it was at length deemed proof against all such banes. Hence mithridate for any kind of antidote.

I came across the usage in an exquisite piece of pastoral-sentimental among the Essays and Characters of John Stephens (1615). Included in his Arcadian picture of the Shepherd is this passage:

> He comprehends the true pattern of a moderate wise man; for as a shepherd, so a moderate man hath the supremacy over his thoughts and passions; neither hath he any affection of so wild a nature, but he can bring it into good order, with an easy whistle. The worst temptation of his idleness teaches him no further mischief, than to love entirely some nut-brown milkmaid, or hunt the squirrel or make his cosset wanton. He may turn many rare esteemed physicians into shame and blushing; for whereas they, with infinite compounds and fair promises, do carry men to death the furthest way about, he with a few simples preserves himself and family to the most lengthened sufferance of nature. Tar and honey be his mithridates and syrups; the which, together with a Christmas carol, defend his desolate life from cares and melancholy.

A cosset was a pet lamb and gave us our verb for fondle, pet, or spoil. (See note on Cosset.) Wanton here is a verb meaning to gambol or frisk.

The English countryside in English letters has strange contrasts. Either it is moon-blanched, hag-ridden, and resounding with the eldritch shrieks of plucked mandragora or else it is the basking-ground of idyllic shepherds with their simple minds immune from the corruptions of the Court and with honey and tar their simple mithridates against a physical infection.

MARMALADE

MARMALADE appears to issue from melimelum, the honey-apple. The earliest marmalade was usually made of quinces. A seventeenth-century traveller, driving from Cambridge to London, took with him macaroons, marmalade (quince) and wine, which suggests a sweet tooth and a sticky meal on the road. The same gentleman's accounts show further fellowship of marmalade and sweet-cakes. Marmalade could be made of every fruit. Cherry marmalade was the old form of our (too rare) cherry jam. In the eighteenth century a Marmalade Madam was another name for a strumpet. *The London Spy,* who spelled them Marmulets, named them so. The word could also be an adjective and applied to the human heart, signifying soft and sweet. But now it has become limited in range to the conserve made of oranges or lemons. A pity. A Marmalade Madam, whose heart was by no means marmalade, strongly suggests a relentless daughter of the game with an eye to all her chances.

I think the derivation from melimelum must be maintained against the pleasant theory that Mary Queen of Scots, when queasy, used to ask for this kind of confection to relieve her. 'Marie malade', her Ladies would say. Hence marmalade. Believe it or not.

METICULOSITY

'WITH the utmost meticulosity' is a recent pomposity for 'with the greatest care'. Meticulous is, I suppose, a word which has so completely changed its meaning of timid that the proper one is almost wholly forgotten. Indeed, one of my dictionaries marks the definition 'timid' as 'obsolete'. Since a timid man may go warily, meticulous came to mean cautious, careful and then precise. So it has actually passed into the lingo of military communiqués. A meticulous commander is no longer a panicky one; he is a model of forethought.

As purveyors of turgid prose it would be hard to beat the generalissimo of today. Here is one example of what may be called MacArthurese. 'In defiance of all internationally recognized obligations of war declaration before initiating belligerency.'

So nobody starts a war now: they initiate belligerency. Further we had this from the same High Command. 'Both in the advance to the north and the subsequent withdrawals to the south the tactical deployments on the correctly assessed cold realities of the military situation as it actually developed have been meticulously according to the directive it was charged to implement.'

'Meticulously according to the directive it was charged to implement' is certainly an imposing variant on 'strictly according to orders'.

Exercise for students. Translate into War Office English (or American) the old brief phrase 'sealed orders'. The good examinee would, I suppose, introduce some polysyllabic Secret Directives demanding total meticulosity of implementation.

Since writing this I have noticed an American military order concerning fat men in the forces. They are termed 'obese personnel'. I shall remember that when next I see Falstaff on the stage.

MICHING

MICHING is skulking, hiding, or thieving. Perhaps Herrick had both shades of meaning in mind when he wrote

> A cat
> I keep, that plays about my house,
>   Grown fat
> With eating many a miching mouse.

Hamlet's 'Miching mallecho' is usually interpreted as secret mischief.

'Shall the blessed sun of heaven prove a micher and eat black-berries?' asked Falstaff, thinking rather of trespass.

The same poem of Herrick's, by the way, has a curious verb for the fruitful hen.

> A hen
> I keep, which, creeking day by day,
> Tells when
> She goes her long white egg to lay.

Herrick, like Clare, two centuries later, is a great minter of words. Out of his treasury tumble ancient and modern pieces. His 'Once a virgin flosculet', for example, is a very classical bud, but Herrick sometimes sets Latin moving on tiptoe instead of using the heavy Roman tread.

MIFFY

In his 'Marginal Comment' in *The Spectator* Sir Harold Nicolson once wrote:

> I have been conscious on previous voyages to and from the United States that, whereas the approach to New York is unequalled in dramatic splendour, and whereas the Customs buildings on arrival were neat and well-arranged, our own front door was miffy and ill-kempt.

I had only vague ideas about the word miffy and so looked it up in *O.E.D.* A miff, I learned, is a 'fit of peevish ill-humour'. Arbuthnot wrote of Lady Harvey, 'She is in a little sort of a miff about a ballad that was wrote on her'. The verb miff has been used both transitively and intransitively for to give or take offence. ('To peeve' is perhaps our equivalent in modern slang.) Miffy, as an adjective, means touchy, easily offended. Sir Harold employed it, apparently, to mean squalidly offensive:

as such it seems to be his own invention – and a nice one. I do not feel miffy about his usage.

When I put this to him, he kindly allowed me to use his reply.

> I did not use the adjective 'miffy' to mean, as you suggest, 'squalidly offensive'. I used it merely to mean 'shabby'. No associations with the eighteenth-century meaning of the word were present in my mind. I have always heard the word used in horticultural parlance of plants which develop blackspot, or hang untidily and unproductively on their stalks. In this sense the word is used to mean something between 'sickly' or 'ragged'. I feel sure that horticulturalists would confirm this use of the word. But if I have invented this meaning I am not in the least repentant since the word conveys, in its tone of voice, exactly the impression which is needed. Of course it may be that the word is purely a family word which we have misused for years. We shall go on misusing it.

So, after that, shall I.

MIM-FOLK

I LIKE mim to describe the pursers of lips, the too demure of speech and of behaviour. In a Scots poem 'Said the Spaewife' (fortune-teller) Dorothy Paulin has employed it vigorously.

> Said the auld spaewife to me –
>   'Never be humble!
> Lads'll tak' the rough o' your tongue
>   An' never grumble;
> But the thing nae man can bide,
>   An' he be human,
> Is that mim-moothed snivellin' fule,
>   A fushionless woman.'

Fushionless is insipid, feeble.

Another of the poets quoted in Douglas Young's anthology of *Scottish Verse 1851-1951*, the Rev. Dr. Walter Chalmers Smith used it effectively in his tributary verses to Miss Penelope Leith.

> Last heiress she of many a rood,
>   Where Urie winds through Buchan braes –
> A treeless land, where beeves are good,
>   And men have quaint old-fashioned ways.

Of Miss Leith he noted,

> The quaint old Doric still she used,
>   And it came kindly from her tongue;
> And oft the 'mim-folk' she abused,
>   Who mincing English said or sung:
> She took her claret, nothing loth,
>   Her snuff that one small nostril curled;
> She might rap out a good round oath,
>   But would not mince it for the world.

Since my own ancestry is of well-beeved Buchan in Aberdeenshire I am naturally attracted by this portrait of the gay Miss Leith, for whom history ended with Prince Charlie and all Whigs were damned, although that part of Scotland was not greatly drawn by the Jacobite call. According to her poet, she broke all the decencies of a Victorian Sunday in Buchan by cosily playing whist while the Whigs were 'psalm-snivelling in the wind and rain' – the mim-folk!

Mrs. Gaskell in *Sylvie's Lovers* mentions a complaint that 'Wenches are brought up so mim nowadays: i' my time they'd 'a thought na' such great harm of a kiss.'

MINIBITION AND MINIBUS

I READ in an official brochure that their Twenty-first Anniversary Conference and Minibition was held by the Purchasing Officers Association amid the agreeable surroundings of Harrogate. Presumably a Minibition is a Minor Exhibition or a display suffering from modesty about its size. (Thus a Minor Exhibitioner of a University might bring himself up-to-date by calling himself a Minibitor.) On the Conference side of the Minibitionist activities was a discussion led by the 'Anglo-American Productivity Council's Production Control Team'. Why so lengthy? This is sadly out of tune with Minibiting. Could not this group be suitably reduced to Prococo? Their precise subject was 'Practice and Trends in American Procurement'. Procurement has a sinister sound, but it has become unimpeachably respectable. Does this title mean anything more than American Buying Methods?

Are there, I wonder, any Majibitions or Maxibitions? I cannot discover that our great-grandfathers spoke of the Crystal Palace Maxibition. The Purchasing Officers should annex this word, if word-patents are available outside the range of branded goods: otherwise the Psychologists, if they too, in frantic pursuit of brevity, become manipulators of the verbal telescope, will be using Maxibition for Major Inhibition and Minibition for some less infuriating frustration. Since trade is now so much inhibited by controls, the Purchasers might like to have their minibition both ways. I am sure that the word minimal was much heard in the speeches of Prococo. To lecture on the minimal impediments to the most efficient procurement by Purchasing Officers is much finer Conference English than to talk about the least hindrance to good buying.

The gathering had its social round and joys of sightseeing. 'For the Ladies. A Coach Tour via Blubberhouses Moor to Bolton Abbey, returning via Ilkley Moor where coffee will be served.' Doubtless full-sized coaches were needed for those Bolton-bound, but had the volunteers been few they could have travelled in a minibus. In the nineteenth century this charming term was actually applied to the tiny version of an omnibus and even, playfully, to a cab. It would be a sign of minikin modesty to say that you are just off by minibus to see a minibition.

Minikin is a good word for anything small and nice. It had a special musical reference to the thin string used for the treble of the lute. Marlowe wrote:

> I cannot lisp, nor to some fiddle sing
> Nor run upon a high-stretched minikin,

and Pepys told of a Mr. Caesar who had a pretty experiment of 'angling with a minikin, a gut-string varnished over'.

A minikin-tickler was a general term for a fiddler, but minikin was also a pretty thing or creature of any kind. Minikins mince it in old songs of love and are linked with manikins in terms of affectionate regard for life's atoms and midgets.

MISBELIEVE

As a noun of assembly, obviously useful. I have already quoted a medieval list of Carving-terms (period of Henry VI) which reminds one how much the kitchens of that epoch depended on the fowler. But why the precisians of the pantry insisted on a new knife-word for capon, mallard, heron, crane, goose, swan, peacock, curlew, pheasant, quail, rail, plover, pigeon, and 'al smalle berdys' I cannot think. This form of verbal extravagance apparently gave great satisfaction. The carver 'disfigured' a peacock. It is a term applicable to the carving of many, whatever their victim. The medieval frushing of birds, the displaying, dismembering, disfiguring, unlacing, unbracing, and all the rest of it, came from an overflowing larder.

But what has all this to do with misbelieve? Nothing, except that the list of carving-terms is followed by some jocose nouns of assembly in addition to the familiar 'Byldyng of rokes (rooks), murmuration of stares (starlings)' and so on. This list includes a 'nonpaciens of wyves' and a 'misbeleve of paynters'. That wives should be thrawn, as the Scots say, is natural enough. (What a wonderful word is 'thrawn-gabbit', i.e. twisty-mouthed, sour, and peevish. 'A testy of wives' would not be a bad term of this order.) But why were 'paynters' mentioned as the most untrustworthy of men? Other artists have told far bigger lies. But a 'misbelieve' should be retained. As a journalist (and proud of it)

I hesitate to suggest 'a misbelieve of reporters' or even of 'columnists', though I must confess to the title being occasionally just. But what about a Misbelieve of Ministers for Question Time in the House of Commons?

MITHER AND DISJASKIT

CHESHIRE appears to be a richly inventive as well as a stubbornly retentive county in its matters of vocabulary. Or is it simply that it produces more word-lovers who want their favourites to live on and kindly let me know it? Doubtless other shires keep that fine slab of sticky sound, slutch, for mud, and share with England's Deeside mither (to rhyme with neither) for pester. One who was told in his boyhood to stop mithering people explains it as a telescoped version of muddle, rile and bother. I suppose that it is a cousin of 'moider' which is still used with much the same sense over a fairly large area. 'Botheration' has a plentiful outfit of descriptive terms.

There is, for instance, disjaskit. This has dictionary status with the limiting remark that it is Scottish. But it is a Somerset man who writes to me on its behalf. *O.E.D.* limits its use to broken and decayed things. It is doubtless a corruption of the Latin disjectus, most familiar in the neuter plural, 'disjecta membra poetae'. But disjaskit is now quite as much used of disturbed people and their states of mind as of scattered and untidy things. It means put out, distraught, depressed, mithered and moidered, and is too good to lose.

Doddled is another word in the vocabulary of fuss and frustration. It is sometimes a form of dawdle, but it can also be applied to activity. I have been shown its use in letters about a century old as a variant for bothered. 'I really cannot be doddled to do it.' 'You had better go and get dodded', is, or was, the North Country suggestion of a hair-cut. And perhaps the answer was 'I can't be doddled'. Trees when lopped were dodded and became doddards. The use of Dod or Dodd for a bare summit like a shaven skull is familiar to lovers of the Lake District. It is exactly similar to the use of maol, which signifies a bald mountain in the Highlands of Scotland. The great Glas Maol which you pass on the way to Braemar from the south would be Green Dodd in Cumberland.

Doddypoll means a blockhead rather than a bald head. It sounds a friendly word. Such a fool would be one of Shakespeare's 'allowed fools' whose motley was a licence to jest with more or less impunity.

MIZZLE

'IT was on a murky October day that the hero of our tale, Mr. Sponge, or Soapy Sponge, as his good-natured friends called him, was seen mizzling along Oxford Street, winding his way to the West.' Mizzling, here, is disappearing: at least so the dictionaries say. But can a man be seen vanishing? Well, he can be seen about to vanish, fading out, and perhaps that is what Surtees had in mind. To me mizzling seems a good term for sauntering, moving slowly like the kind of rain that is called mizzling.

Mizzle, incidentally, is a word with a rich number of meanings. It is a very old variant of drizzle. 'Now gynnes to mizzle, hye we homeward fast' is Spenser's precautionary advice – to potential rheumatoids? To mizzle is also to confuse. The ancient sot was mizzled with his wine. It can be an alternative to muzzle. As a noun it is a form of measles, and so a child can be 'mizzled', i.e. covered with spots. These usages are mostly scarce and antique or a piece of local dialect. But in one sense or another the word hangs on and does not, like Soapy, go mizzling out of sight.

MOPPET

MOPPET is an affectionate form of mop or moppe, which was applied as a termination to the name of fish. A cod-mop was a codling; a whiting-mop was a young 'un of that unexciting tribe so curiously doomed by cooks for ever to chase their own tails. It now seems strange that moppe or moppet should have become a term of human endearment, because we do not feel so tenderly about fish as did our ancestors. We call our dear ones honey or peach, kitten or flame, or any form of flower. But we tend to shrink from the imagery of the aquarium. Sprats and shrimps we reserve for unbiddable boys. Who would think of his beloved in terms of the minor clupeoids or call his Amaryllis his sardine, his elver, his stickle-back, his parr or his prawn? Yet such was the old way. 'I called her Moppe,' wrote Puttenham in *English Poesie*, 'understanding by this word a little pretty lady or tender young thing, for so we call fishes.' Moppets and Poppets have been the darlings of light comedy down the ages. Poppet is a corruption of puppet or doll and I am not sure that to call a young woman a doll seems any more complimentary than to view her as a tiddler. Moppet, however, comes amusingly and agreeably to the ear. It was applied jocosely to effeminate men and Horace Walpole several times dismissed such manikins as moppets.

MORT

WILLIAM HARRISON in his *Description of England* (1587) observed, on the subject of rogues and vagabonds, that a gentleman called Thomas Harman had listed twenty-three species of this 'ungracious rabble'. Here is Harman's catalogue of idlers and 'nips':

The several disorders and degrees amongst our idle vagabonds.

1. Rufflers   2. Uprightmen
3. Hookers or anglers   4. Rogues
5. Wild Rogues   6. Priggers of prancers
7. Palliards   8. Fraters
9. Abrams   10. Freshwater mariners or whipjacks
11. Dummerers   12. Drunken tinkers
13. Swadders or pedlars   14. Jarkmen or patricoes

Of the women kind.

1. Demanders for glimmer or fire   2. Bawdy-baskets
3. Morts   4. Autem morts
5. Walking morts   6. Doxies
7. Dells   8. Kinching morts
9. Kinching coes

Dover Wilson quotes this in his *Life in Shakespeare's England* and adds some interpretations. The ruffler was a pretending rogue, claiming service in the wars and showing as an honourable scar the cicatrice of a tavern brawl. Uprightmen were top-rankers in roguery. Hookers and anglers carried a staff with a hook in reserve, with which they lifted desirable articles. Priggers of prancers were horse-thieves; palliards were beggars in patched cloaks. Abrams pretended madness in order to raise alms (Edgar's device in *King Lear* would put him in this class, easily recognizable by an Elizabethan audience), Fraters were fraudulent collectors for charity, freshwater mariners were bogus sailors, dummerers pretended to be dumb, and jarkmen or patricoes were sham-clergy offering false marriages. Patrico is Pater Cove.

Now, by-passing the nicely entitled bawdy-baskets, we arrive at the morts. Why mort became a term for a girl nobody seems to know. A walking mort was a female vagabond, autem morts were married, Dells were virgins, and doxies were morts neither married nor virgin. Kinching morts would now be less picturesquely called 'juvenile delinquents, female'. Kinching coes are the same, masculine. Kinching is the equivalent of the German kinder or kindchen. The term lived on in English thieves' cant and Fagin's London knew the kinching-lay, i.e. the robbing of children sent out on errands. Demanders for glimmer or fire are described as false claimants to fire losses. But might not they also be people asking for a light or warmth (and light and warmth were not so easily come by in those days) and then stealing from their benefactors?

It is a formidable list and many of the terms have lived on. Mort seems to me the strangest; it is such a deathly name for a lively young party. Flagitious as the mort may have been, at least she was not likely to be at death's door, slow, crippled and cadaverous.

MOU'

ONE of the trials of English-speaking poetry has been the ugliness of the word mouth. The mouth is the implement of that speech which separates us from the animals. It is part of love's armoury. It ought to have a name of beauty. But it has not. Mouth, being so mean, is deserted for lip, itself no beauty. Lip is hardly a fine-sounding word, but at least the poets can do something with it.

> Take, oh take, those lips away
> That so sweetly were forsworn.

The plaintive a's of the first line disguise the thin sound of lips and the rolling o's and r's of forsworn end the couplet with beauty and lead one rejoicing on. But suppose it had been

> Take, oh take, that mouth away,

the lyric would have been struck dead in a moment. Swinburne tried to make music of mouth, but his

> Sweet, red, splendid, kissing mouth

and the like have a certain vulgarity. Mouth can be sanctified and have piety's imprimatur.

> God be in my mouth
> And in my speaking.

But for the pagan gods, for Aphrodite and her train, it will not do. Here lips more suitably intervene.

The Scots have tried to ease the problem with their mou'. It smacks of the field and the farmyard certainly, but it has the gentleness which the ugliness of mouth denies. Browning's use of Minikin-mou' shows that an Englishman could see the point. Scottish poetry is naturally rich in mou's. Take this, for example, of Miss Marion Angus,

> My beloved sall ha'e this he'rt tae break,
> Reid, reid wine and the barley cake,
> A he'rt tae break, and a mou' tae kiss,
> Tho' he be nae mine, as I am his.

or, again, in the warning of the loneliness that comes to women,

> The ghaist o' a kiss on yer mou'
> An' sough o' win' in the rain.

Spectral love may haunt a mou': it would hardly linger on a mere mouth.

MUCKENDER

WHAT a frank word for a handkerchief is muckender! (I take leave to doubt the polite ascriptions of its origin to a place-name.) Perhaps it has been too frank in its catarrhal suggestion to survive in centuries which have grown in gentility. It is the kind of word you expect to find in Ben Jonson – and do.

> Be of good comfort; take my muckender
> And dry thine eyes.

This is spoken by Turfe, a Kentishman, and the word may thus be deemed pastoral by its author. But it had its place in aristocratic English, or at least in lordly incivilities. The Earl of Dorset (1706) wrote of a playwright of his time:

> For thy dull fancy a muckender is fit
> To wipe the slabberings of thy snotty wit.

One gathers from this that the Earl might have applied a muckender to his own somewhat 'snotty' notions of dramatic criticism.

MUFFISHNESS

MRS. LYNN LYNTON, who wrote about the 'The Girl of the Period' in the *Saturday Review* in the 1860's and is properly quoted by Dr. Willett Cunnington in his anthology called *Women*, observed of this creature – always behaving wrongly to the critics of every age – that she painted her face and made unbounded luxury her only aim.

> The Girl of the Period has done away with such moral muffishness as consideration for others, or regard for counsel and rebuke. It was all very well in old-fashioned times, when fathers and mothers had some authority and were treated with respect, to be tutored and made to obey, but she is far too fast and flourishing to be stopped in mid-career by these slow old mortals; and as she lives to please herself, she does not care if she displeases everyone else. . . .

Does the word fast for raffish still survive? I never hear young men about town called fast now, but I do hear financiers called swift.

Mrs. Lynton then added:

> If some fashionable *dévergondée en evidence* is reported to have come out with her dress below her shoulder blades, and a gold strap for all the sleeve thought necessary, the

Girl of the Period follows suit next day; and then she wonders that men sometimes mistake her for her prototype, or that mothers of girls not quite so far gone as herself refuse her as a companion for their daughters. . . .

Dévergondée en evidence is superb. Muffishness was a favourite Victorian term for softness and effeminacy. Since the muff at sports was one who caught a crab while rowing or missed 'a sitter' and got bowled for nothing at cricket, the muffish were 'softies'. Dean Farrar's schoolboys thought diligence at work a sign of this muffishness, just as Mrs. Lynton, a decade later in the same period, regarded muffishness as a favourite term of contempt among the brazen hussies whom she castigated for their mixture of paint and self-exposure.

A different kind of Muffishness or Muffism, as one authoress preferred to shorten it, was 'walking down St. James's Street on a gusty day in September, in a rough and somewhat shabby pilot coat'. That kind of muffishness became an honourable necessity in years of wars and poverty. To the peaceful, well-to-do Victorians this sartorial muffism was gaucherie comparable to failing at games or falling off a horse. It was scarcely the effeminacy which Dean Farrar and Mrs. Lynton associated with the word.

Muff, as a term of contempt, has a well-established place in English. I was puzzled by it while reading Marlowe's *Tamburlaine* which, though only recently restored to the stage, is an 'alms-basket of words'. Uribassa, who sounds like a bloated and choleric mixture of uric acid and bottled beer, exclaims:

Besides, King Sigismund hath brought from Christendom
More than his camp of stout Hungarians,
Sclavonians, Almains, Rutters, Muffs, and Danes,
That with the halberd, lance, and murdering axe,
Will hazard that we might with surety hold.

Marlowe was so pleased with the line beginning 'Sclavonians' that he repeated it, through the mouth of Orcanes, King of Natolia, shortly after, Muffs and all.

Muff was a term of contempt for Westphalians; then for Germans in general; then for all foreigners, including the Russians. Florio wrote of 'swaggering muffes or Dutchmen'. All nations have shown their racial contempts in monosyllabic dismissal of the supposedly minor breeds. The Americans, I fancy, invented 'Wop', the British 'Wog'. The Elizabethans took their pinch of snuff, shrugged their silken shoulders, and muttered 'Muff' as some alien boor trod on their toes or a curious fantastico went mincing on his way.

MUGWUMP

AMERICANS have a vocabulary to match their respect for what Scots sometimes call the High Heid Yin and others the Big Noise or Big Shot. They have drawn on the Japanese Shogun or Tycoon and tycoons of the film or steel-trade are commonly met in journalism. A particularly interesting variant of the tycoon was Mugwump. I say 'was' because Mugwump now means something totally different, being one who backs down or withdraws. A mugwump horse would be one who 'refused' a jump. An American writer recently explained a mugwump as one who sits on the fence with his mug on one side and his wump on the other. But originally Mugwump or Mugquomp was a Red Indian (Algonquin) word for a chief. (Tammany also began life as a Redskin notable.) According to the *Dictionary of American English*, Mugwump was used by John Eliot in his adaptation of the Bible for Indian use. The 'dukes' in Genesis were, for him, mugwumps. Somehow or other mugwumpery was transferred to politics and business and in the New York *Tribune* in 1877 it was noted that

> John A. Logan is the Head Center, the Hub, the King Pin, the Main Spring, Mogul, and Mugwump, of the final plot.

After that Mugwump entirely changed its meaning.

Main Spring has now been so overworked as to be featureless:

it surprised me to find the still popular King Pin used in 1877. The Oriental terms, Mogul, Bashaw, and Nabob have dropped out. We retain, as was said, the Tycoon: also we deal out Aces freely in this connection. It seems a pity that Mugwump lost caste and rank.

MULLIGRUBS

WHY let mulligrubs become an antique only? A corruption, seemingly, of mouldy-grubs, the word first meant a depression, and then a fit of megrims or sometimes a stomach-ache. It is found in the singular and applied to a person. 'Thou art a puffe, a mulligrube, a Metaphysicalle Coxcombe!' wrote Shirley before Dryden went back to the more orthodox 'She is in her mulligrubs'. It is more expressive than megrim, which is English for migraine. The megrim or megrims meant a headache, usually of the sickening, livery kind that descends on one side of the head. Then it means low spirits or even curious desire. Addison linked megrims with whims and freaks. But that sounds all wrong. A megrim should be a heavy article with nothing light and fantastical about it. It is a far sadder word than mulligrubs. 'To lie sick of the mulligrubs' sounds odd and might even suggest the Herodian affliction and death by worm-eating. Or mulligrubs might be some garden-blight. Yet the term also suggests to me an inner warmth, perhaps through its initial resemblance to mulligatawny, which is a Tamil word for pepper-water. Byron linked megrims with dullness.

MUMCHANCE AND MUMPSIMUS

MUM expresses the tightened lip. You cannot shout that syllable. To mum is also to mime or to act. This has led to some confusion. Mumchance originally meant a masquerade: it also meant a game of chance. And then, because the silent 'mum' was remembered as well as the mummer's 'mum', it came to signify silent or tongue-tied. So Lamb had it in that very whimsical essay 'Upon the New Year's Coming of Age':

> Order being restored – the young lord (i.e. New Year) . . . in as few and yet as obliging words as possible assured them of entire welcome and, with a graceful turn, singling out poor *Twenty-Ninth of February*, that had sat all this while mumchance at the side-board, begged to couple his health with that of the good company before him.

Mumchance, thus used, may be deemed an error which has been justified by time and is now established as correct, in other terms 'a mumpsimus'. Mumpsimus is derived from the blunder of a priest who constantly said mumpsimus instead of sumpsimus in reciting the Mass. When corrected, he refused the instruction and continued to use the wrong term. Hence mumpsimus means a habit obstinately held, a mistake which has some sanction of time, or even the obstinate fellow who sticks to the wrong, old way.

MUMRUFFIN

I LIKE this cheerily bedraggled word for a long-tailed tit, the most architectural of our small birds and one who plans his nest as though intending a cathedral. I note that it has attracted other informal names. One of these, according to a *Times* Christmas Quiz, is Feather-poke. I prefer mumruffin, with its suggestion of a quietly roguish little fellow. While on this topic, why, I would ask, was a goldfinch called a chelandry? That nimble-minded young pretender, Thomas Chatterton, while fabricating his medievalisms, gave this example of English 'as wroten bie the gode priest, Thomas Rowleie, 1464'.

> In Virginè the sultry sun 'gan sheen,
>> And hot upon the meads did cast his ray;
> The apple ruddied from its paly green,

And the lush pear did bend the leafy spray;
And pied chelandry sang the livelong day;
'Twas now the pride, the manhood of the year,
And eke the ground was dight in its most deft aumere.

Aumere is interpreted as robe and the pied chelandry as the goldfinch. I think that Master Rowleie might have admitted a mumruffin to his boskage. As a specimen of Ye Olde Fudge Chatterton's lines may be said to take Ye Guerdon.

MUSE-BROW
AND OTHERS

ELIZABETH BARRETT BROWNING has become a popular heroine of stage and screen, but I doubt whether this introduction to Wimpole Street has caused many to discover or revisit the poetry which she wrote there – or anywhere else. She must now be in the forlorn class of the Well-Neglected Classics. Yet *Sonnets from the Portuguese* are more than an exercise in passionate sonneteering. There (in No. XIX) you will find that she thus describes a gift of her adored one's poetic lock:

As purply black as erst to Pindar's eyes
The dim purpureal tresses gloomed athwart
The nine white Muse-brows.

Of course Muse-brow here means a brow of the Muse, but, in view of our modern vogue for brow-estimation, surely a Muse-brow is a word to be retrieved as an adjective for minstrels of imposing forehead. Shakespeare naturally heads the team and, among the moderns, I think W. B. Yeats certainly merited a place.

Mrs. Browning had a sharp pen for the lesser breeds of Muse-brow, the miminy-piminy foot-in-the-grave young men later located by Gilbert in Castle Bunthorne.

In *Aurora Leigh* she observes:

> There are men
> Born tender, apt to pale at a trodden worm,
> Who paint for pastime, in their favourite dream,
> Spruce auto-vestments flowered with crocus-flames.

The last two lines are perfect for a species of Muse-brow Miminy. Auto-vestments now somewhat suggest leather motoring coats, but I have not yet seen these spruced with crocus.

The consideration of Muse-brow led me to reflect on this brow business in general. When did the now inescapable 'highbrow' and 'lowbrow' arrive? Mr. Eric Partridge, chief authority on such affairs, tells me that highbrow came from America at the end of the 1914-18 war and was established in a year or two. Lowbrow followed. Then we had mid-brow, which had become fairly common by 1930. I remember Sir Nigel Playfair, when defending the Lyric Theatre, Hammersmith, from the charge of highbrowism, calling his programme mid-brow. The term was new to me then. The best definition of a highbrow I know is 'a person educated beyond his intelligence'. Some people would be glad to be called highbrows, but not many have such pride of brains. If Muse-brow came into use, would any accept the honour with delight?

Then there is Muse-rid, which is excellent for a hyper-aesthetical young man. But Pope cannot have had the ebullient fantastic but the skinny pedant in mind when he wrote:

> No meagre, muse-rid mope, adust and thin,
> In a dun night-gown of his own loose skin;
> But such a bulk as no twelve bards could raise,
> Twelve starveling bards of these degenerate days.

I suppose the days have, by convention, always been degenerate and poets starveling. Can a man be muse-rid and monstrous? Since I regard G. K. Chesterton as having been, on many occasions, a truly great poet, the answer is 'Yes'. But 'a meagre mope, adust and thin' he certainly was not; nor was his skin a dun night-gown. Mope as a noun might be kept in use; now we talk rather of 'a misery'.

Whether or no we accept Muse-brow, we have to admit, surely, that Highbrow and Lowbrow have been worked to death – with Midbrow insufficiently accepted. Now comes the Egg-head, alluded to by the more learned as the Ovicapitate.

The Egg-head has a smooth, oval head, like one of the elliptical billiard-balls mentioned by W. S. Gilbert's Mikado. This vessel is packed with mental meat which may or may not be in decay. The weakness of the word lies in the possession by so many intellectuals of plentiful and undisciplined tresses: they are as shag-haired as any villain in Shakespeare. Still, there are some nude and glittering domes, wherein great thoughts abound.

Do Egg-heads resent their new name? I quote this from the London *Bookseller:*

> My friend Mr. Miles W. Standish of Forest Gate, a self-confessed egg-head, offers a slogan or rallying-cry for others of that oppressed minority. Though not quite up to Mr. Standish's usual high standard I pass it on freely to more militant campaigners: 'Eggheads of the World Unite: You have nothing to lose but your Yokes.'

But what chance would an Egg-head have in any scuffle? The heavy thatch of the Muse-brow would have its protective power, but the brittle shell of the Ovicapitate is an argument in his case for avoidance of all battle.

We can derive from antiquity some tribute to the value of long-headedness. Is the Ovicapitate very different from the Dolichocephalic (long-headed) Man in the antiquarian's list of types? The Dolichos, we know, preceded the Brachycephalics (short-headed), but they were beaten by the latter's possession of better weapons and the use of iron against bronze and of both against stone. But if the long-heads managed to create the long barrows, the stone avenues, and the great stone circle of Avebury they were considerable planners, weight-lifters, and architects in stone, and so are fit to rank even with the more exalted Ovicapitates.

EDWARD THOMPSON has sung:

> Tramboon and cinnamon:
> Myrrh and myrabalon:
> Tamarind: olibanum:
> Civet and cardamum:

This from the beginning of an aromatic, as well as resonant, poem called 'Bills of Lading'; its theme is the instruction once given by the Honourable East India Company to all Master Mariners. 'We look that our vessels, ere launched on the seas from Ind to Mozambique, be loaden with these.' Then follows a torrent of magnificent spices, herbs, condiments, cloths and Oriental kickshaws of all kinds. Myrabalon, which sounds like a Babylonian miracle, some fruity masterpiece of the Hanging Gardens, is a species of plum. But what are

> Adatas and nassapores:
> Newries and cocatores:
> Percalloes and kastapores:
> Gurrahs and balasores:
> Calamdanes and scrutores?

Again there are listed,

> Hornes of rhenosseries
> Chaubletts and romaulees:
> Soosees: wax of bees:
> Harital and patanees.

Catalogue-poetry of this kind has always been enjoyed by lovers of a good noise since rhythm and rhyming began. It can be done with place-names (Edward Thomas was a master of that map-work), with flowers and herbs (Kipling and Sir Osbert Sitwell pre-eminent), or with Oriental cargoes (Masefield, Flecker, and

Thompson commanding). The glorious word-waterfall that is
'Bills of Lading' can be found in Thompson's *One Hundred
Poems*, a little book containing specimens of a lifetime's utterance
in many moods by a voice insufficiently heard and acknow-
ledged.

NAMBY-PAMBY

AMBROSE PHILIPS, Namby-Pamby to his angry or his laughing critics, may have expected enduring glory for his verses,
but has won it only in a contemptuous nickname. This was
earned, I think, rather by the insipid classicism of his writing
than by his way of life. He was a Whig of the early eighteenth
century and would readily indite a piece to Sir Robert Walpole,
source of power and preferment.

> Votary to publick zeal,
> Minister of *England*'s weal,
> Have you leisure for a song,
> Tripping lightly o'er the tongue,
> Swift and sweet in every measure,
> Tell me, *Walpole*, have you leisure?

'Simply elegant to please', was a line of his. Philips endeavoured
to be that, but he was far from pleasing Pope or Carey. There
was a political reason for their contempt, as there was for his
deference to Walpole who gave him coveted office in Ireland.

'Lo, Ambrose Philips is preferred for Wit', sneered Pope,
whom Ambrose denounced as an enemy of the Government.
Philips quarrelled briskly with Pope and Addison and so created
a certain amount of vigorous sales-resistance to his poetry among
the Tories: and so, by way of their derision, he has given namby-
pamby to our language.

Yet all his writing was by no means of a namby-pamby kind
to be sharply dismissed as milk-and-water, and anthologists have
been glad to quote this version of 'A Fragment of Sappho':

Blest as the immortal Gods is he,
The Youth who fondly sits by thee,
And hears and sees thee all the while
Softly speak and sweetly smile.

'Twas this deprived my Soul of Rest
And raised such Tumults in my Breast;
For while I gaz'd, in Transport tost,
My Breath was gone, my Voice was lost.

My Bosom glow'd; the subtle Flame
Ran quick through all my vital Frame;
O'er my dim Eyes a Darkness hung;
My ears with hollow murmurs rung.

In dewy Damps my limbs were chilled;
My Blood with gentle Horrors thrilled;
My feeble Pulse forgot to play;
I fainted, sunk, and dy'd away.

Here is Augustan English indeed, formal yet impassioned, defeating the accusation that the age of the Heroic Couplet produced verse, not poetry, and that Ambrose composed nothing but 'pamby' stuff. The passage is nicely true to the just meaning of words, especially the line, 'My Blood with gentle Horrors thrilled'. This suggests, not some ghoulish aghastness, but a pricking, quivering excitation. Who could speak of 'gentle horrors' in these days? 'Dewy damps' for a moistening grief is not so good. A correspondent who found this piece copied in an eighteenth-century edition of Alcaeus and Sappho in Merton College library, gives the reading 'Dewy Dumps'. Dump for a fit of melancholy was Tudor English and Philips would have known what it meant. But in the 1748 volume of *Pastorals, Epistles, Odes and Translations*, with a dedication to the Duke of Newcastle signed by the author, the reading is certainly 'damps'. This leads to the further query. When did it become correct English to say rang instead of rung, and sank instead of sunk, as Philips wrote them? These tenses would get him a bad mark at school were he a pupil nowadays.

But we are meandering from namby-pamby, a word which soon pleased far more than the anti-Walpole party and was firmly settled in our language.

NECESSARIES
AND OTHERS

No fictional detective, bidden to the scene of the crime, proceeded to his garage or (of old) his railway terminus without 'tossing a few necessaries into a bag'. Necessaries are never put in bags: they always appear to be hurled there with some violence. It is interesting that the usage should be so old. Among those who have tossed their night-shift, as Highlanders the caber, was Hamlet's Laertes. Bidding good-bye to his father and sister, he said, 'My necessaries are embark'd: farewell.'

Necessaries (for luggage) make several appearances in Shakespeare. Othello's necessaries were unloaded at Cyprus.

When did the tooth-brush join the roll of necessaries? It arrived in English Literature in 1690. But that does not mean that Romeo's Apothecary did not keep a dentifrice or two among his stuff'd alligator and 'old cakes of roses'.

What exactly constitutes a necessary is, of course, undecided. A Victorian climber in the Lake District, James Payn, adventured himself on the conquest of Fairfield, one of the Helvellyn group. Nowadays a youngster would be up and back in an afternoon, sustained only by a cheese sandwich and a bun. But Payn, whose account I derive from G. S. Sandiland's *Anthology of the Lake District*, took the matter seriously, as indeed did all pedestrians assaulting the 'horrid hills' in those days.

> These were the chief of the necessaries which my sagacity procured for our night-bivouac and tremendous ascent: thirty-six bottles of bitter beer, two bottles of gin, two bottles of sherry, one gallon of water; four loaves of bread,

one leg of lamb, one leg of mutton, two fowls, one tongue, half-pound of cigars, four carriage-lamps, and two packs of playing cards. We had also a large tent, which was carried upon the back of a horse. Three men were necessary to pitch this tabernacle and to carry the provisions. About five o'clock in the afternoon we started for the mountains with a huge train of admirers, forming the largest cavalcade that had ever left Ambleside before.

Even so the necessaries were in vain. The assault failed. Rain and wind were victorious.

The necessaries thrown into a bag remind me of other similar words. 'There are two poyntes requisite unto salvacion.' Thus Sir Thomas More. But, when I saw in a shop a placard announcing Religious Requisites, I realized that there were more than two. The phrase Religious Requisites gave me a slight shock, because I had seen this imposing word Requisite applied so widely elsewhere in the service of a general commerce. This is Trade English and does not penetrate the home. No wife would say to her husband, when setting out on a visit, 'Have you packed your toilet requisites?' Yet if the man went out to buy some razor blades, he would probably find Toilet Requisites written large above the counter where the blades are kept. Our English stores abound in Requisites.

The women's fashion-notes make constant reference to Accessories, a word otherwise associated with crime. Accessories are a particular kind of requisite, being required to set off, by their colour and quality, the main garment to the best advantage. Handbags appear to be Accessory Number One, but gloves and shoes seem also to be on the Accessory List. I have never heard a man refer to his necktie as an Accessory, but this kind of thing may happen in the catalogues of the Higher Haberdashery.

Returning from Requisites to Necessaries, I am informed – as a result of watching that universal educator, Television – that Beau Brummell carried on his journeys what he called 'le Necessaire'. This was a gentleman's dressing-case in miniature, with the brushes, razors, unguents, etc., required for maintenance of a fop's position, elegance, and dignity. There is also, in some parts of the country, common reference to 'the Nessy'. For the meaning of that, see later note on Toilet.

ODDLING

THE *O.E.D.* knows nothing of oddling, a word which pleases me by its double suggestion of the lonely and the queer. (Ben Jonson's odling, which probably means cozening, is another matter altogether.) Oddling seems to be the perfect word for certain types mainly to be discovered of old in winter-time, sitting in seaside hotels when patrons are few and prices low, or watching February seas from the shelter on the deserted esplanade. I first met it in John Clare's lines, as sombrely beautiful as woods in December, called 'Emmonsail's Heath in Winter'. He uses it of crows in the plural and one pictures a brace of peevish solitaries whom spring may render more mutually sympathetic.

> I love to see the old heath's withered brake
> Mingle its crimpled leaves with furze and ling,
> While the old heron from the lonely lake
> Starts slow and flaps his melancholy wing,
> And oddling crows in idle motions swing
> On the half rotten ashtree's topmost twig,
> Beside whose trunk the gipsy makes his bed.

A few lines later he has 'and coy bumbarrels twenty in a drove'. Mr. H. J. Massingham's editorial note in *Poems about Birds* explains 'bumbarrel' as a long-tailed tit. This bird, as I noted, was also the mumruffin. Clare, that embodiment of East Midland earth, a piece of heathland animate, spills words in handsome plenty as he wanders across his simple fields and wastes.

OUTRAGEOUS

I LIKE to find outrageous in its original sense of raging outwards. Trent, as North Midlanders still discover to their cost, is a river much given to flooding, and Defoe, whom a Grecian scholar might call a Potamophobe, a dreader of rivers, termed it 'a most outrageous stream'. Arnold Palmer, in his admirable notes to *Recording Britain*, has given more instances of this fear of fluvial 'outrage'. The tumbling Tees, that so decoratively parts Yorkshire and Durham, Defoe called 'terrible', and of the Derbyshire Derwent he wrote: 'That Fury of a River . . . we kept our Distance the Waters being out, for the Derwent is a frightful Creature when the Hills load her Current with Water: I say, we kept our Distance.' Potamophobia indeed!

What exactly did Hamlet mean by 'outrageous fortune'? A fortune, I suppose, that works outward, beyond due limit, like a fury of a river, a frightful creature. The trouble is that while Defoe's precept of judicious distance-keeping is practicable with most rivers, unless you have been silly enough to build a bungalow on easily submersible land, destiny is not so easily dodged. We have got the word outrageous twisted round by now. For example, an outrageous schoolmaster should really be a choleric dominie much given to overflow of censure or of sarcasm. But the phrase would probably be taken to mean a very bad, incompetent schoolmaster. If we say that some cricketer gave an outrageous display, do we mean that he became a Fury and made it prudent policy for the other side to mimic the potamophobe and, Defoe-like, keep their distance? No, such a term now generally describes a poor, incompetent display.

Shakespeare had not really made up his mind about outrage. Sometimes he used it of crime and assault, sometimes of overflowing emotion. His Valentine in *Two Gentlemen of Verona* agreed to live with the outlaws in the forest.

> Provided that you do no outrages
> On silly women or poor passengers

(Who would, at sight, attribute these lines to W.S.?)

In reply to this the Third Outlaw pledged detestation of 'such vile, base practices'. But Prince Escalus in *Romeo and Juliet* commanded the members of his plaguey houses to

> Seal up the mouth of outrage for awhile.

He had cause enough in their outrageous doings.

OVERWEEN

OVERWEEN now smacks of history-book English. 'The king, in his overweening pride', etc. In these days it is always pride that overweens, but there were times when people did their own overweening, that is to say looked and carried themselves arrogantly, and the word might well be restored to the sense in which Aubrey used it of Gwin, the Earl of Oxford's secretary.

> A better instance of a squeamish, disobligeing, slighting, insolent, proud fellow perhaps can't be found. . . . No reason satisfies him but he overweenes, and cutts some sower faces that would turn the milke in a fair ladie's breast.

There was no quicker portrait-painter than Aubrey. He could make a word do a page's work.

PALSY

'SICK of a palsy' strikes at compassion in a way that paralysis does not and palsied age is far more moving than paralytic decrepitude. Sir John Squire amusingly exemplified, in his book *Flowers of Speech*, the potential beauty of the doctor's lingo. In a brilliant Tennysonian and Shakespearean pastiche he wrote:

> How long ago upon the fabulous shores
> Of far Lumbago, all a summer's day,
> He and the maid Neuralgia, they twain,

Lay in a flower-crowned mead, and garlands wove,
Of gout and yellow hydrocephaly,
Dim palsies, pyorrhoea and the sweet
Myopia, bluer than the summer sky,
Agues both white and red, pied common cold,
Cirrhosis, and that wan, faint flower of love
The shepherds call dyspepsia.

But the game can be played both ways. Why not a witches'
coven of infirmities and blains? Might it not too be versified?

What time the hag Psoriasis uprose,
Beckoned her pocky train and called the roll,
Mumpish Oedema, Tetter, Shingles, Scab,
Old Beldam Rheum and slavering Catarrh,
With necklet of carbuncles, warts, and scabs,
Itch, Abscess, Flux and bloated Imposthume.

No, we cannot let Sir John have it all his own way, though he
does well to enlist, on beauty's side, Impetigo, Scrofula and
Eczema, in earlier lines not quoted. I was gratified by his use of
Palsy, which is far too good a word for my atrocious assembly
and quivered tenderly in his catalogue of charming maladies,
his dream of fair plagues.

PARAPHRASE

A CLUMSY Grecian? Perhaps, but to the Presbyterians this is
no mere 'rendering in other words'. The paraphrase – pronounce
it with the first 'a' broad and with a roll of 'r's and you get the
true sound of it – suggests the bare white walls and grave chanting
of a Scottish parish kirk. Why it was deemed necessary to trans-
mute the Scriptures and especially the Psalms into rhymed verse
I do not know : they were good enough, surely, in their ordinary
shape. But these metamorphized incantations, these paraphrases
did we intone when I had a boy's year at Fordyce, Banffshire,

and sat in a family pew under the Rev. James Grant or the Rev. James Anderson, waiting for the indubitable eloquence of the former, waiting also for the latter to display his usual signs of dyspepsia and so temper homily with eructation, waiting also for a splendidly named specimen of bonnet-laird, called Bruce of Bogmuchalls, to answer the Minister's noise with his own, which was a powerful snore. Was there somewhere in those sessions a lad as truly 'whummled' with love as Violet Jacob's 'Tam i' the Kirk'? Here is a poem I cannot read without the fondest of Northern thoughts. Not that I was much addicted to kirk, but the vividness of the poem brings old Grant and Anderson to the ear, old Bogmuchalls to the eye, and much of old Banffshire to the memory. Miss Jacob's Tam is love-bewildered, and no minister, no psalm, no paraphrase can hold his mind.

> O Jean, my Jean, when the bell ca's the congregation
>   Owre valley an' hill wi' the ding frae its iron mou',
> When a' body's thochts is set on his ain salvation,
>   Mine's set on you.

Later on Tam is seen in the third person:

> He canna sing for the sang that his ain he'rt raises,
>   He canna see for the mist that's afore his e'en,
> And a voice drouns the hale o' the psalms an' the
>   paraphrases,
>   Cryin' 'Jean, Jean, Jean!'

Paraphrase is an odd word to fit into one of the simplest and fairest of Scottish love-lyrics written since the time of Burns. And how well it rides in the final stanza!

Violet Jacob has died since I wrote this note, and Scottish verse, now so lively in the vernacular, is her debtor indeed.

PARSNIP

'FINE words butter no parsnips', we are told, and since we are dealing in fine words we must consider the parsnip. But is parsnip itself a fine word? Scarcely. But an odd one and more amusing and attractive than the sickly article it represents – sickly, at any rate, to quite a number of palates including my own. The learned opine that parsnip comes from the Latin *pastinaca* and has attracted to itself the 'neep' or 'nip' found in turnip. The queer-sounding parsnip is 'a biennial umbelliferous plant with pinnate leaves and a pale yellow root'. This root has a sweetish flavour very different from the comparatively astringent tang of the turnip. Parsnip-haters have been long established in the land. In the scene of the play on *Sir Thomas More*, a piece of which has been attributed to Shakespeare's hand and handwriting, some remarks are passed on this theme during a popular discussion (strangely modern) on the influence of Immigrant Aliens. It is complained of these by one Lincoln that 'they eat more in our country than they do in their own' and also that they 'bring in strange roots, which is merely to the undoing of poor 'prentices, for what's a sorry parsnip to a good heart?'

Then one Williamson joins in the abuse of parsnips. 'Trash, trash. They breed sore eyes, and 'tis enough to infect the City with the palsy.' To this Lincoln replies, 'Nay, it has infected it with the palsy, for these bastards of dung (as you know, they grow in dung) have infected us and it is our infection will make the City shake, which partly comes through the eating of parsnips.' Whether the sense be good enough for Shakespeare can hardly be settled by recourse to these few lines: certainly More's final speech, in defence of receiving aliens, is one of high and courteous sentiment and quite possibly of Shakespearean phrase.

The proverb about fine words buttering no parsnips is also uncomplimentary to that root, which has ever lacked friends. Sir

Walter Scott, in *The Legend of Montrose*, mentions the proverb as Southern and Stevenson in his *Book of Quotations* traces it back to the text of a play called *The Citizen* by the eighteenth-century dramatist Arthur Murphy. Wycherley in *The Plain Dealer* had it that 'fine words butter no cabbage'. Parsnips, buttered or plain, may just, I think, be permitted to fill a corner of the stew, if better things be scarce. The trouble is that, once set, they may grow all too generously: the idea that they need a deal of manure is by no means my own experience.

PASSING AND PAY-NAMES

SHAKESPEARE frequently used the word passing as an adverb, and usually it is equivalent to very rather than to almost. I have been asked what Goldsmith meant when he called his village parson 'passing rich on forty pounds a year'. Did he mean surpassingly rich, which is the common interpretation of passing used as an adverb. But in that case the usage, which is complimentary when applied to a lady 'passing fair', is rather foolish as applied to the clergyman's income. Did Goldsmith have in mind 'passing as rich', which would make much more sense? Even with the price levels of eighteenth-century England a forty-pound stipend could hardly be called surpassingly generous or far more than ample. I surmise that Goldsmith used the word without clearly thinking out its exact meaning. Authors frequently do that. Mention of stipend brings to mind the complication of terms that we employ for what Costard in *Love's Labour's Lost* liked to call his Guerdon or Remuneration.

Most people do not object to receiving money: honourable men need not boggle about the name of the reward, if it be honestly earned. Whether their cheque or packet be dubbed pay, salary, or even the dibs or the doings, they value it by the source and the content, not the label. To be salary-earning, instead of wage-earning, may imply slightly more security because longer 'notice' of discharge may be attached to the salary. But, in essence, the payments are *quids pro quo*. And what is wrong with that?

But there are still some who appear to be touchy about receiving money at all, even for good work well done. The Secretary of a Club, for example, often receives nothing so common as a salary: he is presented with an Honorarium. This permits him to write Honorary in front of Secretary, which I take to be nonsense. The man is paid, and rightly paid, for the work which he does to the Club's satisfaction. So why should he shamefacedly pretend to be an amateur? For the sake of Honorarium-addicts I hope that the Income Tax Assessors regard this recompense as fairy gold, an accidental gift, and so untaxable. But I can hardly believe that such clemency exists in a tribe in whom the quality of mercy is, to put it mildly, somewhat strained.

An Honorarium is, according to the informative Mr. V. H. Collins, 'a voluntary payment for professional services'. I do not understand the relevance of 'voluntary'. All salaries are voluntarily paid by the employer: the Club is not forced to use this particular Secretary. The emphasis is surely on the word professional, and there is no shame attached to knowing one's job and carrying it out for money. To ears distressed by any mention of money matters, Honorarium is an escape-word and so smacks of humbug. It may sound fine; but so do fiddle-sticks, properly handled.

It has long been the habit of the genteel to use these escape-words. Why should the parson have a stipend instead of a salary or even, to use the common slang, a 'screw'? The same word has been attached in Britain to full-time magistrates; they are known as stipendiaries.

At what stage does a tip become a gratuity and when does a gratuity soar to the level of a bonus? (A bonus surely ought to be a bonum, since it is a good thing given to a good man and not a good man giving something away.) Bonus has its place in 'officialese' and has been allotted its own adjective bonusable. Mr. Argos, the Surveyor of Taxes, who is usually to be described as a gentleman passing inquisitive, has one of his hundred eyes on the bonusable persons. He means to include these gratuities or bona with their earned incomes and so to knock these benefits very nearly in half. However, not all such bona are always discovered even by Mr. Argos; but the unfortunate incumbent of an English parish, who is now passing poor on whatever stipend he draws, may not keep the full benefit of his Easter Offering. This is a traditional gift, instituted by the parishioners to help ease the strains of his poverty. The parson is now deemed a bonusable worker and taxable as such.

Another word in the category of genteel alternatives to money is Emolument, a term which I should call passing pompous. We have also recently added Incentive to the list and, when asked by somebody to do a job with no fee mentioned, I sometimes politely inquire what is the proposed Incentive. But, so long as the money is real and punctual in its coming, I am little fussed by its titular circumstance. Honorarium, Emolument, Incentive –I care not. Let us cut the cackle and come vulgarly to what was once the oof or the dibs and is now, by way of Broadway, the potatoes or the scratch.

PAVISANDING

A PAVIS was a shield, a pavisade or pavisande a fence of shields. But Kipling made a verb of it.

> Forth she came pavisanding like a peacock, stuft, ruft, stomacher and all.

This cannot have much to do with a pavisande of shields, though it does suggest a lady heavily armoured for the social encounter, a battle-cruiser among *les belles-dames sans merci*. I can picture Queen Elizabeth pavisanding at times and, in a more subtle, insinuating way, Shakespeare's Cleopatra. Among great pavisanders also was Milton's Delilah.

But who is this, what thing of sea or land?
Female of sex it seems,
That so bedeck'd, ornate, and gay,
Comes this way sailing
Like a stately ship
Of Tarsus, bound for th'isles
Of Javan or Gadier,
With all her bravery on, and tackle trim,
Sails fill'd, and streamers waving,
Courted by all the winds that hold them play,
An amber scent of odorous perfume
Her harbinger.

Congreve drew on that maritime form of pavisanding for the entrance of his Millamant and added 'a shoal of fools for tenders'.

PELTING

How many of the young who are dragged through John of Gaunt's speech on this other Eden, demi-Paradise, blessed plot, happy breed, etc., could define the pelting farm which he mentions? One might imagine it to be a holding where pelts or skins are obtained, a sheep-farm. (Those servants of luxury, farmers of silver-fox and mink, were then, of course, unknown.) But pelting was an ancient and rather pleasing epithet for small, trashy, worthless. It is much the same as paltry, which probably has the same origin in palt, an old Scandinavian word for bits and pieces, dross. Shakespeare applied pelting to small streams, small farms, small villages, and petty officers; the last must not be understood in our naval sense. Pelting and paltry are both nicely dismissive adjectives. The very sound of them humiliates the noun to which they are attached. A pelting farm is obviously a hovel with some weedy acres, while a pelting petty officer must be a contemptible little Jack-in-office. It seems a pity that pelting should have lost favour; and paltry, too, is a trifle literary now. We have our own terms of derision in common use for pelting people and paltry things – terms which may be ruder. But are they really more apt and effective?

It is odd that pelting rain should be no paltry downpour.

PERJINK
AND OTHERS

A WHOLE army of Scotticisms follow, so anti-Caledonians are at full liberty, and are even advised, to practise the art of skipping for a page or so. It was observed by Henry Fielding's Jonathan Wild that many men fail in wickedness for want of going deep enough in, a remark which seems to me, as my experience of life grows with the years, to be both accurate in fact and profound in principle. Accordingly, if it be a trespass to pick a few of Scotland's verbal bluebells or king-thistles, I shall not commit the further error of self-limitation to one or two such blooms. Let there be no meagre paddling in the Lallans burn, but a full plunge into that pool of peaty waters. All this arises from a passage in a lecture on 'The Scottish Character as it was viewed by Scottish authors from Galt to Barrie', delivered by James Bridie to the Greenock Philosophical Society and reprinted in his rich volume of assorted sweets and bitters called *Tedious and Brief*. I quote this at length and with the author's following glossary as well as his permission.

Here are some of his words to Greenock:

The Scot, on the other hand, has always taken an almost morbid delight in oddities of mind or behaviour. A remarkable proportion of his vocabulary consists of words which are lightning caricatures of 'character' seen from this aspect. In any railway carriage he can mark his fellow passengers as gaucie, menseful, forfochen, couthie, perjink, cappernoytit, fusionless, dour or douce. It is interesting to reflect what a large proportion of this vocabulary describes character in which mental defect is a prominent feature. The Scots conversation is full of thowless, bloutering nyaffs; of feckless, donnart, doited, havering gowks; of daft, glaikit, foutering tawpies; of snuitit gomerals. Next to the Idiot come the Slut and the Harridan. It would be a mistake to stress this too much. A nation which makes a thorough study of character in its most subtle forms must necessarily be rich in terms of abuse. Much the most effective kind of abuse is the intimate and personal. To call a man a black-guard gives him such a wide range of choice that the sting is dissipated. But, if you call him a rowting sump or a wullie-wallocks and are careful in your choice of epithet, you hold, as 'twere, a mirror up to his defect; you get home.

Apart from the language of denigration, there is plenty in the Scottish tongue to show that here is a race that takes character seriously and has an endless variety to choose from. What applied to the race in general, applied to Scottish writers in particular.

As an absentee Scot, I must confess to some weakness in the finer shades of the Doric, Lallans, Scots, or what you will. The words for fool seemed to explain themselves, but the previous list of adjectives needed interpretation to be fully relished. I consulted Mr. Bridie, who replied with the natural courtesy of a Lowland Scot and a punctuality most unusual in gentlemen of the artistic professions. Here are his definitions, described as 'not official, but the connotations I have heard commonly employed'.

Gawcie (or *gaucie*): 'Handsome' is only part of it. It means also jolly, 'well-put-on', flourishing, euphoric, buxom (if it applies to a woman). It implies a large and jovial sort of grace . . . like a chrysanthemum or a dahlia.
Menseful: Thoughtful. Not so much sicklied over with the pale cast as intelligent and considerate and considering.
Forfochen: Thoroughly depressed. Also implying the battered effect produced by Fortune's buffets, and a tendency to lamentations.

Couthie: Comfortable. Neat. Well-to-do. Opposite of 'uncouth'. An old meaning is popular or kenspeckle.

Perjink: Tidy. Pernickety. Precise.

Fusionless: Sapless. Feeble. Without fusion of the elements.

Cappernoytit: Confused chronically in the intellects. Slightly deranged. This is odd because *Cappernoity* means a mischief-making gossip. *Cabair*, a babbler; *naitheas*, mischief. It is an adjective, of course, in both cases.

Dour: Same as 'dur'. Hard, obstinate, glum, grim.

Douce: Gentle, courteous. Also implies that the douce person never gets rattled.

Glaikit: From *gleogach*, silly. Applied very often to an idiotic appearance, rather than to habits. Burns uses both above words in 'The Unco Guid':

> That frequent pass douce Wisdom's door
> For glaikit folly's portals.

Sumph: Is the right spelling, I think. A heavy, dull, stupid person.

Wullie-Wallocks: An effeminate boy. Also implies silliness.

The allusion to the spelling of sumph was caused by my protesting against Bridie's sump. The latter is a drain. The former, as I remember from boyhood talk in Scotland, is a dolt. 'A muckle sumph' was supposed to be finally dismissive of a person's claims to any grey matter.

The fusion in fusionless is really the same as Shakespeare's foison, which means the sap or strength of a plant or crop, leading to plenty in the field and larder.

Certainly it is a fine list of what Armado called the congruent epitheton. Apply it, for example, to Hamlet. Angered by his gawcies mother's second marriage, the douce and menseful prince turns dour and forfochen, and rails at himself for being fusionless. For safety's sake he pretends to be glaikit, no dull sumph but certainly cappernoytit. He kills the perjink Polonius and is brought a challenge by the wullie-wallocks Osric. So life in Elsinore is scarcely couthie.

Would English be the worse for borrowing from Scottish? Am I really to be scolded?

PERSON

PERSON has had a very odd history. It comes from the Latin *Persona*, which meant the mask of a mummer. So the first person was really a false, unreal person. But history has swung the meaning right round. A film-actor is today announced as 'appearing in person' to signify that he is there in the actual flesh and with no mere fictitious presence of mask or photograph. That is not the only reversal of fortune which has befallen the word. At one time a person meant a great person or what we call a personage. 'As I'm a person!' cries Congreve's Lady Wishfort. But nowadays to call a person a person is usually demeaning and derogatory. 'There's a person who comes in to do the rough work' is genteel housekeeper's English. The old kind of person lingers on Latinly in 'Personae Dramatis', but even by Shakespeare's time person was truly personal, as we would say, in 'Our royal person' and similar phrases. But a hint of the old notion of masquerade or assumed aspect lingers on in Quince's 'to present the person of moonshine' and possibly in Iago's line about Cassio: 'He hath a person and a smooth dispose'. Personnel became a war-time favourite of 'officialese' English. 'Anti-personnel bomb' was one of the larger flowers of this horrid growth. Our ancestors were savage in their attitude to poachers and scattered horrible devices for their capture. But at least they called these things simply and accurately 'man-traps'. Now they would be 'Anti-personnel pincer mechanisms'.

PHAETON

AND OTHERS

'You must know that, one day last week, as Lady Betty Curricle was taking the dust in Hyde Park, in a sort of duo-decimo phaeton, she desired me to write some verses on her ponies.' Thus challenged, Sheridan's Sir Benjamin Crabtree composed, instantaneously, thus:

> Sure never were seen two such beautiful ponies,
> Other horses are clowns, but these macaronies.
> To give 'em this title I'm sure isn't wrong,
> Their legs are so slim and their tails are so long.

The motor car has pushed the phaeton off our roads, but it lasted well. During a boyhood year in the north of Scotland I remember that my father purchased a phaeton and a carriage-horse and hired a boy to look after them. The lad was given (and was proud of) a page-boy suit of the 'buttons' kind. Our phaeton had not the elegance of Lady Curricle's, since the horse was a singleton and no macaroni. But it served for shopping excursions to Cullen and Portsoy, townships hardly in Sir Benjamin's acquaintance.

The old and speedy phaeton was named after the sun-god's son and charioteer. He should be spelled Phaethon by Grecians who mean to be correct: he means shining; his life is a cautionary tale. He asked and received his Sun-Father's permission to drive the parental chariot across the sky. But he could not hold in the horses who deviated, as the totalitarians say of free-thinkers, and came so near the earth as to singe it, thus creating black people on the globe. Zeus, who was perhaps colour-conscious or at any rate disliked major celestial disturbances, took the whole affair peevishly; it never did to be on the wrong side of Zeus, whose powers of transmogrification (yes, that is a dictionary word and as old as 1656) were both drastic and tetchily employed. Phaethon himself was killed by a flash of lightning and thrown into the river Eridanus; his kinsman and fellow-traveller Cycnus became a swan and his sisters, who had yoked the horses, were turned into poplar trees.

That fiery and disastrous escapade had little in common with our plodding Banffshire phaeton, its worthy steed, and its red-headed, silver-buttoned George. But the name at least was heroic and the Hyde Park phaetons of eighteenth-century London (they seemed to have arrived in 1742) were doubtless dashing specimens of 'the four-wheeled, open pleasure-carriage', usually fitted with its seats facing forward.

The names of our old carriages are picturesque and plentiful. The Barouche was a four-seater, half-coverable, in which the two front passengers faced the back ones. The Brougham I find described as 'a one-horse closed carriage with two or four wheels for two or four people'. Both these were nineteenth-century contraptions for private use. The Cabriolet, whence came the public Cab, was a two-wheeled one-horse chaise with open hood. The Curricle was a light two-wheeler of the eighteenth century, parent of the Victorian Dog-cart. The earliest dog-carts were drawn by dogs: but the later vehicle continued to earn the name by supplying room for stowing sporting dogs under the driver's seat. Gigs, Phaetons and Tilburys were linked together by Dickens. There was the Dennet, too, which, like Gig and Tilbury, was a light two-seater. The Fly I remember in boyhood at Cheltenham, where it plied for public use and was sometimes oddly known as a Rat. It seemed the first cousin to a Phaeton. *O.E.D.* defines it as 'a quick-travelling carriage – especially a light vehicle introduced at Brighton in 1816 and originally drawn by men: subsequently extended to any one-horse covered carriage, as a cab or hansom: let out on hire'.

The names of carriages multiplied in the early nineteenth century. Europe contributed to the vocabulary. You could ride in a Frenchman's calash (calèche) and Russia sent the droshky. From Landau in Germany the House of Hanover brought the four-seater of that name.

The inventors or first users usually gave a title to the vehicle, e.g. Brougham, Tilbury, Dennet and Hansom. This last was called the gondola of London by Disraeli's Lothair. It is described as a 'low-hung, two-wheeled cabriolet with the driver mounted on a dickey behind and the reins going over the top'. Then there was the Stanhope, a Regency period one-seater, invented by the Hon. and Rev. Fitzroy Stanhope. The Hansom's larger brother, slow and dowdy, was the Four-Wheeler, more commonly called Growler, whether from the noise of its motion or the manners of its driver I do not know. The Victoria (1870) was a genteel variant on the Phaeton: it had four wheels, a collapsible hood, two main seats facing the horse and a small 'pull-out' stool facing them. Queen Victoria took her drives round Balmoral in a Sociable, with John Brown in the Rumble. Since the original Phaethon was deemed a rebel and came to such a bad end, being both incinerated and liquidated by his celestial father, it would scarcely have been nice for Queen Victoria to be transported in any vehicle so named. But the rash man has not only lived on in the livery stables: he gave matter for lines of Shakespeare which have a typical and haunting beauty. Cries Richard II,

> Down, down, I come, like glistering Phaethon
> Wanting the manage of unruly jades.

Phaethon had struck Shakespeare's fancy: we hear a deal of him and, as a wagoner, he cracks a whip in Juliet's eager fancy.

Glistering Phaethon! Not all the vehicles of that class have deserved the bright adjective. But Lady Betty Curricle's duodecimo phaeton undoubtedly glistered.

Then there were the Chariots, suggesting a raging pace in the arena. I am always glad to meet a chariot in eighteenth- and nineteenth-century novels. The nimble and voluble scout employed by Messrs. Chicksey, Veneering and Stobbles described Miss Bella Wilfer of *Our Mutual Friend* as 'a slap-up gal in a bang-up chariot' when she came to see her papa at the firm's offices. This leaves me delighted with the vision of Bella as another Boadicea, but unable to explain why such terms of violence as 'slap-up' and 'bang-up' should signify warm approval.

Chariots are, by nature, Biblical, Roman and generally antique. The Brythons are said to have put knives on the chariots' wheels and Romans put stakes (of the betting order) on their teams of horses. The translators of the Bible had chariots constantly at the tip of their pen-nibs, Jehovah made the cloud his chariot, and Time's chariot had wings for Marvell. It seems a considerable descent from Jehovah's chariot of cloud and Blake's chariot of fire to the jog-trot of a cab in early Victorian London, but Dickens's novels are full of their rattle-trap progress.

The Times of April 2nd, 1849, advertised a sale by auction of eighty carriages, including Clarences, dog-carts and chariots. The Clarence was a four-seater. There was also in the sale a vehicle called a Britschka, said to be as good as new; it had been discarded by a lady with no further need. The Britschka was equipped with a barouche seat in front and a rumble behind. A rumble was the 'dicky' of those days. It took luggage and the less regarded passengers.

PHONEY

THIS strange term of contempt and dismissal has spread powerfully from America and has almost ousted the once fashionable bogus from usage over here. Bogus, which may have some link with bogy, was an earlier importation from the West. Phoney is usually spelt thus and not with an 'f', suggesting some connection with telephony. But why should a telephoned message be more false or pretentious than a written one? The only explanation of phoney in my acquaintance is that given by Eric Partridge in his *Dictionary of R.A.F. Slang*. Commenting on the various kinds of 'gen' (see note on 'intelligence') he considers 'phoney gen' (doubtful information) and concludes 'Phoney from the American underworld, which adapted it from Fawney, the English underworld term for a ring, the transition being effected by "Brum" jewellery'. The *O.E.D.* gives fawney as a brass ring disposed of as gold. Any other theories? No doubt the victory of phoney owes something to the sound of the word. But why the 'ph'? It is true that such words as fair and famous begin with 'f', but the 'f' sound is frequently contemptuous. Filthy, feeble, fatuous, futile, fiddling, finicky, fatheads and fools are just the folk to be fobbed off with faked and phoney articles. It is unquestionable that phoney is expressive and comes easily off the curling lip.

PICCADILLA

IT had numerous spellings, as did so many people and things of Tudor times. It meant the cut-work of the great Tudor collar: then the collar itself, the vast neck-piece of fashion and display. Excessive people exceeded in their piccadills.

> Her Piccadill above her crowne upreares:
> Her Fardingale is set above her eares.

And so to Piccadilla Hall, a mansion built in the late sixteenth century somewhere near the present Piccadilly Circus. Why the name? Two answers are usually given. One, that the area was then the fringe or necklet of the town, which still hugged the river between Westminster and the City. Two, that Piccadilla Hall was the seat of a jumped-up clothier, who had sold the modish article at high profit; the town thus gave the nickname to all his demesne. Some say the name of the Piccadill-king was Baker; others say Higgins. There is a story that he bought an acre and a half for fifty pounds, on the whole and in the light of the centuries a good speculation. So the name was there and the great herbalist of the time could write, 'The small wild buglosse grows upon the drie ditch bankes about Pickadilla.' Charles II endeavoured to honour his Queen by calling the road, leading west from Piccadilla Hall, Portugal Street. But this pleased neither London pride nor Cockney instinct. The public insisted on having its Piccadilly, and that name became 'Official' during the middle of the eighteenth century.

The voice of the people was certainly in this case the voice of understanding. Piccadilly was a nice invention. The title of Pall Mall to the south started with a courtly game, but suitably began to signify later on the saunterings of those whose day's occupation was to move from Foodle's Club to Poodle's, there to find a new audience for their observations on the Government and the decay of the nation. Piccadilly was obviously a lighter street, gayer, less heavily fortified with red leather armchairs, less garrisoned by those club servants for whom no adjective but 'august' will suffice. It mingled expense with taste, clothes and caviare with books and pictures, and all with delight. Invitations to go down the Strand have been the cry of the pleasuring Londoner, but Piccadilly is a senior claimant for convivial honours. It became, with its absurd syllables, the centre of the traveller's dream of home. A. H. Clough, abroad, idealized even the paving-stones on which our feet have burned and ached on summer days:

> Oh, you flags of Piccadilly,
> Though I hated you, I vow
> I could wish with all my heart
> You were underneath me now.

So the old Tudor collar survives the centuries – and not in London only. Other cities have liked the queer road-name and adopted it.

PICKSOME

I noticed this word in a *Times* obituary of Holbrook Jackson, that keen student of the eighteen-nineties and of good book-production in all ages. To be a picksome man is not, I think, to be a pernickety man: the latter is a fuss-pot or possibly worse. The former is fastidious, and to be thus selective, thus picksome, is plainly a virtue. Do we suggest a fault if we use the adjective fastidious? Surely not. Nowadays we have the slang word 'choosey' invading this range of meanings and the 'choosey' man is certainly regarded as being picksome to a tiresome extent. In this array of epithets for the precise and careful chooser the Scottish perjink is admirable.

Finical and finikin are also useful and attractive adjectives, but they express a distaste for the too sedulous taster, which fastidious does not. I do not know who invented fuss-pot, but it gives a vivid impression of somebody boiling over with 'chooseyness'. One hears the fuss-pot simmering with his whimsical addictions and dislikes. The picksome man, as I conceive him, is cool and works on judgment not on excitement. He ranks with the connoisseur and curioso, not with the finical tribe. A fashionable epithet of the time is hand-picked, to signify carefully chosen. It seems to me silly; especially when applied to candidates for jobs. These the wise employers select mentally, in a judiciously picksome way. The origin of pernickety seems to be unknown.

PIDDLE

THIS is not only 'to make water, now vulgar', in dictionary definition, but to be fussy with one's food, to pick at it and peck at it and trifle with it.

> Give order that twelve pigs be roasted yellow,
> Nine geese, and some three larks for piddling meat,
> And twenty woodcocks.

So did a Jacobean, Simon Tanner, who has the title-part in Middleton's *The Mayor of Queenborough*, order a dinner. Simon also used the verb in its vulgar sense. 'Like beast as I was I pissed out the fire last night and never dreamed of the king's coming.'

Pope, a century later, also trifled thus with his food.

> Content on little I can piddle here
> On broccoli and mutton all the year.

But the vulgar sense has now so far overcome the proper one that the children of today are unlikely to be rebuked for piddling with their dinner.

PLURISY

To the Elizabethans plurisy is a plus-ness, an excess of anything. It is quite a different word from our pleurisy, which is derived from the Greek 'pleuron', a rib, and is defined as 'Inflammation of the pleura, with or without effusion of fluid into the pleural cavity and usually characterized by pain in the chest or side'. Those who have had the affliction know all about that. Our pleurisy of the sickroom can create a plurisy of distress.

The original plurisy, meaning surfeit and overplus, was once commonly used. Shakespeare's

> For goodness growing to a plurisy
> Dies of his own too much,

is paralleled by John Ford's

> Must your hot itch and plurisy of lust,
> The hey-day of your luxury, be fed
> Up to a surfeit?

Those lines, incidentally, might easily occur in the Closet Scene in *Hamlet*. The terminology is identical with Shakespeare's. The dramatists of that period had a tremendous stock of rich reach-me-down stuff for the deeds both of Venus and of Mars.

On the other hand, the sub-Shakespeareans, while they handle this wealth of lusty lingo, usually betray themselves in the end as being less than William. Ford, in the already quoted speech of Soranzo's from *'Tis Pity She's a Whore*, continues:

                    Now I must be the dad
                    To all that gallimaufry that is stuffed
                    In thy corrupted, bastard-bearing womb!
                    Why must I?

To which Annabella replies,

                    Beastly man!

She had a case.

POMP

A GOOD midget word, if you stop to look at it. Surely it dismisses what it describes: the sumptuous, processional rites are aptly snubbed with this monosyllable. 'Our pomps of yesterday' are put aside by the mere use of the little word. Pomps and vanities have been made inseparable, although our world could do with more of the flourish, the tint, the cavalcade. An age more proud of show, addicted to the wonderments of masque and triumph, could use the word more happily.

                    Is it not passing brave to be a King?
                    Oh yes, my Lord, 'tis sweet and full of pompe.

No hesitation in Marlowe's mind where the 'pomps of power' were concerned.

But the English Puritan drew back from pomps and in Cornwall, perhaps elsewhere also, 'to pomp' became a domestic term for to masquerade or to show off. Here is a note from J. C. Trewin.

> Do you know the word 'pomping'? (I rediscovered it when turning up some notes a week or two ago.) My mother used it sometimes when she meant acting (or, loosely, any sort of flamboyant display). It's not regular Cornish dialect, but an old man at Mother's village of Manaccan, in Meneage, during the late 'seventies, used to speak with horror of actors as 'they pompin' folk'; and it seems to have become a local usage. It's rather pleasant. I thought it was the perfect adjective for Mae West.

Cornwall has also kept Marlowe's use of brave for grand: in the Duchy it still means anything big. A brave appetite will get a brave helping. I suggest also that when a circus comes to town with all its bravery (display not courage) it goes pomping down the street. And may not some politicians and other bigwigs be said to pomp?

POW

THE dictionaries turn away from pow. Southern England will not acknowledge it. Burns made it familiar.

> But now your brow is bald, John,
> Your locks are like the snow,
> But blessings on your frosty pow,
> John Anderson, my Jo.

Again, of a limping and bent old man he wrote that he hirples

> Wi' his teethless gab and his auld beld pow.

But it is not just a Scotticism. In Mr. T. Thompson's robust and racy sketches and dialogues of Lancashire life there is often a gathering at the barber's. 'To pow' a man here is to cut his hair, and a nice, crisp term for it too. Pow-wow, for a putting of heads together in counsel and debate, might come from this, but does not. It is one of the Red Man's gifts to his White conqueror. It is odd that, while the Redskin is usually pictured as a serene and silent chieftain, wrapped in tobacco-smoke and silence, one of our most graphic words for a talk should be his. Palaver, another good one, comes from Africa.

PRETTY

I WAS reminded by a note of Sir Walter Scott's that 'the word pretty is, or was, used by the Scots in the sense of the German *prächtig* and means a gallant, alert fellow, prompt and ready at his weapon'. But this kind of practicality also included tricks and wiles and indicated mental shrewdness and agility. Hence 'a pretty wit', which is an earlier arrival than a pretty face. The adjective slid, by way of neatness, from the nimble limbs to the taking features. In Shakespeare pretty is already being used for attractive as well as in its original sense of tricky.

Scotland, more conservative, kept pretty for gallant, long after it had been relegated to wits' corner or the ladies' beauty parlour in England. Said Bailie Nicol Jarvie of the Highland cattle-thieving: 'A thing deplorable in any Christian country – the mair especially that they take pride in it and reckon driving a spreagh (which is, in plain Scotch, stealing a herd) a gallant, manly action and more befitting of pretty men – as sic reivers will ca' themselves – than to win a day's wage by ony honest thrift.' The nineteenth century turned pretty into considerable and dealt in pretty sums and pretty pennies, gambling with which will bring men to a pretty pass.

Pretty, for the fair-way of a golf-course, is dated by the *O.E.D.* as a creation of 1907. I should have guessed that it was much earlier. Presumably the phrase 'sitting pretty' comes from, or is at least linked with, the vision of a golf-ball nicely cocked up and awaiting a long, straight sweep from the pretty to the green. Such a stroke would be pretty in the *prächtig* sense as well as pretty to the eye.

PRIME

PRIME can be a verb meaning fill or charge or a noun with a special significance in fencing. Usually it is an adjective and one of strangely limited employment. It has been commonly applied to one kind of Minister, many kinds of meat, and certain kinds of mover. It used to be the butcher's darling, adorning and commending the steaks beside the market naphtha-flare or pinned upon the massed mutton of the Flesher's Saturday Night, with limbs set 'steadily shoulder to shoulder' – like the Boys of the Old Brigade – or legs all in order – as in a troupe of dancing girls. It is odd how certain trades annex certain epithets. Prime has long been the prime favourite of British butchery. It is amusing that the word Primates should refer to Archbishops as leaders of the Church and to Apes as leading mammals.

Then there is 'in the prime', as applied to the lives of men and women. Gordon Hewart, late Lord Chief Justice, once defined this prime as the age of fifty-five. This was consolation to many and would have staggered an Elizabethan who regarded two-score as an age of wrinkled ruin. Shakespeare, who talked frequently of youth's sweet prime, was jostled by a rough wind in May into brooding over summer as a tenant shortly to be evicted and was likewise set aghast by the siege of forty winters, digging deep trenches in the brow. Bernard Shaw, on the other hand, as a good Methuselist, put 'the prime' away up in the centuries and nearly lived up to his own prescription. There is ugly use of prime for lecherous in *Othello:* 'Were they as prime as goats.' But mostly prime rides in good company, with the leading citizen, the sweet of the year, and the best of the carcass. Do vegetarians answer prime beef with 'prime cabbages'? I think not.

PROPAGATE

SAID Romeo

> Griefs of my own lie heavy in my breast
> Which thou wilt propagate.

He is close here to the original meaning of propagate, 'to fasten or peg down slips of plants for growth, to multiply plants by layering'. Hence it later meant to breed one's kind and later still to diffuse one's news. And so to the ever-present propaganda. I hate using the word propaganda, but it is now very difficult to avoid.

Propaganda in our time suggests dishonest persuasion, yet it had a most august and holy start in life, when Pope Gregory XV founded his Commission of Cardinals as a *Congregatio De Propaganda Fide*. For the word was first applied to persons or systems rather than to doctrinal instruction. 'Any association, systematic scheme, or concerted movement for the propagation of a particular doctrine or practice' is one of the definitions. In our time propaganda has become impersonal and signifies chiefly the ideas propagated and the process of propagation. Hence, by back-formation, the verb to propagand, which is a sorry use of the original Latin, if you wish to be strict in these matters. It should, of course, be propagate; but that has become chiefly physical in meaning.

There are plenty of slang terms for propaganda now. I note that an outburst of propagandist statements by Stalin was dismissed by an American Senator as 'The old malarkey'. I have no idea what malarkey actually signifies. Damon Runyon's Broadway argot included 'the old phedinkus', which has a Grecian savour. Malarkey, in the same way, has a Latin-sounding first syllable. When the narrator of one of Runyon's yarns observed in Mindy's restaurant that he was afflicted with the tender passion, the 'I' of the story confessed that 'For me love is just the old phedinkus'. The same voice often spoke of 'the phonus bolonus' and I surmise that phedinkus meant much the same to him and that malarkey is cousin to boloney and phedinkus too.

Boloney comes from the famous Bologna sausage and was Polony in Cockney usage: then it still meant a reputable sausage, but the American boloney refers to malarkey and phedinkus, not to honest pork. Just as propaganda has fallen from the affairs of faith to the less desirable work of the politician, so has tasty sausage-meat descended to the status of a fraud. Phonus Bolonus is the ultimate fate of the gardener's honourable propagation.

PURDONIUM AND TORALIUM

I was reminded of Purdonium, which is Auctioneer's English for a coal-scuttle, by a correspondent who told me of Toralium, which is similar lingo for an eider-down. Latin *torus* (bed) gives the latter its veneer of scholarship, but the origin of Purdonium is a mystery, unless it is somehow based on Greek 'pur' (fire), in which case it should be Pyrdonium. The *O.E.D.* admits Purdonium but not Toralium. Does Purdonium survive in catalogues? Perhaps not, for my memory of its grave splendour comes from boyhood. The jargon of salesmen has many fascinations. House-agents' English is an everlasting treasure. Toralium as well as Purdonium should be on the inventory list of (may I suggest) 'Tudor-Style Bijou Bargain in Essex Highlands. Facing South with fine views over E. London. Veritable Sun-trap. L'pool St., 35 mins. Handy three stations, two golf-courses, eight cinemas, greyhounds (two tracks), foxhounds (two packs), and super road-house. Suit City gent. with sporting tastes'. Or again : 'Six Centuries of Romantic History, but still standing in own grounds, Nobleman's Period Seat. Stately Baronial Home-County Gem, completely renovated, just on market. Wealth of old oak and modern plumbing. All usual offices on ducal scale. Eight Luxury Bath-rooms. Timbered park a picture. Company's and ornamental water. Forty mins. City, House of Lords, Shaftesbury Avenue.'

A Purdonium is hardly a luxury, but it does its best to sound as much. The use of the word 'luxury' as an adjective ('Blonde Dead in Luxury Flat') saves a little space, but, for me, it always raises a question. At what point does a mere Flat become a Luxury Flat? Presumably, when it has more than two Luxury Bath-rooms. And when does a mere Bath-room become a Luxury Bath-room?

PYRAMID

PYRAMID is a fine soaring word in an iambic line, especially with the Greek plural in four syllables, as in Cleopatra's cry,

> Make
> The high pyramides my gibbet.

Here was Parson Woodforde's idea of an 'elegant' dinner:

The first course was, part of a large Cod, a Chine of Mutton, some Soup, a Chicken Pye, Puddings and Roots, etc. Second course, Pidgeons and Asparagus. A Fillet of Veal with Mushrooms and high Sauce with it, roasted Sweetbreads, hot Lobster, Apricot Tart and in the Middle a Pyramid of Syllabubs and Jellies. We had Dessert of Fruit after Dinner, and Madeira, White Port and Red to drink as Wine.

After this he reports 'we were all very cheerful and merry'. What would happen to us now? Have we lost, in our hard times, all stomach for such a fight? That hot lobster in the middle of it all! How much was it polite to miss? My impression is that most of the diners had a dip at most of these concoctions. Pyramidal times!

QUARELET

A WORD of three syllables, denoting something cut from a quarrel, which was the old word for a quarry as well as the lasting word for a brawl; thereafter it meant any kind of stone or gem. Quarelet certainly is rare, but it comes up shining in Herrick,

> Some ask how pearls did grow
>> And where?
> Then spoke I to my girl
>> To part her lips and showed them there
>> The quarelets of pearl.

Pearl would seem to be the last kind of gem to be associated with quarrying; but let that pass. It is strange that so nice a word for stones and jewels should have slipped through the fingers of authors habitually eager for an attractive synonym.

QUINSY

A STRIKING word for a nasty business. It has been suggested to me that quinsy, a very painful and dangerous swelling in the throat, is connected with quince, 'a hard, acid, yellowish pear-shaped fruit' whose bitterness may have constrictive results. (Quinine is another matter, being an alkaloid product, both chemically and verbally, of cinchona.) The dictionaries do not link quinsy with quince, but attribute it to the Greek word for a dog-collar, cynanche. The Greek dog, cuon, has given us, then, both cynic, the philosopher who carried his contempt of worldly pleasure so far as to go and live in a tub or kennel, and quinsy, because a collar can be to a dog what an inflammation of the throat can be to man, namely a pain in the neck.

QUODLIBETARIAN

'NOT long ago,' said Sir Max Beerbohm in his Rede lecture upon Lytton Strachey, 'I heard that agile and mellifluous quodlibetarian, Dr. Joad, saying in answer to a questioner who wanted to write good letters that anybody could write good letters; one had but to think out clearly what one wanted to say, and then set it down in the simplest terms.' The advice was criticized by Sir Max, who believes that a true gift for writing is something more than lucidity. He is generally considered to prove the truth of this belief in his own writing. Meanwhile, what is a quodlibetarian? A quodlibet (Latin for what-you-will) is a question in philosophy or ethics set as an occasion or exercise for argument. A Brains Trust is largely engaged with quodlibets. Sir Thomas More wrote of the quodlibets before 'a pot parliament', which is indeed a complimentary title for a public-house argle-bargle. Quodlibet has sprouted some imposing stems. Quodlibetical is an epithet which I shall reserve for several of my friends, one of whom, on being casually told that it's a fine day, would certainly retort in the Joadian manner, 'That all depends on what you mean by the word fine and what you mean by the word day. Do you mean a total absence of rain for twelve or twenty-four hours?' And so tenaciously onward. There is a verb 'to quodlibetificate'. My friend deserves it.

RACY

RACY means, in the first place, characteristic of the native. Charlotte Brontë wrote of Yorkshire families as being 'racy, peculiar and vigorous'. Racy came to be used of all distinctive things, especially in relation to soil and locality. The ordinary reader, on first seeing the word, is apt to confuse it with racing and think of something swift. There is, indeed, some connection with the two kinds of race here, because fast can mean raffish as well as speedy. (Is this usage disappearing? Does anybody under sixty now speak disapprovingly of 'a fast girl'? The rates of this kind of motion have risen so sharply that the word seems a trifle tame. We have moved on to more vigorous dismissals.) 'Racy of the soil' is generally applied to language and conversation, and by racy talk, I imagine, is meant something not altogether reputable, at least where the phrase is used by solemn persons.

I came across racy not long ago while turning out a drawer and discovering an ancient wine-merchant's catalogue. What a lingo the craft has employed! The vintners' English still has a pleasing variety of words and of application of words. 'Full-bodied, stout, shows great breed.' This referred to a Clos de Vougeot, not to a Champion Clydesdale. 'Exhibits great finesse' was used of a white Bordeaux and not of a bridge player. 'Medium body, elegant, very ready' might fitly describe a young woman or a motor car. It did, in fact, describe a claret. 'Smooth, vinous, very high-class' suggested to me an advertising agent. But it was the description of Château Cos d'Étournel, 1928, from the region of St. Estèphe. The words 'stylish and racy' brought to the mind's eye a perfectly brogued and tweeded beauty photographed at some Point-to-Point Steeplechases with shooting-stick and leathery friend. They belonged, in fact, to a Rhine wine.

RAMEKIN

In a *Times* Fourth Leader called 'Under the Hammer' there was some pleasant scrutiny of 'The Valuable Contents of the Mansion'. One Sale Catalogue put together 'Peafowl, Antique Man Traps, Garden Statuary'. Obviously, as they say, here was 'something to go for'. In our years of incessant and violent burglary the Antique Man Trap, though the setting of it is, I suppose, illegal, must have its appeal for those who put a rough security before a nice legality. The leader-writer, enjoying his catalogue, adds, 'Its style, though sedate, is rich. Cassones and torchères, ottomans and fauteuils, tazze and tureens and ramekins, garnitures and purdoniums – we feel ourselves transported to a world of rather exotic opulence.'

I have previously noted the word purdonium as a stately piece of Auctioneers' English for a coal-box; ottomans, fauteuils and tureens are familiar articles of luxury or use. (The tureen, though it sounds lordly, has a humble origin, being 'terrine', the earthenware pot.) Torchères we can guess at. They might be brandished by the new-fangled torch-singers who afflict our nightly revels. (A Torch Singer is a terrible creature, at least as defined by Wilfred Granville in his *Dictionary of Theatrical Terms;* he describes her as a sentimental songstress 'who shines her torch in the face of a male in the audience', thus embarrassing him and amusing others.) A Tazza is a shallow ornamental bowl supported on a pedestal. Cassones elude me. Are they the same as caissons or chests? Garniture has, I suppose, some particular significance for Auctioneers, but, in any case, it is a nice word for appurtenances, the dressing of a dish or of a man. Dryden's phrase 'Men of feather and garniture' employs it prettily.

Now for ramekin. *O.E.D.* interprets it as 'a small quantity of cheese with bread-crumbs, eggs, etc., usually baked and served in a special mould'. But the 'cheese, bread-crumbs, eggs, etc.' would be in a curious state of decomposition if kept for the sale which eventually follows the decay of the Gentleman's mantrapped Estate or of the Nobleman's peafowl-strident Seat. So, the ramekin must here signify the special mould itself and not the mouldy fungus growing upon its surface. However, in this Penicillin Age we have been well instructed never to be harsh to a fungus or to brush off a mould as though it were a pestilence. Far otherwise. The decaying ramekin may yet bring us something of astonishing power to heal and save.

REABLE

'ABLE' is a good simple verb (as well as adjective) and one which speaks for itself. Indeed, it is a pity that it does not speak for itself more often nowadays. 'If God shall me able', wrote the diarist Evelyn and I do not see how the wishful hypothesis could be better expressed. 'I'll able 'em,' cried Lear at Dover amid his inclusive denunciation of rascal beadles, usurers, corrupt justices, and scurvy politicians. I have been reminded of this kind of able by a powerful defence of 'reable' as a substitute for the long, cumbrous, ubiquitous rehabilitate, a word I have often wished out of our language.

In place of rehabilitation I have suggested simply mend or cure, of bodies, and mend or restore, of things and buildings. But reable, originally a term for the legitimizing of a bastard, does give the idea of physical restoration clearly and briefly and I am very glad to know that it is now being used by some medical men. If we have disable, why not reable? We have not yet got to 'dishabilitation of personnel' to describe disablement of workers.

Sir Edmund Spriggs, a great physician of language as of body, writes to me:

The Ministry of Labour and National Service, following upon the Disabled Persons (Employment) Act, 1944, 'to enable the general public readily to identify officers engaged on this special work' arranged that 'they should be known as Disablement Rehabilitation Officers (D.R.O.)'. This seemed to me a terribly repetitive term and I wrote letters to one or two friends in authority about it.

I now hear from the Ministry of Labour that it has been decided to alter the title to 'Disablement Resettlement Officer', which is an improvement. As a Reabled person would naturally be resettled I am not sure that 'Reablement Officer' would not say it all in two words.

I am not discussing the word 'Rehabilitation' as regards houses and decayed organizations, though I should for them prefer the word 'Restore'; but in medical matters I suggest humbly that 'Reable' is better than 'Rehabilitate', and I am glad to see that the words Reable and Reablement are now being frequently used in the *Lancet* and other journals, although the longer words still cumber many documents, official and otherwise.

Sir Edmund also sent me a copy of some amusing and ingenious verses which appeared under the signature 'Anon' in the *Lancet*. They dealt with the adventures of Able Seaman Abel among the rehabilitators of his dishabilitation. They ended thus (the 'orotund' term referred to is dishabilitation):

> But Abel is an Englishman; and stabler
> Then to countenance so orotund a term.
> When disabled, he's reabled by an Abler –
> As, when able, A. B. Abel will confirm.

Orotund, by the way, strikes me as a pleasant, booming kind of adjective, justly applied to pompous polysyllables. It was sometimes applied to clearness and fullness of rhetoric in a complimentary manner, but much more often to resonant verbosity. The 'Disablement Rehabilitation Officer' is a triumph of official orotundity, a species of terminological carbuncle properly pricked by the *Lancet*. So more strength to the reablers and also to those who preserve able itself as a verb meaning to strengthen and empower.

REBARBATIVE

In a wireless talk on play-going, delivered in October, 1945, Sir Max Beerbohm defied the general ruling of the B.B.C. that the style and vocabulary employed should be conversational and easily comprehended of all. Listen to this, for example,

> The dramatic critics of that time were a less sophisticated race than the present one. They were a race of cheerful hacks. They did not see eye to eye with their argute Scottish colleague, William Archer, on the merits of 'A Doll's House'. Even A. B. Walkley, though he of course recognized the magnitude of Ibsen, found Ibsen rather rebarbative; and Bernard Shaw, though promptly Ibsenite, had not yet become a dramatic critic.

Argute for shrill, clear, or keen is, perhaps, not too difficult and has a fair amount of literary authority.

But rebarbative? The *O.E.D.* is unhelpful, calling it a rare word and defining it as crabbed, unattractive. Why? Because of the dressing back or curtailing of the beard? Of course Ibsen was largely bearded, but, if rebarbative in dramatic method and philosophy to Walkley, he was by no means rebarbative in facial style. The only example of this epithet given in the *O.E.D.* applies the epithet to a lady! The place in which it so occurred was an article (authorship unspecified) in the *Saturday Review* of 1892. 'Max' was then twenty. Was he already practising in the paper which he was later to adorn with such grace and constancy? It is the usual practice of scholars, when handling ancient texts of doubtful authorship, always to assume that usage of the same rare word suggests, or even proclaims, the same hand. Is Max our only dealer in rebarbativity?

REFOCILLATE

REFOCILLATE is rare, but commoner than focillate, meaning to refresh or reanimate. Presumably it is related to focus, the hearth, and means renew the fire. Coleridge liked to have his spirits refocillated and there is a nice use of it in Aubrey's *Life of William Prynne*, whose zeal for scholarship did not disdain refocillation through a frequent recourse to what is now commonly known as wallop:

> About every three houres his man was to bring him a roll and a pott of ale to refocillate his wasted spirits. So he studied and dranke, and munched some bread; and this maintained him till night; and then he made a good supper. Now he did well not to dine, which breakes off one's fancy, which will not presently be regained: and 'tis with invention as a flux – when once it is flowing, it runnes amaine; if it is checked, flowes but *guttim*: and the like for perspiration – check it, and 'tis spoyled. Goclenius, professor at —— in Germany, did better; he kept bottles of Rhenish wine in his studie, and when his spirits wasted, dranke a good rummer of it.

We most of us know that sinking feeling which beset the learned Goclenius. Nowadays sherry or a whisky and soda are commoner refocillants; but a good rummer of Rhenish sounds well enough to me.

RODOMONTADE
AND OTHERS

ONE does not expect Belloc to go wrong with a word, but surely in the following passage from *The Path to Rome* he seems to use rodomontade – as I believe it should be spelt – to signify a flimsy excuse, a fantastic fabrication. He may have confused it with 'romancing'.

> So I thought of how I should put myself right with those people. I saw that an elaborate story (as, that I dressed thus for a bet: that I was an officer employed as a spy, and was

about to cross the frontier into Germany in the guise of a labourer: that my doctor forbade me to shave – or any other such rhodomontade): I saw, I say, that by venturing upon any such excuses I might unwittingly offend some other unknown canon of theirs deeper and more sacred than their rule on clothes; it had happened to me before now to do this in the course of explanations.

But Rodomontade is uproarious boasting. Rodomont was the vaunting Saracen in Ariosto's 'Orlando Furioso'.

Rodomontade has fullness of sound and an imposing air. One form of military exhibitionism, often resented by civilians, is the deliberate use of a special vocabulary to create wonderment among listeners or readers. That, of course, is a vice of all professions. Captain Fluellen was a great one for the lingo of the text-books of war, and his kind continued in the eighteenth century to be a target for the indignant essayist.

In past centuries the Englishman at home, being, or purporting to be, a plain, blunt fellow, censured the lingo of the young soldiers as being Frenchified and Italianate, pretentious 'mounseer' stuff. The new jargon of artillery and engineers was continually derided by our John Bulls of the stay-at-home squirearchy. Addison's Sir Roger complains of dispatches from Marlborough's men containing this sort of thing:

> I had the good Fortune to be in that Regiment that pushed the *Gens d'Armes*. Several *French* Battalions, who some say were a Corps de Reserve, made a show of Resistance; but it only proved a Gasconade, for upon our preparing to fill up a little Fossé, in order to attack them, they beat the Chamade, and sent us *Charte Blanche*. Their Commandant, with a great many other General Officers, and Troops without number, are made Prisoners of War and will I believe give you a visit in England, the Cartel being not yet settled.

Sir Roger added,

> The Histories of all our former Wars are transmitted to us in our Vernacular Idiom, to use the Phrase of a great Modern

234

Critic. I do not find in any of our Chronicles, that Edward the Third ever reconnoitred the Enemy, tho' he often discovered the Posture of the French and as often vanquished them in Battle. The Black Prince passed many a River without the help of Pontoons, and filled a Ditch with Faggots as successfully as the Generals of our Times do it with Fascines. Our Commanders lose half their Praise, and our People half their joy, by means of those hard Words and dark Expressions in which our News Papers do so much abound.

But an earlier protestant against the military lingo had at least the retort legal. Sir John Davies wrote in 1598:

> Gallus hath beene this Sommer in Frizeland,
> And now returned he speakes such warlike wordes,
> As if I could their English understand,
> I fear me they woold cut my throate like swordes.
> He talkes of counter scarphes and casomates,
> Of parapets, of curtenays, Palizados,
> Of Flankers, Rauelings, gabions he prates,
> And of false brayes and sallyes and scaladose,
> But to requite such gulling termes as these,
> With wordes of my profession I reply,
> I tell of foorching, vouchers, counter pleas,
> Of whithernames, essoynes, and champarté,
> So neither of us understanding either,
> We part as wise as when we came together.

RUFFLE

ONE of the chief occupations of journalists in war-time is finding polite names for set-backs and disasters. How well accustomed readers everywhere must have grown to strategic retirements, movements to prepared positions, elasticity of defence, and tactical regroupings on more favourable ground. While reading the history of Bonnie Prince Charlie's fatal campaign in 1745 and 1746 I came across one of the most charming of these euphemisms. On the night of Culloden, Macleod, the Prince's aide-de-camp, wrote from Gortleg to Cluny MacPherson:

> Dear Sir,
>   You have heard no doubt ere now of the ruffle we met this forenoon . . . Dispatch is the more necessary that His Highness has something in view which will make amends for this day's ruffle.

Well, there was no panic there. But ruffle! At least a thousand of the scanty Highlanders were dead and many were doomed to slaughter in the next few days. Of course there could be no 'amends for this day's ruffle'. The game was up and Charles Edward Stuart knew it: he could tell a ruffle from a rout. Brave in his own defeat and escapade, he never mustered the clans again. The ordinary ruffle is a disturbance or upset. It is gentle enough as a rule. The placid waters of the lake, the tranquil contents of the mind, these are the matters of berufflement. Ruffles of another kind once flowed round the neck or adorned a cavalier's boot-top. But ruffling, on the whole, is a tender process, far short of calamity, and has little in common with a Culloden. Amid all our admissions and mitigations of enforced retreat in 1940, no ingenious sub-editor ever thought of mentioning 'a ruffle in the Low Countries'.

SANCTIMOODY

THIS engaging word I owe to a friend's report of rural tavern-talk. Sometimes there bubble up from the subconscious, stimulated by a pint of beer, such verbal felicities as this. Were not Sankey and Moody great evangelists and surpassingly righteous? Is not the sanctimonious fellow also inclined to dark looks and moody ways? Very well, then sanctimoody is the adjective for him. 'Thou concludest,' said Lucio, 'like the sanctimonious pirate that went to sea with the Ten Commandants but scraped one out of the table.' Captain Hook and Smee between them had their sanctimoody aspects. But we need not limit so grand a condemation to the sea-dogs. Sanctimoody is good enough for such land animals as the great Dickensian humbugs.

These rustic confusions with happy results are fairly common and sometimes lead to satire quite beyond the notions of the speaker. Of a rich gentleman who had just taken and altered an old farm, a labourer said to me, 'He's had it all remoderned'. The word remodern is delightful in its ironic reflection on the vanity of vogues and the transience of the up-to-date. An accidental sarcasm, but most pregnant.

SCOBBERLOTCHER

THE *O.E.D.* knows only of this strange monster that it may be connected with Scopperloit, an old word for leisure or idleness. Scobberlotcher I found along with some other weird terms of abuse. It occurs in Aubrey's description of that 'don of might', Dr. Ralph Kettell, President of Trinity, Oxford, in the sixteen-forties. Here is the passage:

> Dr. Kettell, when he scolded at the idle young boies of his colledge, he used these names, viz. Turds, Tarrarags (these were the worst sort, rude rakells), Rascal-Jacks, Blind-cinques, Scobberlotchers (these did no hurt, were sober, but went idleing about the grove with their hands in the pocketts and telling the number of trees there or so).

Scobberlotchery does not seem, on the whole, to be a desperate form of dissipation. Nowadays it might pass for a prelude to silviculture. Rake-hell I always like, especially in its adjectival form, rake-helly. The learned inform us that rake-hell does not mean a hell-raker, but comes from an Old English adjective rakel or rackle, meaning disorderly. But does it matter? Anyhow, the rake-hells and scobberlotchers won't care.

Kettell, who had 'a terrible gigantique aspect with his sharp grey eies', was not always ferocious. True, he was 'irreconcileable to long haire' and would carry 'a paire of cizers in the muffe which he commonly wore' and with these pounce on the super-fluous tresses of his more hirsute undergraduates while they sat in hall. But he 'sang in a shrill, high treble' and he had a humane cure for tippling and a shrewd knowledge of how to 'keep the boys at home':

> He observed that the houses (i.e. Colleges) that had the smallest beer had most drunkards, for it forced them to go to the town to comfort their stomachs: wherefor Dr. Kettell always had in his College excellent beer, not better to be had in Oxon: so that we could not goe to any other place but for the worse and we had the fewest drunkards of any howse in Oxford.

It is a fascinating picture that Aubrey gives of his College. Did he ever acquire the curious vice of tree-counting in the grove with hands in pocket? Was he a Scobberlotcher in the President's eye or was he – perhaps worse – a Tarrarag? Or even a Blind-cinque?

SCURRYFUNGE

HERE is an extract from a letter of William Cowper to Lady Hesketh.

> I know not my dearest Coz that I have anything to trouble thee about save half a dozen tooth-brushes; Mrs. Unwin will be much obliged to thee also for a black Summer cloak *untrimm'd*, because Hannah is making a trimming for it. Two of the brushes abovesaid must be for inside scurry-funging, viz – they must be *hook'd*. These wants satisfied, we have no other commissions with which to charge thee. The stiffer the brushes the better.

I know no history of the tooth-brush: if it does not exist, it should be written. I expected a chronicle of tooth-scrubbing in the *History of Everyday Things in England* by Marjorie and C. H. B. Quennell, but could not find one.

Scurryfunging, with its suggestion of scraping away fungus, is a fine, grim term for dental scouring and suits the stiff, hooked article for which Cowper asked. It is interesting to note that there were then different species of brush available: he wanted two of the potent scurryfungers and four other, presumably gentler, weapons.

SECRETARY

How often does the user of the word secretarial think of it in terms of deep confidence? Indeed, the fact that we have to employ the phrase 'confidential secretary' shows how far the original meaning has disappeared. (Really, one might as well talk about a culinary cook.) The Secretary of State was the man who held the secrets of the nation and any secretary's first business was rather to keep his mouth shut and ears open than to write and file letters. Hence secretary was applied to any conniver at privacies, especially to darkness. In an anonymous seventeenth-century poem of passion, drawing obviously on Latin sources, I came across the word in that connection.

> Let us begin while daylight springs in heaven
> And kiss till night descends into the even,
> And when that modest secretary, night,
> Discovers all but thy heaven-beaming light
> We will begin revels of hidden love
> In that sweet orb where silent pleasures move.

Izaak Walton, calling Sir Francis Bacon the Great Secretary of Nature, did not mean that he took down and wrote out Nature Notes.

SECURITY

WHAT a tyrant this word has been in our time! Security censored our letters and our news, condemned us to Stygian darkness, robbed us of sign-posts, maps, cameras. The word, incidentally, has been a total traitor to itself, since in Latin and at first in English it meant without care, easeful, feckless. So Shakespeare had it several times. 'Page is an ass, a secure ass', said Ford. Hamlet Senior was murdered in his 'secure hour'— there we get the contradiction of meaning at its most extreme. Macbeth's witches also proclaimed doctrine most odious to modern Governments.

> And you all know, security
> Is mortals' chiefest enemy.

How then did the word swing round so much that a man's secure hour could really be his safe one? One can argue it out like a Shakespearean clown.

> 'And if a man be careless, then, argal, he must be free from care.' 'Ay, marry is he.' And if he be free from care, then he stands in no hazard, for danger is a care. So your careless man is one out of hazard and your secure man is your safe one!'

So security moves on from the risks caused by neglect to the immunity from risk caused by taking thought or even by being remote. Adonais in death was secure 'From the contagion of the world's slow stain'. 'Security be our watchword,' cried the Elder Pitt. Shakespeare would hardly have understood that. Finally the word ends in the strong-box of the lawyer and the financiers as token of financial safety. And thence to the Home Office and all the engines and apparatus of hush-hushery. Did ever a term so stand upon its head?

SHADES AND SHADOW

THESE symbols of dark, sad and transient things naturally crowd our poetry and the latter word especially adorns it. It is strange that the extra syllable should add so much poignancy, but certainly it does so. The meaning of the two is sometimes, but not essentially, the same. Shadows are what the shade creates, but, in fancy, much more. A shade can be a ghost.

> And oft between the boughs is seen
> The sly shade of a Rural Dean.

A Dean's shadow would be that of a living man. So from this spectral suggestion 'the shades' became a synonym for the lower world or Hades. And for that reason, I suppose, the word lingers above the cellars of elderly taverns, which still occasionally invite your descent to their Avernus, The Shades. These, I think, always signify an underground 'snug'.

'Man walketh in a vain shadow.' 'What shadows we are and what shadows we pursue.' Substitute shade for shadow and the feeling is lost. The final -ow contributes powerfully to the idea of futility and evanescence. 'He has outsoared the shadow of our night', sang Shelley over Adonais. The second syllable of shadow not only helps the scansion. It tolls the bell.

Shadow was a particular favourite with Shakespeare. It was not only a technical name for the covered part of his stage: it declared his notion of his own profession's unreality, but not, for that reason, of its inutility. Art, especially theatrical art, is a shadowing of life and the shadow is perhaps more beautiful and moving than life itself, as the shadows of evening are often more beautiful than the bright radiance of the day. When the Athenian rustics are acting their rough comedy at the end of *A Midsummer Night's Dream* Duke Theseus rebukes some boorish mockery of the mummers by saying, 'The best in this kind are but shadows – and the worst are no worse if imagination amend them'. There is a whole philosophy in that astonishing sentence,

'The best in this kind are but shadows!' Remember that, Master Kemp. Take heed of your ephemeral calling, Master Burbage. And again, in the epilogue, when Puck begins the actor's apology with

> If we shadows have offended

the word, with its picturing of dim, thin creatures flitting in their insubstantial pageant, tears at the heart. Macbeth, too, mingled it with the player's impermanent craft,

> Life's but a walking shadow, a poor player,
> That struts and frets his hour upon the stage,
> And then is heard no more.

Then there is the haunting beauty of Sonnet 53.

> What is your substance, whereof you are made,
> That millions of strange shadows on you tend?
> Since every one hath, every one, one shade,
> And you, but one, can every shadow lend.
> Describe Adonis and the counterfeit
> Is poorly imitated after you;
> On Helen's cheek all art of beauty set,
> And you in Grecian tires are painted new.
> Speak of the spring, and foison of the year;
> The one doth shadow of your beauty show,
> The other as your bounty doth appear;
> And you in every blessed shape we know,
> In all external grace you have some part,
> But you like none, none you, for constant heart.

Oscar Wilde cited these lines in support of his view that the recipient was an actor. But no actor plays millions of parts and that first couplet remains as baffling as it is beautiful. Yet the general intention of flattery without loss of dignity is plain.

Shakespeare was constantly playing with the word shadow, which often is almost equivalent to a portrait.

> For since the substance of your perfect self
> Is else devoted, I am but a shadow
> And to your shadow will I make true love.

That is spoken by Proteus in *The Two Gentlemen of Verona*, but its sentiment might occur in the Sonnets. Shadow for him was an attractive because an elastic word; it has itself so many shadows as well as shades of meaning.

Cleopatra, when becoming philosophical in the praise of her dead lord, cried out

>   Nature wants stuff
> To vie strange forms with fancy: yet t'imagine
> An Antony, were nature's piece 'gainst fancy,
> Condemning shadows quite.

Shadows here are the creations of the artist, which natural man, in miraculously begetting an Antony, has far outranged. But they were also shades or ghosts;

>   then came wandering by
> A shadow, like an angel, with bright hair.

Shadows are actors and spectres, creations of the mind and even, in the person of Simon Shadow and his fellow-conscripts, faint copies of the martial man. Sir Thomas Browne summed up the inclusiveness of shadows.

> Life itself is but a shadow of death and souls departed but the shadows of the living. All things fall under this name. The sun itself is but the dark *simulacrum* and light but the shadow of God.

The word shadow has thrown infinite magic upon our literature.

SISSERARA

THIS from *Tristram Shandy*:

'But 'tis no marvel, continued the corporal – seeing my Uncle Toby musing upon it – for Love, an' please your honour, is exactly like war, in this; that a soldier, though he has escaped three weeks complete o' Saturday night, – may nevertheless be shot through his heart on Sunday morning – It happened so here, an' please your honour, with this difference only – that it was on Sunday in the afternoon, when I fell in love all at once with a sisserara – it burst upon me, an' please your honour, like a bomb – scarce giving me time to say, "God bless me".'

Sisseraras or, more commonly, Sassararas, began to ornament the English language in Tudor and Jacobean times. But they are not bombs. In Tourneur's plays a man could be 'fetched up to Heaven with a Sasserara'. And there, in its early form, the curious, picturesque and resounding term is most accurately used. For a Sassarara is a writ of Certiorari, much confounded by the popular tongue. So 'with a Sassarara' came to mean 'with a vengeance' or rapidly and violently. Not only were lovers seized by their passion with a sassarara, but nuisances would be sent packing with the same expressive noise. So in *The Vicar of Wakefield*, where my edition prints Susserara, the innkeeper's wife said:

'I am sure she has been here a fortnight, and we have not yet seen the cross of her money.' 'I suppose, my dear,' cried he, 'we shall have it all in a lump.' 'In a lump!' cried the other: 'I hope we may get it any way; and that I am resolved we will this very night, or out she tramps, bag and baggage.' 'Consider, my dear,' cried the husband, 'she is a gentle-woman, and deserves more respect.' 'As for the matter of that,' returned the hostess, 'gentle or simple, out she shall pack with a susserara. Gentry may be good things where they take; but for my part, I never saw much good of them at the sign of the Harrow.'

It is interesting to note that the 'colour of her money' as we should now say, was then the 'cross of her money'.

SLAISTER AND SLOOMY

SLAISTER is not much used in England, but it may have a hold in the North as well as in Scotland. A slaistery thing is unctuous and defiling. To slaister is to paint or colour ill. Vulgar little vamps slaister their faces. It gives a rich and odious suggestion of bad, greasy make-up and of lips crudely incarnadined; also of vulgar decoration of a room or person. To call wet, mud-making weather slaistery seems almost flattering to the adjective. A slaister-kyte is a foul feeder. I thank 'Ximenes' of the *Observer* for bringing slaistered into one of his puzzles; it deserves to be more widely known and used.

What is the Southern English equivalent? Bedaubed is not nearly so effective, since slaistered suggests the slap-dash use of paint in a showy or sluttish way. I have come across the adjective bejezebelled; that is a more portentous form of slaistered. A person of some quality who has overdone her preparation for conquest could be accused of bejezebellery; but no person of any quality could be slaistered. It is a word for wantons of the meaner sort.

The girl who has slaistered herself is trying to avoid looking sloomy.

In a book review in the *News Chronicle* Frederick Laws used the adjective sloomy, claiming, justly, that it had the blessing of the dictionary. It means sluggish, spiritless, dull and certainly would suit some of the volumes which arrive on a book-reviewer's desk. It has an agricultural and Scandinavian origin; it was used, 'of grain not properly filled', and so, I suppose, empty of vitality. Above it appears sloom, meaning a gentle sleep or slight doze, what the Scots call a 'dwaum'. To those coping with a sloomy tome an ensuing sloom is natural. A nice pair of dictionary neighbours.

Tennyson's *Northern Cobbler* spoke of 'sloomy Sally'.

SLEAZY

IN one of the fourth 'leaders' in *The Times* I read 'In most of us the word hinterland suggests something stern and wild. It has the ring of a challenge. Beyond the sleazy, tropical port, beyond the semi-derelict railhead in the foothills of the plateau, out there, under the pitiless sun, stretches the hinterland, illimitable, imponderable, and inadequately mapped. It is—so at least we have instinctively supposed—a much tougher proposition than the interior'. I have surmised the author to be Peter Fleming. (I specialize in surmising the authorship of *The Times* fourth leaders by their vocabulary, quotations and general play of wit.) Mr. Fleming has made an extensive study of hinterlands in South America and elsewhere; he has also a very sure hand with words. But I was puzzled by sleazy. In the context I felt that it might be a telescopic form of slummy or sluttish and greasy. In that connection it seems to me an admirable adjective for a certain kind of tropical harbour.

But the dictionary tells me that it is thin and insubstantial; it is especially used of cloths and fabrics. So the leader-writer was visualizing a mere row of shacks and huts. But sleazy sounds wrong for thin; it oozes fatness of a nasty kind. A sleazy person is not, for me, a starveling, but one whose diet contains rich proportions of garlic and *fritto misto*, consumed with a cheap Chianti.

The leader on hinterlands pointed out that this word of menace has now become a tame piece of Planners' jargon. It is, for them, an 'urban sphere of influence'. Thus all our towns of any size, i.e. the unsleazy ones, have hinterland environs. 'The main difference in this respect between (say) Basingstoke and the

Belgian Congo being that the Belgian Congo's hinterland is inside the Belgian Congo – whereas Basingstoke's hinterland is outside Basingstoke'. This is hard on the old romantic hinterlands of the novelists with their lone trails and sparse populations of despairing squatters and occasional decayed aristocrats who had been taken cheating at cards or passing 'dud' cheques and had retired to save the family's name from further degradation. I would expect to find sleazy (in my sense) types in a hinterland, but in planned Britain the hinterland mainly sprouts villas, garages and olde Tudor tea-shoppes.

SMIRK

SMIRK is a good old word for neat and trim, cousin to smikker which is a casualty in England but still, in a similar form, is the ordinary word for pretty in Denmark. We can hardly now dissociate smirk from a knowing, leering glance and to find a 'Smirk Butler' in Herrick is no doubt particularly pleasing because of its hint of a Davus, even of a Jeeves. The Smirk Butler appears in the parson's robustly sensuous Nuptiall Song or Epithalamie on Sir Clipseby Crew and his lady ('To bed, to bed, kind Turtles') and is described as eager to express his wit in the arrangement of napery and even as striving to catch her ladyship's eye. I have a feeling that Sir Clipseby may have found it necessary to be rid of the fellow before long and to find a rather less smirk successor. What did Herrick mean exactly by 'smirking wine'? Smiling, bubbling? Here is the passage.

> If smirking wine be wanting here,
> There's that which drowns all care, stout beere.

Wycherley used smirk with the odious sense that we attach to it, attributing to one of his characters 'the canonical smirk and filthy clammy palm of a chaplain'.

SNEAP, SNOB, AND SNUB

FEW words have stood on their head more completely than snob, which began as a shoemaker, was 'town' as opposed to 'gown' in Cambridge, and so generally proletarian. 'A person belonging to the lower ranks of society: having no pretensions to rank of gentility.' Then it became exactly the opposite, 'A person admiring, apeing, and pretending to gentility.' Nobody knows the origin of snob. Everybody, especially the foreigner, likes to use it. 'Très snob' has endeared itself to the French, even as an expression of praise and delight. Could not a Gents' Suiting be labelled in the window 'Très snob'?

Words beginning in 'Sn' frequently betray contempt. So, if snobs are fawning creatures, they are exceptions to the rule. But when the snob is spurning or rebuking his supposed inferiors, he conforms to the habit of his first letters. Here is a catalogue of proud, contemptuous 'Sn's' – sneer, snib, snicker, sniff, sneap, snotty or snooty, snub, snuffy. Sneap is the most dignified of these, a word of pedigree as well as of pride. Falstaff used sneap for rebuff: 'I will not undergo this sneap without reply.' The adjective sneaping was employed for a pinching or withering quality in the weather:

> Biron is like an envious, sneaping frost
> That bites the first-born infants of the spring.

(Sneaping winds in Scotland are also snell, another 'Sn'.) It is regrettable that snub should have so far grown in favour as to make us forgetful of sneap. Alison Uttley in her book of a north-country childhood's memories writes:

> Anyone who had been snubbed or repressed into silence before other people was said to have been 'sneaped'. A haughty woman would sneap another, an overbearing man would sneap his wife, the wintry-wind sneaped us to silence.

248

Snirrup or snurp is (or was) a Northern term for turning up the nose.

> As seun as she fund I depended on labour
> She snirpt up her nose and nae mair leuked at me

occurs in a Cumbrian ballad.

SPAWL

WHAT is spawling? Presumably a noisy clearing of the throat. A remarkable cure for it is described in John Aubrey's brief life of Walter Rumsey:

> He was much troubled with flegme, and being so one winter at the court of Ludlowe (where he was one of the councesellours), sitting by the fire, spitting and spawling, he tooke a fine tender sprig, and tied a ragge at the end, and conceited he might putte it downe his throate, and fetch-up the flegme, and he did so. Afterwards he made this instrument of whale-bone. I have oftentimes seen him use it. I could never make it goe downe my throat, but for those that can 'tis a most incomparable engine. If troubled with the wind it cures you *immediately*.

Ludlow is an enchanting place, but I am not sure that a wild December in the company of Rumsey although he was 'an ingeniose man and had a philosophicall head' would have been altogether pleasant. I have no liking for spawlers, the most vehement of whom I have discovered to be in action in European hotels after the hour of waking. (We Britons are, in the main, blessedly behind the field as competitors for the Spawling Cup.) John Aubrey, though unable to apply Rumsey's case to himself, had a servant called Marc Collins who, he says, made the implement incomparably better than Rumsey himself:

The Judge sayd he never sawe any one use it so dextrously in his life. It is no paine, when downe your throate; he would touche the bottome of his stomach with it.

By a coincidence I came across spawl with quite a different meaning immediately after writing this. I was rereading that late and fanciful novel by Thomas Hardy, *The Well-Beloved*, and found this of the building ways in Portland.

Like all the gardens in the isle it was surrounded by a wall of dry-jointed spawls.

There was nothing dry about Aubrey's notion of a spawling fellow.

SPRUNKING AND SPRUSH

ROSE MACAULAY in her anthology 'The Minor Pleasures of Life' quotes *The Ladies Dictionary* (1694),

This sprunking is a Dutch word, the first, as we hear, of that language that ever came into fashion with ladies.

The instances of the sprunking then employed indicate that it meant personal titivation. John Evelyn wrote

Now therefore spare in the next place
The pocket sprunking Looking-Glass;
And that the cheeks may both agree
Plumpers to fill the cavity.

There was much use of cosmetics and scents prescribed and then

Thus rigged the Vessel, and equipped,
She is for all Adventures shipped.

Montaigne recorded the bitter pains of sprunkery in Paris.

I have seen some swallow gravel, ashes, coale, dust, tallow, candles and labour and toyle themselves to spoile their stomacke only to get a pale-bleake look.

A desperate flight indeed from rosy rapture. The Scots have their own word for sprunking. It is sprushing.

I learn from Dr. Agnes Mure Mackenzie's *Scottish Pageant* that 'the piece of joyous devilment called Johnnie Cope' was written by a Lothian farmer, Adam Skirving, after the rout of the English army under Cope by Prince Charlie's men at Prestonpans.

> Cock up your beaver and cock it fu' sprush,
> We'll ower the Border and gie them a brush,
> There's somebody there we'll teach better behaviour,
> Hey, brave Johnnie lad, cock up your beaver.

> Sawney was bred wi' a broker of wigs,
> But now he's gone southward to lather the Whigs
> And he's to set up as their shopman and shaver,
> Hey, brave Johnnie Cope, cock up your beaver.

Sprush is even better than spruce for jaunty neatness. It is full of spit and polish. Trig, which may be a development of trick, is another good Scots word for neat. If a man has been called perjink, trig and sprush there is little more to be said of his nattiness.

SPUNGY

SPUNGY, or as we now spell it, spongy, always strikes the eye and ear. Its softness of sound perfectly suggests the absorbency of its nature. Long before Mr. Soapy Sponge was invented, human sponges had been sucking up liquor or money or advantage. Portia, declining to be married to a spunge, referred to drink, but Hamlet called Rosencrantz a spunge for soaking up the king's rewards and for being in turn squeezed dry. Hector in *Troilus and Cressida* said:

> There is no lady of more softer bowels,
> More spungy to suck in the sense of fear...

But Lady Macbeth meant drunken by spungy, when she described the well-dined and well-wined chamberlains of the king:

> When in swinish sleep
> Their drenchèd natures lie as in a death,
> What cannot you and I perform upon
> The unguarded Duncan? What not put upon
> His spungy officers?

Elsewhere Shakespeare uses spungy of weather and climate. April and the South are both spungy to him. With his love for verbs beginning with 'dis' he makes Enobarbus say in his despair:

> The poisonous damp of night disponge upon me.

When Donne was bidding his mistress remain in England and warning her against the foreigner, he observed:

> Nor spungy, hydroptic Dutch shall thee displease
> If thou stay here.

Hydroptic does not apparently refer to the moist eyes of the Old Soak, but to his generally dropsical condition. In the same elegy, by the way, Donne describes our nearer neighbours as

> Men of France, changeable chameleons,
> Spitals of diseases, shops of fashions,
> Love's fuellers and the lightest company
> Of players which upon the world's stage be.

The Dean of St. Paul's had not a smooth pen nor did he rhyme with grace. But he could be as sharp in his censure as profound in his morbidity of contemplation. And 'changeable chameleons' is a phrase to suit much of recent French history.

Coming to our own time, we have one of Sean O'Casey's characters crying, 'This spongy leaden sky is Dublin: these tomby houses is Dublin too – Dublin's scurvy body. And we've Dublin's silver soul.' After which the young lady, perhaps a little spongy in another sense, spits.

SQUIGGLE

THE squ's suit slanting movements. We have squint, with the Shakespearean squinny, and squirm. (A squiny, however, or squinancy was a quinsy of old.) The dictionary says that to squiggle is to 'writhe about', another form of squirming. I associate it with handwriting, and especially with the illegible signatures of the Squiggle family.

What is maddening in the conduct of these Squiggles is that they are not, as a rule, bad writers in general. They will send you a quite legible letter and then end with an indecipherable mess where the name should be. Here indeed is a 'writhing about'. It is as though a wasp had fallen into the ink and then, maddened, had squiggled over the paper.

Why does Squiggle squiggle in this way? Is it an overwhelming modesty which makes him feel that he is so trifling a creature that it really cannot matter whether his name be read or not? Or is it an overwhelming vanity which makes him feel that the world must recognize his mark? There are those who sign, Napoleonically, with a single letter. That suffices. In the same way Squiggle may believe that his inky scrawl is enough. The world should know it and be suitably impressed.

Often these letters need an answer and then one has to pore and ponder, look through the page to see how Squiggle makes his letters when he is not just squiggling, and so waste much time and trouble. Some writers compose cryptograms throughout; the medical profession includes many such, if their prescriptions be taken as evidence. Chemists, I suppose, know in advance much of what is being ordered; if not, they must have taken courses in deciphering as part of the apothecary's training.

There are sound-squiggles too. Specialists in this are the boys who 'page' names in clubs and hotels. They wander about making vague and plaintive imprecations, as though calling upon a Mr. Myah-Myah, always Mr. Myah-Myah. It is not surprising that this squiggle-scream rarely evokes any response from the chattering or sleeping figures to whom it is addressed. There is also the Squiggle Introductory, uttered by the hostess who presents one as Mr. Mum-Mum and leaves both parties completely ignorant as to whom they are meeting.

We have all sinned as Squigglers in some form or degree. My correspondents on verbal matters often take infinite trouble – with everything but their signatures. I am deeply grateful for their information and for their corrections of my errors. I do my best, with my secretary's aid, to interpret the queer splotch that is sometimes the signature. A grateful reply is needed. Can the Squigglers blame me if I write on the envelope, over the address,

A. Blank Squiggle, Esq.,

and leave it at that?

STOLCHY
AND OTHERS

STOLCHY, meaning trampled into mire, I found in Edmund Blunden, Suffolk's singer and the worthy editor of John Clare, both being bards so earthy and ethereal at once.

> When groping farms are lanterned up
> And stolchy ploughlands hid in grief,
> And glimmering by-roads catch the drop
> That weeps from sprawling twig and leaf...

This, I take it the East Anglican, form of the word is much better than the more general 'stoach' and 'stoachy'. Kipling wrote of fields 'stoached with sliding hoof-marks'. But the 'l' is sovereign. It powerfully stiffens the mire and expresses all the squelch and struggle of a walk across November clay.

When I once used the word 'stolchy' a correspondent reminded me of the Scottish and Northern English 'clarty' which appears to mean much the same thing.

Queachy land always sounds to me as though it should be

heavy clay, stolchy stuff. One can almost hear one's boots queaching as one drags them out of the tenacious mire. Perhaps it should be wet chalk-land rather than clay, for a piece of well-sodden chalk beats all British soils in the horrible combination of the slippery and the sticky. But queachy is not primarily a muddy term. First of all, it is woody, shrubby, bosky. The Elizabethan dramatists, but not Shakespeare, have quite a deal of queach (noun for thicket) and of queachy (or bosky) ground in their scenery. But, as is perhaps natural in our climate, where there's a shrubbery there's a puddle too, and queachy begins, under pressure of our wet westerly winds, to be swampy after all.

There is much to be said for remembering slottery in November,

> Now that the fields are dank and ways are mire,

as Milton wrote to his 'Lawrence of vertuous father vertuous son'.

Slotter is old English for dirt (hence slut) and the fifteenth century called dirty folk 'slotterbugges', which is a lively anticipation of the recent 'jitterbugs' and gives it medieval precedent. 'Sl' is a favourite beginning of our mucky words. Slobber, slub, slubber, slubberdegullion (a variant for slotterbugge which occurs in Butler's *Hudibras*), slime, sludge, slur, slush – they go squelching nicely along on the clarty, stolchy, slottery way.

SUCCEDANEUM

HERE is a good thumping alternative for a substitute. It met the eye as I was making *Dombey and Son* the companion of a bed-ridden week. Captain Jack Bunsby of the *Cautious Clara* was encountered by Captain Cuttle and Florence Dombey wearing 'a dreadnought pilot-coat and a pair of dreadnought pilot-trousers whereof the waistband was so very broad and high that it became the succedaneum for a waistcoat, being ornamented near the bearer's breastbone with some massive wooden buttons like backgammon-men'. Another succedaneous article of this kind has been the oriental Cummer-bund. In an age of drastic clothes-rationing, either by coupon or by height of price, the three-piece was commonly reduced to the two-piece suit in men's wardrobes; the waistcoat in Britain was succeeded by the pull-over or Cardigan, which has the merit of general service. But nobody now would portentously talk of his woolly as a waist-coat-succedaneum.

There is an adjective succedaneous. It would be nice to see a masculine noun of this kind applied to relief-men in sports. In cricket-scores we read, when a succedaneous fielder has made a catch, 'Caught Sub. Bowled Googler'. Cricket scores have now to be abbreviated more than ever. To read 'Caught Succedaneous', would be a handsome change. But I suppose it would be cut to 'C. Succ., B. Googler' which is not so imposing to the eye.

SWANKY

THIS from the late Gavin Bone on Anglo-Saxon poetry: 'It is the strange consonant combinations of which we have no speci-mens in modern English which seem to us savage and uncouth. For instance, "wl" at the beginning of a word, e.g. Wlanc, which seems as odd as the "ng" at the beginning of some African words, or "sth", "shth" at the end of a verb. Actually "wlanc" (pro-nounced with its "a" far back) is a splendid word for its meaning, which is "proud". We have felt the advantage of such a word in modern English and have conscribed "swanky" from one of the dialects. "Wlanc" is a more serious word, but with the good elements of "swanky".'

The dialect from which swanky was 'conscribed' was his own Scottish. The swanky lad is not a figure of up-to-date pavement slang imported from the U.S.A., but a Scottish 'jo' of consider-able antiquity. Mourning the Scottish dead ('The English, for ance, by guile wan the day') Jane Elliot wrote in her farewell to the lads 'cauld in the clay', of whom all Scotland was 'wlanc':

> At e'en in the gloaming, nae swankies are roaming,
> 'Bout stacks with the lasses at bogle to play:
> But ilk maid sits drearie, lamenting her dearie –
> The Flowers of the Forest are a' wede away.

A game of Bogle must have been a kind of Bogey-Bogey romp, bogle being a spectre, bug-bear, or scare-crow.

SWINK

It is odd that Shakespeare missed the rustic Swink, meaning labour, both as noun and verb, and sometimes used as a verb meaning to 'drink or carouse'. Spenser had used it and Milton's 'swink't hedger' remains familiar. Francis Thompson described 'The Poppy',

> lethargied with fierce bliss
> Hot as a swinkèd gipsy is.

I am assured that it is still in use on the Cotswolds, and a Tewkesbury friend also recounts a surviving use of the superb past-participle, forswunk. Could any word better express the collapsing state of one who has been all day at some hot and galling drudgery of house or land?

> I trenched and hoed and weeded

sang A. E. Housman, not, I surmise, having done anything of the sort. If indeed he had so turned from Latin texts to garden-tools, he would certainly have been forswunk. Trenching and hoeing and weeding are genuine swink.

SYLLABUB AND TATNAM

SYLLABUB, or sillabub (sometimes syllybub), was a dish of milk curdled with wine and given various flavours. Is the word, or the article, ever served up nowadays? One hears of syllabubs in Early Victorian England: Tom Brown knew about them and so did the Surtees folk. One meets them commonly in the accounts of Restoration pleasuring. An outing in the gardens usually led to a syllabub for two before it proceeded to become a more serious escapade. This, from Wycherley's *The Gentleman Dancing Master*, gives a handsome list of the recreations awaiting the London miss in 1672, that is if she had more freedom than the young ladies in the play:

> HIPPOLITA: Not suffer'd to see a play in a twelve month!
>
> PRUE: Nor to go to *Punchinello* nor Paradise!
>
> HIP: Nor to take a Ramble to the Park nor Mulberry-garden!
>
> PRUE: Nor to *Tatnam-Court* nor Islington!
>
> HIP: Nor to eat a sillybub in new Spring-garden with a Cousin!
>
> PRUE: Nor to drink a Pint of Wine with a Friend at the Prince in the Sun!
>
> HIP: Nor to hear a Fiddle in good Company!
>
> PRUE: Nor to hear the Organs and Tongs at the Gun in *Moorfields!*

The allusion to Tatnam-Court is interesting, since that abode of bliss left its name behind. (Mulberry-garden was replaced by Buckingham Palace.) The long, cumbrous, and now meaningless name of Tottenham Court Road is an odd survival. When the early London tubes had conductors to open and shut the train-gates they had to warn the passengers by announcing the next station. In this case it soon became 'Torra Corra next' and Torra Corra lives upon the tongues of bus-conductors. Tothill, Toten-hall, Tatnam or Tottenham Court was a famous manor on whose grounds Fitzroy Square was ultimately built. But, while it remained a nobleman's seat until the middle of the eighteenth century, it had long been surrounded by pleasure-gardens and famous for its syllabubic confections. There is a reference in Ben Jonson to 'courting it to Totnam to eat cream' and in 1648 people were fined a shilling a-piece for drinking at Tattenhall Court on the Sabbath. Gay wrote of spring, when

> Love flies the dusty town for shady woods,
> Then Tottenham Fields with roving beauty swarm.

The Adam and Eve was a great beer-garden of that area and the name still lingers, but without benefit of gardens, at the corner of Euston Road. None the less the view of Hampstead heights seen on a summer evening from 'Torra Corra' is still one of the sylvan surprises and delights of London, a syllabub for the senses.

TARDLE

THOMAS HARDY did not often write a full Wessex dialect in the manner of Barnes and most of his poetry is far more Latinate than rural in its choice of terms. But occasionally he broke into Dorsetshire narrative (as in 'The Bride-Night Fire') and then what a cascade of good words ensues! Young Tim espies his Barbree, who has escaped into the orchard from the flames and is 'bivering wi' fright'.

> Her cwold little figure half-naked he views
>   Played about by the frolicsome breeze,
> Her light-tripping totties, her ten little tooes,
>   All bare and besprinkled wi' Fall's chilly dews,
> While her great gallied eyes through her hair hanging loose
>   Shone as stars through a tardle o' trees.

Tardle for a tangle, anything that blocks and retards, is excellent. It surely need not be reserved for vegetation nor should it be isolated in the West. For everybody knows what a tardle of work is and can have no other noun for it that is half so expressive. To say that you have a tardle of stuff on your desk expresses a confusion of papers that will certainly keep you at the office for hours. What other word, meaning a hindrance that expresses delay, says so much so briefly and expressively? In his more solemn prose Hardy would have used some such cumbrous phrase as 'arboreal impediment' instead of 'tardle of trees'. I am second to none in reverence for the author of the Wessex novels, but I often feel that he would have bettered his own excellence if he had cut out the Latinate, periphrastic way of writing to which he was so often prone (e.g. 'ecclesiastical edifice' instead of church) and given us more old Dorset. His vocabulary, in fact, was sometimes a tardle of words. When less learned and genteel, and more local, his lexicon was full of simple riches. One notes in these verses the use of Fall for Autumn, which America has retained with its usual conservation of the ripest English.

TAWDRY

TAWDRY is a cousin of Tantony, the latter, as I noted, being a shortened version of St. Antony and applied to the smallest pig of a litter. Tawdry, in the same way, is St. Audrey and began its new life as a piece of lace. 'Come,' says Mopsa, in *The Winter's Tale*, 'you promised me a tawdry-lace and a pair of sweet gloves.' It is obvious from this that there was nothing tawdry about the original tawdry-lace: it was a covetable article. The usual explanation is that St. Audrey believed herself to be punished for wearing rich jewellery round her neck: accordingly she took to wearing a collar of fine lace as a precautionary and ethical device. The tawdry-lace of the sixteenth and seventeenth century was a treasured article and Wycherley could call a Tawdry Rogue 'well-dressed', but it began to decline in quality, became showy, and was linked with cheap vanity. Hence our own adjective tawdry. St. Antony is hardly insulted by association with a nice little pig: but we have been certainly treating

St. Audrey with injustice. Another view is that tawdry came from the gew-gaws sold at Ely Fair on St. Audrey's Day. And what of gew-gaw? The learned say it is a duplicated form of 'gifan' to give, the impolite suggestion of this being that presents are usually trash. Anyhow it is no bad term of contempt, and Dryden made it an effective adjective.

> Give to your boy, your Caesar,
> This rattle of a globe to play withal,
> This gew-gaw world.

Gew-gaw never had any favourable aspect, but tawdry's youth was even saintly.

THRIBBLE

A NICE word for making do and muddling through. I came across it in a passage by Richard Brome, one of Shakespeare's successors. He introduces into his play a nobleman, who is organizing a play. He seems to reply to Hamlet's speech to the player and to justify 'gagging'. Brome (c. 1590–1653) was an associate of Ben Jonson and may have enjoyed a retort to Ben's great rival.

The nobleman says,

> My actors
> Are all in readiness, and I think all perfect
> But one, that never will be perfect in a thing
> He studies: yet he makes such shift extempore,
> (Knowing the purpose that he is to speak to)
> That he moves mirth in me above the rest,
> For I am none of these Poetic Furies
> That threats the actor's life, in a whole play
> That adds a syllable or takes away.
> If he can thribble through and make delight
> In others, I am pleased.

An accommodating nobleman certainly, but what the author thought of this thribbling is another matter.

I cannot discover whether thribble was a particularly theatrical word or whether it was of general use. If it was theatrical, the players are foolish to have lost it. It is curious how many stage-terms survive from Shakespeare's time and have never, presumably, been out of use. The prompter prompted for Burbage as for Sir Laurence Olivier. Benvolio in *Romeo and Juliet* talks of the 'without-book prologue, faintly spoke after the prompter'. The book, i.e. the script of the play, was even then the book. Parts were studied, until the actor was perfect or word-perfect as happens now. Webster's Flamineo in *The White Devil* has a magnificent farewell to the life which he has used so ill. 'I go', he says, 'to study a long silence.' The surprise of silence, instead of part, is superb. If thribble was commonly employed then, the more folly to let it go, for it is a most expressive term, with its suggestion of an improvised dribbling of the lines. We have most of us seen some wretched actor, caught short of his words, thribbling faultily and showing his distress. Perhaps Brome's kindly nobleman would have pardoned even that – provided the fellow showed some invention.

THRILL

JOURNALISM, as I have already noted, seizes on the short word, seizes and soon works it to death. 'Thrill' has been one of its most unhappy victims. Originally it meant a shiver down the back and the adjective thrilling was applied to things shiversome on the grand scale. In Shakespeare thrill is tremendous. 'I have a faint cold fear thrills through my veins.' We should shudder at that. In Claudio's magnificent speech on the terrors of death, thrilling, now tagged to any tawdry event or stage-surprise, properly takes its place.

> Ay, but to die, and go we know not where;
> To lie in cold obstruction, and to rot;
> This sensible warm motion to become

A kneaded clod; and the delighted spirit
To bathe in fiery floods or to reside
In thrilling regions of thick-ribbèd ice,
To be imprison'd in the viewless winds,
And blown with restless violence round about
The pendent world;

Thrilling there comes in like a whip-lash of East wind – or did to an Elizabethan. When Charlotte Brontë wrote of 'thrilling pains in her back' she meant agony. Thrilling has retained its dignity and power in some modern poetry. In Kipling's 'Sussex',

Here through the strong and shadeless days
The tinkling silence thrills.

This splendidly mingles the sheep-bells and the stab of sun upon the treeless chalk. In Laurence Binyon's famous poem 'For the Fallen'

Solemn the drums thrill: Death, august and royal,
Sings sorrow up into immortal spheres.

But the 'boosters' of the Entertainment Industry, as well as the hard-pressed sub-editors seeking a short word for excitement, have effectively murdered thrill by now and are pathetically striving to revive it with emphatic prefix. I recently read a puff of a film with 'A Thousand Super-Thrills'. As if that helped!

TIDDLE

In the eighteenth century 'to tiddle' was to fidget over or to cosset. One tiddled with one's more precious belongings. A child would be asked to stop tiddling with his toys or with his food at table. This leads to the question why tiddler became slang – or even general – English for a small creature. The term has been applied especially to a small fish, or stickle-back, the latter being named after its prickly-finned back. The small boys whom I see so blissfully engaged in the shallows of the pond on Hampstead

Heath, where Shelley is said to have sailed boats for the Leigh Hunt household, are quite certain that tiddlers are their natural prey. And how they tiddle away in the mud in order to land the tiny wriggling prize in the jam-jar! So tiddler is now used (almost as much as toddler, I think) to signify the human shrimp, nipper, or urchin.

Urchin itself leads to some tiddling with verbal research. A hurcheon was a hedge-hog and a sea-urchin is a sea-hurcheon, but why the resulting urchin should have been applied to small boys is difficult to follow. Probably the explanation runs this way. The hedge-hog hunches himself up. So, of hard necessity, does a human hunch-back and urchin was one term for this kind of unfortunate. As the hunch-back is usually smaller than the average man, so the word urchin was next applied to boys, even those small enough to be toddlers or tiddlers.

The common English nicknames for small men are Tiny or Tich, the latter, of course, being a lingering tribute to the dwarfish frame and large humours of Little Tich, the music-hall comedian, famous for tiddling with his gigantic boots. So the little and beloved Kentish bowler, Freeman, became Tich to the cricketing crowd. It frequently happens that certain letters or pairs of letters are associated with certain ideas. 'Ti' seems now to be the natural beginning of small matters and small people. For example, I always think of Tim as a small man and I suppose that is a common habit, the result in part, no doubt, of Tiny Tim in *A Christmas Carol*. To this the objector may mutter, 'What about Titanic?' but Titans have come monstrously clumping into our world from the classics and I can immediately retort with tit (originally a very small horse and now a species of bird essentially small), tit-bit (a tiny as well as a tasty morsel) and tittle, familiar associate of jot. Jot was the Greek Iota or letter i and the tittle was the tiny dot on top of it; so a tittle came to stand for any diminutive article or piece of an article. Thus the union of 'ti' with minuteness certainly seems to be well established – but I have tiddled with the subject long enough.

TINKLE

'GIVE me a tinkle', says the modern, inviting telephony. It is a gentle word for a ring, its derivation obviously coming from the sound of metal lightly struck. Yet tinkle has occurred in tremendous passages. Isaiah, for example, explained that,

> Because the daughters of Zion are haughty and walk with stretched forth necks and wanton eyes, walking and mincing as they go, and making a tinkling with their feet,

the Lord would smite these ladies with scabs on the scalp and other physical penalties. The offence given was due to their gauds, catalogued as follows: Bravery of tinkling ornaments about their feet, cauls (hair-nets), round tires like the moon, chains, bracelets, mufflers, bonnets, ornaments of the legs, head-bands, tablets, ear-rings, rings, nose-jewels, changeable suits of apparel, mantles, wimples, crisping-pins, glasses, fine linen, hoods, and veils. On the whole, these tinklers of Zion seem to have been well-equipped vessels of vanity.

Hence tinkling, especially of cymbals, became the special token of vain performance.

> A crowd is not company and faces are but a gallery of pictures and talk but a tinkling cymbal where there is not love.

Milton echoes that judgment of Bacon,

> Speaking of human frailty and vanity, we are but crackt cymbals, we do but tinckle.

Tinkling has always seemed to me too small, too dismissive a term for the melody of church-bells heard across country. Theirs is very different music from the jingle of anklets so obnoxious to Isaiah. But it has been beautifully used of sheep-bells. Everybody knows,

> Now fades the glimmering landscape on the sight,
> And all the air a solemn stillness holds,

Save where the beetle wheels his droning flight,
And drowsy tinklings lull the distant folds.

Gray redeemed tinkling from the company to which the grave moralists condemned it.

Presumably a tinker was so-called because of the tink-tink he made when mending pots and pans. The Scottish form of tinker, which is tinkler, emphasizes the name's origin among the appropriate music of that craft. In Scotland tinkler, when abbreviated to tink, became a term of contempt. 'Just brute tinks!' Isaiah, so contemptuous of tinkling in ladies, would have seen the point.

Who wrote,

Nor in obscurèd purlieus would he seek
For curlèd Jewesses with ankles neat,
Who, as they walked abroad, made tinkling with their feet?

The answer is John Keats.

TIRRIVEE

WE have had tantrums with us for about two centuries and the origin of that word remains obscure. I like the Scottish equivalent which has deservedly found its way into some English dictionaries, that is, the tirrivee. Jamieson attributes tirrivee to the French *tirer* and *vif;* your tirrivee is something evoked and then darting out in lively fashion. I came across tirrivee again in Neil Munro's *John Splendid:* that tetchy cavalier, his martial and vagabond hero, a Campbell with a D'Artagnan's temper, was for ever in a tirrivee himself or causing tirrivees in others. From a tirrivee or tantrum the progress was towards a tulzie or tuilyie, which was a quarrel, and so on to a brulzie or bruilyie, which was an affray. (The Scottish language was remarkably rich in the lingo of insult, resentment and violent reaction.)

In places where artists work together and tempers and temperaments are violent the word tirrivee would certainly be useful. It is friendly and disarming and would come well from a theatre manager's or producer's appeasing lips. 'Now, please, my dears, no tirrivee. It can all be arranged quite simply. I can fix everything to suit you both. No tirrivee.' Peacock called such treatment of the tantrums 'demulsing'. It is absurd that tirriveeism in the arts should occupy so much of important people's time and cause the diversion of so much skill and energy into demulsion, but there it is. Man is born to sparking, to be *tiré* and *vif*, and so companionable a term as tirrivee lets off his failing lightly.

I am told that in Sussex the verb create can mean to cause a tirrivee. 'If it is said that a man is "fair creating", it is a South Down warning to keep out of his way. But creating is also common theatrical slang. Few series of rehearsals can be carried on without somebody creating before he or she 'creates' the part.

TITTUP

'You do not really think, Mr. Thorpe,' said Catherine (Miss Morland of *Northanger Abbey*), 'that James's gig will break down?'

'Break down! Oh Lord! Did you ever see such a little tittupy thing in your life? There's not a sound piece of iron about it, it is the most devilish rickety business I ever beheld.'

Jane Austen's tittupy may have something to do with a verbal confusion, as *O.E.D.* suggests, and to a contraction of tip-up-etty. But tittupy is also prancing or mincing, when applied to horses.

A tittup was a hand-gallop, then a curvet or half-turn of a horse. Then it was applied to human beings of an over-sprightly or affected gait. Was Agag perhaps a tittuper? From the verb we get a noun for a prancing miss or hussy. To call a girl a tittup in the eighteenth century was to designate a young lady with a mincing carriage and a strong desire to attract attention. So Sir Walter Scott wrote of the 'titupping misses' among the beaux at St. Ronan's Well.

He might, by the way, have called a tittup of this order 'a

piece'. This sounds like a modern vulgarity but is, in fact, a seventeenth-century usage. Bishop Gauden, who shed *Tears of the Church* in 1659, thus described the miseries of the cloth amid parochial embranglements:

> What complyings and cringings must this poore perplexed Minister use to fence himself against the crafty agitations of his spitefull neighbours and those pragmatick pieces who in every corner doe hover over the heads of Ministers, as Kites doe over Pigeons.

I find pragmatick (i.e. busy) pieces a pithy and a pungent term. While on this theme, it is worth noting that a tittup could, without loss of period idiom, have been engaged in 'picking-up'. There is nothing modern about the pick-up girl. Defoe discovered her in the lordliest form in the Assembly Rooms of Bury St. Edmunds (*Tour of Great Britain*, 1724). He found it alleged in a book called *Familiar Letters* that 'the daughters of all the Gentry of the three countries come hither to be picked up, in a way of speaking I never before heard any Author have the Assurance to make use of in Print'.

The tittups!

TOILET

HERE is a curious progress of meanings. The toilette was originally a piece of cloth used for wrapping up clothes; it was also the towel or protective coverlet placed by the barber round the shoulders of his clients. From this it became the linen covering a dressing-table; then it was the table itself and all its appointments, the munitions of Venus. So Pope used it of Belinda,

> And now, unveil'd, the Toilet stands display'd,
> Each silver Vase in mystic order laid.
> First, rob'd in white, the Nymph intent adores,
> With head uncover'd, the Cosmetic pow'rs....
> From each she nicely culls with curious toil,
> And decks the Goddess with the glitt'ring spoil.
> This casket India's glowing gems unlocks,

And all Arabia breathes from yonder box.
The Tortoise here and Elephant unite,
Transform'd to combs, the speckled, and the white.
Here files of pins extend their shining rows,
Puffs, Powders, Patches, Bibles, Billet-doux.

It is interesting to learn that Belinda counted her holy writ in the plural.

So, in the age of the fops and belles, toilet came to mean not only the implements of beauty but the procedure of making-up. It could also signify a dressing-room reception of visitors or dress and decoration in general.

Finally America, in its search for exalted titles for the common 'convenience', a search which has given us the admirable Comfort Station, seized Belinda's toilet as one of its lavatory-labels. In this practice the polite sections of the European world have followed the Western lead. But when Pope wrote that 'the long labours of the toilet cease' he was not referring to ultimate victory over intestinal stasis. A small boy, with whom I was walking on Hampstead Heath, suddenly stopped on the fine ridge that looks across to Highgate and politely inquired, 'Is there a toilet here?'

He never uses the term 'nessy', to which I have made previous allusion: it is, I think, more common in the North than in the South.

TREACLE

A CORRESPONDENT who is a devotee of old shop signs sent me the following from Cornwall:

> Bibles, Buckets and Boots,
> Godley Bukes and Grinding Stones,
> Trousers Testaments and Tea-Kittles,
> Everything to buy and sell here
> Except Treacle. Best prices paid
> For Whale-Bone Staze.
>
> J. W. NINNIS.   1835

The strong objection to treacle taken by the devout Mr. Ninnis set me thinking about that queer word. It began its English life as triacle, and meant an antidote for a bite. Salves and treacles went as much together as pills and potions, and the saving power became spiritual as well as physical so that it was possible to talk of the Sovran Treacle of sound doctrine, following the common medieval usage of treacle as a means of salve and salvation. The name of Jesus was called 'holsomest tryacle' by Lydgate. (Triacle or treacle used for balm gave its name to the Treacle Bible.) Then treacle flowed out of the pulpit on to the counter and left the apothecary's for the grocer's shop. It became 'the un-crystallized syrup produced in the process of refining sugar'. Also 'an inspissated saccharine juice obtained from trees and plants'.

So treacle, which had once been the symbol of strong, curative, cleansing power, became the common metaphor for suggestion of cloying and sickly matters. It was the eighteenth century that set treacle oozing on the downward path and reaching its present 'sticky end', as the slang phrase goes; a sticky end, but not a bad one, for a good dollop of treacle or of the gentler 'golden syrup' is an article generally approved, and the 'treacly puddin',' of which Jay Laurier used to sing with such relish in the music-halls, is an excellent comfort on a wintry day. Shakespeare never used treacle for salve, and as a sweetmeat it was still unknown in his time. The Tudor for lollypop was 'candy' and here, as so often, the Americans have kept the old usage. Talk of candy never seems quite normal English in England, but Shakespeare used candy as an adjective ('What a candy deal of courtesy') and also the verb discandy for melt away or desert. Candy was commonly a verb for sweeten or crystallize in Tudor English.

Treacle has also been used as a verb to denote a sticky kind of trickle. This from Suffolk—an old woman speaking: 'I axed passon, Passon do ye give me a pew under your pulpit. There's Mrs. Robinson and Mrs. Smith sit right afront of me, and by time your sarmon treakle through them two, that do sound

wonnerful poor stuff, that there really do.' We have all heard
speeches – don't let us put all the blame on the clergy – that
treakled through the audience in just the same way.

TROLLOPE OR SLAMMERKIN

DURING a visit to a provincial church in 1756 Cowper records
the spectacle of 'several negligées, with furbelowed aprons,
which had long disputed the prize of superiority; but these were
most woefully eclipsed by a burgess's daughter, just come from
London, who appeared in a Trollope or Slammerkin, with treble
ruffles to the cuffs, pinked and gimped, and the side of the petticoat drawn up in festoons'.

Here dress-making dances its verbal minuet. Let us trace the
steps backward. I have always liked the look of the word
festoons, the garlands of a festival. Since we live in a period much
addicted to Festivals and can hardly arrange a couple of concerts
without somebody calling the affair by the high Festival name,
we should be free with our festoons. Festoons of petticoat are a
nice conceit. A festoon was also, in architecture, a carved ornament. 'Flora and Boys in *alto relievo* supporting festoons', to
quote Horace Walpole, was part of the dignity of a mansion.
Nowadays it suggests something in a more grandiose pantomime
or spectacular revue – possibly on ice; but let Flora be: I cannot
read of festoons without delight.

Gimping, too, excites a pleasant curiosity. 'Silk, worsted, or
cotton twist with a cord or wire running through it.' Pinking is
a fencer's word. The duellist pinked a body with a thrust: the
dress-maker ornaments by perforating little holes. Pinking the raw
edge of silk was scalloping a pattern on it. And so to Trollopes.

The Trollop was a sluttish woman before she was a rakish one.
Carelessness of attire was later connected with laxity of conduct.
Shakespeare, though he never used the word, had the arch-trollop
in the Audrey of his Arden, who, denying sluttishness, thanked
the gods that she was foul; to that Touchstone observed that,

271

with foulness present, sluttishness would come hereafter. From the untidy trollop came the trollope or trollopee, a loose garment in which the trollops might trollop about – for the noun has its verb. Then the carelessly worn wrapper of the slut was elevated to be the negligée of the elegant. A lady could ask for her trollopee without loss of dignity. It was, as Cowper observed, Church-worthy and Sunday-go-to-meeting attire.

I do not know whence the family name of Trollope came, but we may reasonably imagine an ancestress who earned the title from supercilious neighbours. She need not have been an Audrey, but rather one who played up to Herrick's notion of the careless charmer.

> A sweet disorder in the dress
>   Kindles in clothes a wantonness;
> A lawn about the shoulders thrown
>   Into a fine distraction.

With a 'tempestuous petticoat' and 'ribbands to flow confusedly' he pictures the trollope-de-luxe who, a century later, would have donned a trollòpee.

Slammerkin is, likewise, a word of double application. It means both the slatternly woman and the loose covering she may like to wear. (The favourite initial letters for untidiness are plainly indicated by sloppy, slouching, sluttish, and slatternly slammerkins. Idleness comes into the same alphabetic category with slothful, sluggish, slumping slummocks.) It is not known whether John Gay's Mrs. Slammerkin of the *Beggar's Opera* gave a new name to the trollop and the trollopee or whether these derived their slammerkin title from the character in the piece, as Grundyism came from Mrs. Grundy who was another party of the play. She was mentioned in Thomas Morton's *Speed the Plough*, which is very rarely revived in these days.

It was a finely echoing boudoir in which milady could cry out for a slammerkin or trollopee.

TRUCKLE AND TRUCKLE-BED

READING that General Eisenhower had 'slept in his truckle-bed', I remembered how truckle-beds had appeared in old stories of my boyhood's pleasure. Yet I was vague about the article. What precisely was it? What exactly earned it the name of truckle? Had it anything to do with the Scots trachle or trauchle, which means to tire out, with trauchle also employed as a noun for hard toil. So 'he went off to his trauchle' wrote Lewis Grassic Gibbon of the slaving crofter, greedy for more earth, in his fine short story of land-hunger called *Clay*. Was the trauchle-bed that of a poor, tired man? No, truckle-bed does not mean the labourer's simple cot. It was the small trolley-bed on truckles or castors which used to be pushed under the large standing bed, with which it was frequently contrasted. The lower party had the truckle. 'To bed all alone and my Will in the truckle-bed' (Pepys). The old-style tutor could expect nothing better. Bishop Joseph Hall (1574-1656), in his amusing picture of the usher in private service, explained that:

> A gentle squire would gladly entertain
> Into his house some trencher chapelain;
> Some willing man that might instruct his sons,
> And that would stand to good conditions.
> First, that he lie upon the truckle-bed
> Whiles his young master lieth o'er his head.
> Second that he do on no default
> Ever presume to sit above the salt.
> Third that he never change his trencher twice.
> Fourth that he use all common courtesies:
> Sit bare at meals and one half rise and wait.
> Last, that he must never his young master beat,
> But he must ask his mother to define,
> How many jerks she would his breech should line.
> All these observed, he could contented be
> To give five marks and winter livery.

(Jerk, of course, is here a cut with the cane.)

From the inferior position of the truckle-bed, under the standing-bed, came the idea of truckling as acting in an inferior way, fawning, surrendering. Truckle was also a verb for sleeping in a lowly way, but the usage has vanished. Hall suggests that the truckle-bed remained under the standing-bed, but its name hints strongly that it was pulled out. If the beds remained one on top of the other, the gentleman below must have had a stuffy night, but our ancestors usually preferred the snug to the snell in the matter of aeration.

TWACH
AND OTHERS

THAT excellent poet, Lord Herbert of Cherbury, wrote of a twaching kiss in a poem so complete in its survey of osculation that it must be amply quoted,

> Come higher Womankind and all their worth,
> Give me thy kisses as I call them forth.
> Give me the billing-kiss, that of the dove,
>   A kiss of love;
> The melting-kiss, a kiss that doth consume
>   To a perfume;
> The extract-kiss, of every sweet a part,
>   The kiss of art;
> The kiss which ever stirs some new delight,
>   A kiss of might;
> The twaching smacking kiss, and when you cease
>   A kiss of peace;
> The music-kiss, crochet and quaver time,
>   The kiss of rhyme;
> The kiss of eloquence, which doth belong
>   Unto the tongue;
> The kiss of all the sciences in one,
> So 'tis enough.

Quite enough kisses. But not, perhaps, enough of Lord Herbert's hand and fancy.

Even the larger Oxford Dictionary knows nothing of twach, a verb which must be left to speak (or kiss) for itself. But I am grateful for being driven to the Twa's, since there I find Twatchel, an earthworm, Twattle, meaning chatter, and Twattle-basket for chatter-box. Now that basket has become a shunt-word for bastard in English slang and popular humour the term Twattle-basket dismisses a prattling bore with even greater vigour.

TWEATE

PEOPLE who are fond of words have a perpetual banquet spread for them in any garden. Kipling gave a musical expression to an obvious truth when he wrote that our flowers 'sing themselves': it was the kind of statement which he could easily prove in rhyme by marshalling the examples, dittany, elecampane, and the rest. What of the fishmonger's slab? The commoner sea-fish, cod, haddock, hake, etc., fall heavily on the ear. The fresh-water fish are also unlucky in their naming. Trout, for example, a creature dapper and dappled, lithe and swift beyond description, demands a far more expressive title. So squat and absurd is trout that we apply it in slang to foolish old folk. To call somebody 'a silly old trout' is not rude only to the object of the remark. It is an insult to the liveliest of creatures and the lively water in which he ruminates and darts.

The coarse fisherman's monosyllabic prey, pike, chub, dace, perch, roach, bream, etc., are scarcely the stuff that poetry is made of, but the old rhymers could make a ballad of an angler's basket none the less. John Dennys, that happy water-poet of England's Middle-West, has this, for example, when discussing the Worm as Bait (date 1613):

> And with this bait hath often taken been
> The Salmon fair, of River fish the best;
> The Shad that in the Spring-time cometh in,

> The Suant swift, that is not set by least.
> The Bocher sweet, the pleasant Flounder then,
> The Peele, the Tweate, the Batling, and the rest;
> With many more that in the deep doe lye
> Of Avon, Uske, of Severne and of Wye.

This has brought me to Tweate (or Twaite) with which I headed the note. The Shad is a 'clupeoid' fish of which the British species are the Allice and the Tweate. (Clupeoid means small river fish akin to the herring.) Shad, I am told, come up the Severn as far as Tewkesbury. But let us not become too learned. As far as exact identity goes, we may leave 'the Bocher sweet' and also the Batling to the erudite piscators. We shall be happy to roll the words upon our tongues. Peele, Tweate and Batling, what an admirable firm of accountants or solicitors! They would be perfect for handling the business of The Worm Fishers' Club, a society which I have secretly longed to form, especially when enjoying (free) the saddle of lamb and claret of the Fly Fishers. Was it wrong of a pampered guest to resent the Club's seigneurial disdain of any methods but their own? My idea of fishing is to catch something in order not to look a fool – and the sooner done with all this tangle of line, hook and trouble the better. Worm fishing, when you have cajoled or hired a small boy to get the worms, is the simplest way out. When Worm Fishers have their place in Pall Mall, the immortal memory of John Dennys shall be drunk. Incidentally, if any maker of plays or films lifts the firm of Peele, Tweate & Batling from this page, I stipulate only that Tweate shall be played by Mr. Robertson Hare.

UMBER

ALL through winter Britain abounds in exquisite tints. Blake's 'green and pleasant land' has become brown and russet. The bare, ruin'd choirs have their sombre splendour of tint as well as of form. But the writer who endeavours to paint this glory in words finds himself with a galling scarcity of satisfactory epithets of colour. Dun is a dull word and sepia smacks of the paint-box rather than of the vivid beauty of woods in winter. I have a liking for umber, which may or may not be connected with the Latin word for shade. That connection has long been lost: to Shakespeare umber was a pigment for staining things and disguising the complexion. ('And with a kind of umber smirch my face.') Now it has come to signify brown in general and its depth of sound suggests a like depth of colour-tone. For Housman,

> Wenlock Edge was umbered
> And bright was Abdon Burf
> And warm between them slumbered
> The smooth green miles of turf.

The adjective not only delights the ear: it helps to drench the stanza with the more sombre pigments of our coloured counties. Umber, I am told, is one name for a grayling, which by its swift, underwater movement acquires the dark look of a shadow.

This leads me to umbrage. Why not restore to umbrage its proper meaning of shadow? Now it seems always to bear its later sense of disfavour and, there too, it is in disfavour, or at least in mockery. Who talks of 'taking umbrage' except as a joke? But umbrage, in its true significance, is a good, black, shadowy term for suggesting a dense covering of leafy or needled branches. Milton's

> When highest woods impenetrable
> To star or sunlight spread their umbrage broad

drives into the dark heart of silvan gloom. Hamlet used umbrage for the shadow of a man and any word in Hamlet's vocabulary has a prescriptive right to endurance. For adjectives there are umbratile and umbrageous, umbrous and umbrose. Umbrageous is the most common. Carlyle's Teufelsdrockh, that ingenious and impassioned spinner of words, moved on 'umbrageous lawns'. Umbratile will not do now. It too unhappily suggests the pert trade name of a patent waterproof hat. Umbrageous might also be a telescoping of umbrage with outrageous and is not right for quiet, shady places. Umbrose hints at a man called Ambrose in a pet. Umbrous is best. Meanwhile we have to recover umbrage from its status of a slightly comic alternative to 'dudgeon' and put it back among green thoughts beneath the trees.

UMPER

IF you should find in an ancient text, with ancient spelling, the word umper, you do but meet with an early version of the white-coated arbiter of ins and outs at a cricket-match. Lyly's Euphues was made an umper to decide in some contest. Does anybody know why the footballers refused to have umpers and preferred referees? The summer games, cricket and lawn-tennis, are faithful to the Norman umper while the winter sports of football and hockey are refereed. Racing men, neutral in this issue, abide by their Stewards' decision.

I called an umper a Norman because in French, and in a muddle, lies his origin. Professor Ullman in *Words and Their Use* points out that

> Erroneous analysis may detach a sound from one word and add it on to another in its immediate vicinity. In English, the indefinite article has been particularly exposed to this treatment. An apron developed out of a napron, Old French naperon, 'napkin', an adder comes from a nadder, an auger from a nauger, an umpire from a numpire, Old French nomper 'peerless, odd man'. In all these cases, the initial n- of the next word was taken as belonging to the article. The reverse has occurred in a newt from an ewt and a nickname from an ekename, where -n of the article has been added on to the next word. A similar shift is responsible for 'for the nonce', earlier for then once.

A nadder sounds certainly more venomous than an adder; the latter has a suggestion of blameless clerkdom. Indeed, to nadder might be a good verb for to sting. Theatrical producers and their actors can, if they wish to be precise, talk about a napron or a napkin stage. So the umpire is the exceptional man, the nonpareil. I have in the past done some service (of dubious competence) as an umper, and then I regarded myself as a drudge considerably put upon. It now appears that I was awarded loftier status. I was being unique.

UNCUMBER

MARTHA was 'cumbered with much serving'. There is a good weight about the word. The weeds cumber the ground and sin cumbers the earth. Marc Antony announced, over Caesar's gashed and bleeding body, that domestic fury and fierce civil strife 'would cumber all the parts of Italy'. There is a roll of drums about such cumbering. The brief cumber is, I think, more effective than our encumber, which has largely replaced it; certainly the negative uncumber is preferable to the clumsy disencumber. I owe to the word-learned 'Jackdaw' of *John o' London's Weekly* the discovery that Uncumber is a name and a holy one too. There is in Westminster Abbey a statue of St. Uncumber. This lady, orginally of royal Portuguese descent, has the double distinction of being both a saintly and a circus type. For she was a bearded woman as well as a benefactress of wives; her particular power was to get rid of unsatisfactory husbands. She also seems to have had a curious and somewhat farmyard appetite, since the usual offering, made by distressed wives in search of conjugal relief, was a gift of grain. Of St. Uncumber Sir Thomas More observed that 'for a peck of oats she would provide a horse for an evil husband to ride to the devil upon' and there are other references to the oat-offering. The functions of St. Uncumber have now been largely taken over by those legal gentlemen who cumber themselves with wigs.

Cumber as a noun for trouble or distress has disappeared. Sir Walter Scott used it in his 'Coronach':

Fleet foot in the correi,
Sage council in cumber,
Red hand in the foray,
How sound is thy slumber!

When I first noticed it I thought that it might be a Scottish version of chamber, since counsels, councils and chambers are so often linked together. The old spelling of corrie, the hollow in the mountain-side where the deer shelter and feed, is now as rare as is the use of cumber as a substantive. Why did this kind of cumber vanish while the verb remained? It is a useful, expressive word and we must all have felt some time that we were in a devil of a cumber.

I fail to see why James Hogg's couplet in a poem to a Skylark,

Bird of the wilderness
Blithesome and cumberless

should qualify for inclusion in that agreeable Anthology of Bad Verse, *The Stuffed Owl*. To me cumberless is an excellent adjective for the certainly soaring and presumably carefree bird.

USKY

THE Gaels' 'Uisge Beatha' (water of life), is familiar to us by the rather mean name of whisky. It first became usquebaugh and by 1770 the English were calling it (and calling for it) by the word we now know. But, for a while, in the early eighteenth century, when Wade's men were exploring and road-building in the Highlands, the term hovered at an intermediate stage as Usky, a stage which has its own suitability and attraction. Usky was the spelling used, for example, by Edmund Burt, an officer of engineers who wrote letters from the North of Scotland about 1730, explaining the deeds and pleasures of the natives. They give, he said, to their children of six or seven years as much usky at a nip as would fill a wine-glass. Evidently this strengthened young heads and stomachs for the serious drinking of later years. When some of Burt's fellow-officers audaciously entered upon an usky-drinking-match with the locals, the Highlanders were easy victors and left the field without loss, whereas the English casualties were severe. Here is Burt's chronicle of the ruin. 'One of the officers was thrown into a fit of gout, without hopes; another had a most dangerous fever; a third lost his skin and hair by the surfeit.' The fourth competitor went 'yellow' in the slangy modern sense. 'When drunkenness ran high, he took several opportunities to sham it', and so, presumably, preserved his looks, locks, and hide.

It seems to have been a good party on the whole. One has heard of curious effects produced by a carouse, but a case of simultaneous depilation and depellation is new to me and should stand high among the cautionary tales for the reckless practitioners of absorbency. The standard of consumption in the Highlands, as Burt saw them, was imposing. 'Some of the Highland gentlemen,' observed this Gael-watcher, not denying them the title of gentry, 'are immoderate drinkers of usky, even three or four quarts at a sitting.' Burt himself was an anti-usky man, believing that 'this spirit has in it, by infusion, the seeds of anger, revenge, and murder (this, I confess is a little too poetical), but those who drink of it to any degree of excess behave, for the most part, like barbarians, I think much beyond the effect of any other liquor'. Life in 'the lone sheiling of the misty island' was not, in those days, dry. The collector of customs at Stornoway told Burt that 'One hundred and twenty families drink yearly 4,000 gallons of this spirit and brandy together, although many of them are so poor that they cannot afford to pay for much of either, which, you know, must increase the quantity drunk by the rest.' Burt did not, however, clinch his argument by relating the statistics of murder to those of usky-gallons drunk. It seems a little odd that 'uisge beatha', the spirit of life, should have been the name for a fluid so lethal. In any case, for the kind of skin-destroying, hair-uprooting tipple that Burt describes, usky seems to be an apter, because a rougher, name than whisky.

There were other spellings. A Scottish Gentleman, who visited the Highlands in 1737, was so delighted by the work of Wade, Burt, and their men in the civilizing of the country that he made his obeisance in a poem of a thousand lines.

> And thee, O Wade, shall coming Ages bless
> Whose prudent Care did give the Scheme Success, etc., etc.

At one of the banquets of celebration given after the building of another Highland bridge, the poet says that the workers

> Then beef and pudding plentifully eat
> With store of cheering Husque to their meat.

He also alludes to the 'Houses of Intertainment' set up for the travellers.

> With Corn and Grass, enclosures all around,
> Where fitt Supplys, for Men and Horse, are found.
> There various Meats and Liquors too are got,
> But Usqueba must never be forgot.

Those travelling over Wade's roads in 1944, as I had the pleasure of doing, at least over part of them, were not so lucky with their meats and liquors. Certainly Usqueba was not forgot; but, no less certainly, it was never as much in the glass as it was in the mind.

VAIL

Does anybody vail now – in the sense of taking off his hat or making obeisance? Or does anybody 'take a vail' in its old meaning, that of a noun to designate an extra payment or tip? Milton would have understood a waiter or a cab-driver who refused to vail until he got his vail and any eighteenth-century gentleman would have vailed to another who vailed to him – except Pope's Aristarchus (mask for the mighty scholar Bentley),

> His Hat, which never vail'd to human pride,
> Walker with reverence took and laid aside.

Shakespearean monarchs use this word, should occasion come for removal of the hardware hats of their profession,

> None that beheld him, but, like lesser lights,
> Did vail their crowns to his supremacy.

Again time comes for La Pucelle,

> When France must vail her lofty-plumed crest
> And let her head fall into England's lap.

Vailing descended from plumes and coronets to the humbler headgear of gentry and even commoners. Now that so many men wear no hats at all, there is less need than ever for this nice little word.

VAPOURS

DOES nobody ever have the vapours now? Are all our young ladies for ever vapour-free? Few maladies have had so expressive a name. Vapours were supposed to be exhalations of the organs rising to affect the brain and to agitate the nervous system. Crudely put, wind. Well, wind round the heart sounds poetical enough and Miss Beatrice Lillie has made a song of it in her finest vein of hilarious gravity. But such vapours can mean agony of the most material kind. Falstaff attributed 'crudy vapours' to the brain, vapours to be dispelled by the wise through plentiful addiction to sherris-sack. One knows that 'crudy vapour' feeling, even if the rather sickly potion suggested strikes one as a far from proper remedy. We would rather prescribe a more astringent carminative to suit the sharper palate of a spirit-drinking age. Falstaff might have enjoyed better health on whisky and soda than on sherris-sack.

Vapours, of the climatic kind, have a more melancholy charm than mere mist. I disagree with Hamlet's naming of the globe as a 'pestilent congregation of vapours'. The word is too good for such world-dismissive talk. Pestilent congregation of fogs, certainly. But vapours, no. Tennyson knew better:

> The woods decay, the woods decay and fall,
> The vapours weep their burthen to the ground.

That is essential autumn. And of course the Bible translators saw the value of its sound. 'For what is your life? It is even a vapour that appeareth for a little time and then vanisheth away.'

I like vapouring, too, for idle, fantastic talk. Celia Fiennes, that undaunted traveller of the William and Mary roads of England (or what passed for roads), wrote of a fellow-traveller who 'drew his sword and vapoured' when some imagined peril was at hand. She meant that he had blustered, or perhaps only twittered, not that he swooned. Nowadays politicians often talk of one who gets up and 'waffles'. Waffle has only dictionary status as a batter-cake to be eaten hot with butter or molasses. It is also a good invention for empty talk, but not, I think, as sharply descriptive as the old word, vapouring.

VERMIN

THE case of vermin raises the interesting question whether the meaning of a word can affect the value of its sound. Association of ideas must, I suppose, break in: but it is against all logic that a word should be deemed ugly because of the nasty thing to which it is applied. Most of the unpleasant articles have, as a matter of fact, titles unpleasing to the ear. No charm of sound is attached to dung, offal, sewer, smell, stench, stink, sweat, and so forth. But the issue was raised in the case of vermin. Robert Hichens, in his autobiography, recalls this conversation with Sir Max Beerbohm. (It was Max's habit to call Hichens 'Crotchet'.)

One day he said to me, 'Do you think, Crotchet, a word can be beautiful, just one word?'

'Yes,' I said, 'I can think of several words that seem to me beautiful.'

'Ah?'

A pause.

'Then tell me, do you think the word "ermine" is a beautiful word?'

'Yes,' I said, 'I like the sound of it very much.'

'Ah?'

Another pause.

'And do you think "vermin" is a beautiful word?'

The answer, as I see and hear it, is that vermin is quite an attractive, if not a beautiful, word. Its origin among worms, its transference to 'rats and mice and such small deer', does not alter the fact that it is, in sound, close neighbour to the rich vermeil and vermilion: both these ride well upon a poet's line. Supposing vermin had a loftier, even leonine, significance and we met such a verse as,

> Where mighty vermin of the forest roar,

should we dismiss it as contemptible? Ermine (Erminea Mustela) is a name for the unpleasant stoat. As the Max-Crotchet conversation suggests, it comes well off the tongue as well as looking well in places of ceremonial assembly. And vermin takes the ear no less.

VESUVIAN

DOES any member of the Old and Bold still call a match a Vesuvian, a term which paid fiery and handsome honours indeed to the eruptive splutter of a fusee? Matches were Vesuvians to Ouida and her Guardsmen:

> The hangings of the room were silken and rose-coloured, and a delicious confusion prevailed through it pell-mell— box-spurs, hunting-stirrups, cartridge-cases, curb-chains,

muzzle-loaders, hunting-flasks, and white gauntlets being mixed up with Paris novels, pink notes, point-lace ties, bracelets, and bouquets to be dispatched to various destinations, and velvet and silk bags for bank-notes, cigars, or vesuvians, embroidered by feminine fingers and as useless as those pretty fingers themselves.

This astonishing den belonged to

> ... the Hon. Bertie himself, second son of Viscount Royallieu, known generally in the Brigades as 'Beauty'. The appellative, gained at Eton, was in no way undeserved.

Of this Beauty it was later stated:

> His features were exceedingly fair, fair as the fairest girl's; his hair was of the softest, silkiest, brightest chestnut; his mouth was beautifully shaped; on the whole, with a certain gentle, mournful love-me look that his eyes had with them, it was no wonder that great ladies and gay lionnes alike gave him the palm as the handsomest man in all the Household Regiments. ...

Lionne is a nice 'appellative' that we appear to have dropped.

What seems so odd now is the effeminacy in which the Hon. Bertie, himself most masculine of taste if not of appearance, appeared to revel. Nowadays he would have been terrified of being given the 'appellative' of Spenser's 'prettie paunce' (more vulgarly 'screaming pansy') had he thus appeared and surrounded himself with such curious elegance. Beauty on Horse Guards' Parade combined the 'martyrdom of cuirass and gorget' with carrying no masculine 'muckender', but a 'dainty filigree handkerchief, all point, embroidery, and perfume'. But, however velvety or silken the texture of their Vesuvian and bank-note receptacles, Ouida's he-men were of a 'he-ness' awesome, intense, and unchallengeable.

VILIPEND

'On George's intercourse with Amelia he put an instant veto – menacing the youth with maledictions if he broke his commands and vilipending the poor innocent girl as the basest and most artful of vixens.' This of Osborne Senior in *Vanity Fair*. Vilipend is not a word often met to-day and Thackeray seems to have used it wrongly in this instance. To vilipend is, in derivation, to hold cheap or think poorly of any one. It does not imply more than opinion. But it came to be used as an alternative to vilify, which is to dishonour, disparage, and abuse in an active way, transcending a mere intellectual disdain. Thackeray's vilipend might well be vilify, for it is obvious that the odious old Osborne did not keep his opinions to himself.

It would be better to reserve vilipend in order to signify only mental depreciation and to use vilify for actual and practical aspersion. In any case, vilipend is worth retaining. It has a fine gravity. As one who has been engaged in various forms of critical journalism for many years, I was glad to be reminded of this sounding term and I think it should be employed with exactitude. Many a time have I vilipended a piece of work without feeling the urge and need (or perhaps lacking the energy and courage) to vilify it. It is a nice distinction.

VIRITOOT

What is a viritoot? Something at least to which the gayer maidens of the Middle Ages brought the 'brisky juvenals' of the male sex. Consider this, from *The Miller's Tale*.

> This Absolon knokketh al esily,
> And seyde, 'Undo, Gerveys, and that anon.'
> 'What, who artow?' It am I, Absolon.'
> 'What, Absolon! For Cristes sweete tree,
> Why rise ye so rathe? ey benedicitee!

What eyleth yow? Som gay gerl, God it woot,
Hath brought yow thus upon the viritoot;
By seinte Note, ye woot wel what I mene.

But do we ourselves wot well what this superb word indicates?

The glossary of the Globe Chaucer dodges it altogether. But it interprets Verytrot as quick-trot, and implies that a Viritoot is a Very-trot. Other editions give viretote and then leave that unexplained. I like to think of viritoot as a Chaucerian spree or jaunt, made in the flush of spring and early manhood. In any case it is a gorgeous creation: let us recommend viritooting to the young and the 'gay girls' who can provoke it.

WALLOP

WALLOP has a strange assortment of meanings. It appears to come from French 'galop' and first means light and speedy motion. Thus it was used by Allan Ramsay in his *Up in the Air*:

Now the sun's gane out o' sight,
Beat the ingle and snuff the light;
In glens the fairies skip and dance
An' witches wallop o'er to France.

Then wallop began to mean a heavier motion. (Both our fighter and bomber aircraft once, like the witches, walloped over to France in one sense or the other.) Next the heavy movement became really clumsy, as in walloping along, and then it moved on, as a noun, to mean a blow. It would be understood as a helping at table, 'a good wallop of pudding'. (Perhaps a confusion with dollop, a word of Nordic origin for clump or lump.) Finally it has become slang for mild beer and many a bar resounds with demands for a pint of wallop. Why?

WAME

WEEM is a cave in Scotland and from it come womb and wame. The latter is Scottish and Northern for stomach, and how well it suggests queasiness therein! The very sound of it has a hint of undulant unrest. Scottish popular poetry rumbles with wames.

> Food fills the wame and keeps us livin';
> Though life's a gift no' worth receivin',
> When heavy dragged wi' pine and grievin';
> But, oiled by thee
> The wheels of life go down-hill, scrievin',
> Wi' rattlin' glee.

'Thee' refers, of course, to John Barleycorn. Burns writes of the City Gent as 'Purse-proud, big wi' cent per cent, and muckle wame'. So we would expect Burns to have the word wame expanding warmly in his 'Lines to a Haggis', but there he spoke of swelling kytes which

> Are bent like drums;
> Then auld guidman, maist like to ryve,
> Bethankit hums.

'Kyte' is still used in vulgar English for a belly. 'Every night, blow out your kyte with boiled beef and carrots', roared Harry Champion in the music-halls of my boyhood.

Robert Fergusson used wame simply for the front of the body in his praise of 'Braid Claith', respectability's uniform. He counselled the aspirants to prosperity and fame to

> Hap them weel, both back and wame,
> In gude Braid Claith.

The same poem, incidentally, has the nice word 'gawsy' for consequential. The barber spark, when done with 'scrapin' wark', goes out on the Sabbath trig and gawsy, 'in gude Braid Claith'. George Douglas Brown in *The House with the Green Shutters* describes that home of disaster as 'planted firm and gawcey'. That story, by the way, is not only a notable piece of tragedy, but a treasury of Southern Scottish speech.

Returning to wame, I have been delighted to find it as a verb, indicating acute gastric distress. A-wameling in the passage quoted may be in confusion with the more common wambling, which means both to stagger about and to feel nausea. Both staggering and vomiting seem to be implied by an eighteenth-century Scottish traveller in her diary's description of a voyage to the Continent. She was a Mrs. Margaret Calderwood, who went from Scotland into England and on to Brussels in 1756:

> Marinasa the opera dancer was in the company, and a companion of his, a Swiss, who was either a singer or a dancer. ...All the company were sick, less or more, for first we plyed down the river with a cross wind, tacking every half hour till the tide was spent, and about three o'clock afternoon, when we were off Orford, on the coast of Suffolk, we were obliged to cast anchor; which was no sooner done than everyone fell a-wameling, as the ship did, and there was such sighing and groaning in the two cabins, as I never heard the like.
>
> At the upper end of the cabin, a bed lyes across the stern, in that lay the Swiss dished up like a boiled salmond (for it has no cover over it), sick to death; on the right hand of it lay the almost expiring dancer; on the left lay the old lady; at her feet lay I as quietly as I could; on the side with the dancer lay Mr. Webb; John Rattray was laid before my bed, with his head on a clog-bag and his feet in the state-room.

A dreadful scene. 'A-wameling' both for the tossed vessel and its spent voyagers is express and admirable; the 'boiled salmond' is a curious simile, but striking.

WAN

DIM has been given inclusion. Shall wan remain behind? A beautiful word for all pale, lack-lustre things, it throws a shadow wherever it strikes. What better entry than that first line of King Henry IV, now wearing the murdered Richard's crown?

> So shaken as we are, so wan with care,

But, apart from the everlastingly wan stars of romance and the wan maids more lovesick than any of Castle Bunthorne, my chief reason for bringing in this frail monosyllable is desire to cite the exquisite use of it in the Scottish ballad of Fair Annie, which begins with what is surely the cruellest stanza in all such doleful story-telling.

> It's narrow, narrow, mak your bed,
>   And learn to lie your lane;
> For I'm gaun owre the sea, Fair Annie,
>   A braw bride to bring hame.
> Wi' her I will get gowd and gear,
>   Wi' you I ne'er gat nane.

When the 'braw bride' was brought in:

> Fair Annie served the lang tables
>   Wi' the white bread and the wine;
> But ay she drank the wan water
>   To keep her colour fine.

The wan water! There is a splash of magic in that.

WANHOPE

THE 'wan' words—the prefix signifying want or wane—have faded away. But wanhope, for despair, seems exquisite now; no doubt the added notion of wanness in colour as well as of waning gives special poignance to the word. R. C. Trench, Archbishop of Dublin, in his book on *English, Past and Present*, collected a number of these 'wans' – wanthrift, wanluck, wanlust, wanwit, wangrace, wantrust. They rarely survived Middle English: the cause of their disappearance is hard to comprehend. Mention of wanwit recalls 'witwanton' used as a verb in the sixteenth century. The Scots were more retentive. They had a beauty of this kind in 'wanwauchtie', unable to take the hearty draught. (Waucht must be known the world over through Burns's guid-willie waucht, the dram of kindliness.) 'He's unco wanwauchtie that scunners at whey', is an old Scots proverb. Scunners, for the benefit of the English, meant dislikes or shrinks away from.

WANION

WANION or waniand means 'in the waning of the moon' and the moon is deemed to wane unluckily. Hence 'with a wanion' meant with a curse or with a vengeance. So it occurs once in Shakespeare: 'Come away or I'll fetch you with a wanion.' It became possible to wish a wanion on to a person as a form of pest. It sounds too agreeable a word for this despiteful usage, but nearly everything connected with the moon acquired an unfortunate sense at one time. Nowadays we are more tolerant; sentimental balladry and music-hall lyrics have made the moon a symbol of happy romance as well as of frustrated yearning. So a wanion might come back to favour if anybody would use the word.

WANTON

I HAD always thought that wanton had much to do with wandering, but apparently it is Old English for untrained: hence it means ungoverned or rebellious. Mankind has ever taken two directly conflicting views of the unschooled and ignorant state, i.e. that it is either blissful innocence or abominable sin. Thus the beautiful word wanton came to be used in two contradictory

292

senses. Usually it implies cruel, lascivious aberration: Shake-speare constantly employed it so. A notable example is in the wonderful picture of the Dark Lady in *Love's Labour's Lost:*

> A whitely wanton with a velvet brow.
> With two pitch-balls stuck in her face for eyes.
> Ay, and by heaven, one that will do the deed
> Though Argus were her eunuch and her guard.

So the plays are full of wanton lads with wanton blood and of maids no colder or more staid. But the innocent wanton, betoken-ing the state of nature, is also there. Listen to Friar Lawrence (sometimes a bore, but here at his best):

> Here comes the lady: O, so light a foot
> Will ne'er wear out the everlasting flint;
> A lover may bestride the gossamer
> That idles in the wanton summer air
> And yet not fall; so light is vanity.

What could be more sinless than the breath of June? Herrick could think of wanton purity, claiming to sing of cleanly wantonness. Another of his century, Quarles, used wanton to signify a gracious meandering. In his 'Divine Rapture' he obviously thought of wanton as wandering:

> E'en like two little bank-dividing brooks
> That wash the pebbles with their wanton streams,
> And having ranged and search'd a thousand nooks,
> Meet both at length in silver-breasted Thames,
> Where in a greater current they conjoin.
> So I my Best Belovèd's am: so He is mine.

Reflection on this. Did Charles pronounce conjoin conjine – or is it just a false rhyme? His subsequent rhymes with mine are twine and coin. One gathers coin was kine to him.

Further, what a change of tint the Thames appears to have undergone! How often does the Thames seem silver-breasted now? I have always been puzzled by the colours attributed by the poets to English rivers, especially the southern ones, whose normal hue is a dull, muddy brown. Milton, for example, calls Sabrina (the Severn) 'glassie, translucent and coral-paven'. Our oozy English streams certainly have a romantic effect upon their bank-side minstrels. Often the 'wanton streams' are seen through colour-tinted glasses and so move in silvery splendour far different from the dun floods of our acquaintance.

Making all allowance for the pollution of our streams by our industrialism, I still find it difficult to believe that the wanton (or wandering) Trent was ever argent. Yet Shakespeare wrote of it as 'smug and silver' (smug is smooth of surface, not of manner, in this context).

Recently I passed, during a winter train-journey, through Burton-on-Trent, that fountain of the best of our beers. It is, to the casual glance, a town of chimney-stacks which might be turning out diesel oil or chemicals rather than the sovereign brews of Bass, Worthington, Marston and others. The Trent had splashed itself over the spungy fields and covered them, under a grey sky, with dark and squalid pools. Even in June is there a silver Trent?

Returning to London, Spenser, composing his richly worded 'Prothalamion', explained that he

> Walkt forth, to ease my payne
> Along the shore of silver streaming Themmes,
> Whose rutty bancke, the which his River hemmes,
> Was painted all with variable flowers.

The poet's colour-painting is as variable as those blossoms. For later 'the flood' has become Christal. Apparently the only thing whiter, or at least more silvery than the river was the plumage of the swans, whose 'fayre plumes' the benignant Themmes did not wish to soil with 'water not so fayre'.

Such, apparently, was the prospect just outside the Temple and the Strand and on adjacent reaches of the river. We have certainly altered the setting. But still I cannot believe that the stream was ever as 'christal' as all that.

WAY-WISER

THERE were reproduced in *Country Life* not long ago two photographs of Perambulators or Way-wisers; one was on loan to the Dorchester Museum, the other is in the possession of the Salisbury Museum. The former is the larger and more handsome; it is also more distinguished in early ownership – or rather tenancy. It was pushed from Sherborne to Crewkerne by Dorothy Wordsworth, who had it as part of the equipment of a furnished house called Racedown. It must not be supposed that she was taking a baby for this strenuous walk. She was perambulating not only in the sense of walking, but of measuring the distance as well. She satisfied her curiosity while she took the air.

The way-wiser, to keep the good Saxon term for the classical Perambulator, was a single wheel with handle and with a recording clock attached. The latter was capable of marking distances. The instrument was certainly in use during the seventeenth century and is mentioned in Evelyn's *Diary*. Mr. Macnaghten, author of the *Country Life* article on way-wisers, believes that Christopher Saxton, who mapped every county in England and Wales about a century before that, must have had his perambulating machine. The specimen which was trundled along by Dorothy Wordsworth was made by Thomas Wright (1711–86), Instrument Maker to His Majesty. It is beautifully fashioned, as the photograph revealed, a charming piece of craftsmanship in metal and wood. The Salisbury way-wiser is simpler, but no less gracious.

One would naturally like to have the word way-wisdom for the practice of road-measurement. But the 'wise' part of way-wiser comes from the German 'weisen' to show. It is a wegweiser, but most happily Anglicized. Perambulators remained way-wisers until mid-Victorian times, when the modern 'pram' arrived. Perambulator for stroller, not on wheels, has been retained by James Bone in his books of delighted and delightful topography, *The London Perambulator* and *The Edinburgh Perambulator*.

WELKIN

THE Welkin still rings in writing of 'ye olde' kind. But nobody would now use that word seriously. The welkin came to us from the S.E. as weolkne and weolkyn, meaning a cloud. Then the cloud became the arch of heaven and the sky itself. Then, to the all-seizing genius of Shakespeare, it was a sky-blue adjective. I came across it in *The Winter's Tale:* cries Leontes to Mamillius,

> Come, sir page,
> Look on me with your welkin eye: sweet villain!
> Most dear'st: My collop!

(Scots know all about collops from eating them minced. A collop is a slice; so a child, being a slice of life, can be a collop too.)

Poets, when calling the sky the welkin, have as a rule regarded it chiefly as a sounding-board. The welkin does not merely ring. In Marlowe it also howls and cracks. Marlowe, incidentally, in *Tamburlaine* gives a fair anticipation of a flying-bomb aloft:

> As when a fiery exhalation,
> Wrapt in the bowels of a freezing cloud,
> Fighting for passage, makes the welkin crack.

I regret the passing of welkin from the common speech and script of to-day. Especially does the adjectival welkin seem a loss. After all, we use blue for so many things that another word for this colour would be valuable. 'Feeling a bit welkin this morning?' 'Yes, sir, I'm afraid we kept it up last night till all was welkin.' 'Rough house?' 'Well, some of the stories were a bit welkin.' How hard do we work our blues!

WHIFFLE AND TRUNCHEON

COUNTLESS students of Shakespeare must know, for annotation's sake, the passage in the last Chorus speech of *Henry V.*

> Behold the English beach
> Pales in the flood, with wives, and boys,

Whose shouts and claps out-voice the deep-mouthed sea,
Which, like a mighty whiffler 'fore the king,
Seems to prepare his way.

Whiffler here is a man-at-arms who keeps back the crowd. Such services are much in demand in our times when film-stars take the public air or are expected to attend a function. But our police must whiffle back the fancying crowds with only a truncheon in quiet reserve and no recourse to clubs, halberds, javelins or arquebuses. Borrow, in *Romany Rye*, talked of the last of the whifflers hanging himself for lack of occupation 'since the discontinuation of Guildhall banquets'. No need for such despairing self-slaughter nowadays. The film-star has altered all that. And monarchy, let the film-stars admit, can make our modern and gentle whiffling necessary upon occasion. We still have 'mighty whifflers 'fore the king' – and before queens and princesses too.

To whiffle was first of all applied to the light action of the wind. People could be whiffled 'on every wave of doctrine'. It was also used intransitively to mean hesitate, jink or evade. Because of the breath of wind a whiffler could be a smoker. Because of the lightness of the breath a whiffle could be a trifle and a whiffler a trifling, empty, chattering and dilly-dallying fellow. Gravely Carlyle announced that 'life is no frivolity or hypothetical coquetry or whifflery'. It is a queer coincidence that makes the term for a robust constable and inescapable warden or janitor also apply to trifles light as air.

The modern British whiffler has his truncheon; this article appears to be a thing sliced or broken off. The French keep tranche for slice. Here is oddity again. The word signified originally a fragment or shaft of a weapon rather than the weapon itself. It became a staff of office or the whiffler's baton. The broken particle was magnified in time to become the source of broken heads, just as the light-weight whiffling ninny was transmuted to the substance and authority of a powerful guard and constable.

WINE-DARK

Y EATS wrote:

> At wine-dark midnight in the sacred wood,

and the adjective works powerfully, though I cannot remember a midnight of exactly that hue. Wine-dark is the customary translation for the Homeric epithet applied to the Aegean Sea, which I have visited entranced, but did not find to be an empurpled flood. Radiantly, gloriously blue, yes; but scarcely claret or port, Samian or Chian – to be more local in the vintage. Yet the sound and suggestion of wine-dark do evoke in the mind the richness of the Archipelago where European civilization rose, like Aphrodite, from the waves. The surge of wine-dark waters in a line of poetry now inevitably brings to fancy the isles of Sappho and Alcaeus. Yet that aspect of nature which to me is truly wine-dark, or at least wine-misty, is much more native. I mean our English woods in winter.

In the Chilterns, the naked beech-woods of the short and misty days seem to me even lovelier than when they wear the tenderest greenth of May or blaze to heaven in October's frost before, consumed, they cast their leaves to earth. Day after day in the dark months the woods, especially the copses of birches and other smaller trees in the hollows, yield a tint of the utmost delicacy for which I think we have no proper word. It lies upon them like bloom on fruit; sometimes it seems to be given off and to take the air, like a visible essence, a fume, an emanation. This colour is not quite purple: yet it is richer than any brown. Umber is an epithet that somehow comes near to it. On December walks, when

> Trod beside me, close and dear,
> The beautiful and death-struck year,

I have fancied that tawny, as applied to port-wine, is just this shade. Certainly the exquisite effluence of the wintry spinneys reminds me of a rather light port drawn from the wood. So I would not call these noble groves of the chalk ridges and bottoms wine-dark; but wine-vaporous would not be inaccurate. Winter after winter I have walked amazed at the fine hues of the long timbered slopes, but never lovelier than when the leaf has fallen. Their browny-purple is as soft as the coo of their doves in spring and indeed has something feathery about it too.

WISEACRE

THIS ought, one feels, to be a complimentary word, since the acre suggests some width of wisdom. But the wiseacre is not the man whose 'mind to him a kingdom is', not the seemingly spacious intellectual but a pretentious fellow, assuming a wisdom that he does not possess. He was originally a wise-sayer. But, just as the soothsayer began life as one who speaks sooth, i.e. the real truth, and then was degraded to mean a charlatan who, in prophecy, made a guess at the truth, so the wiseacre was also put down a peg or two and his sagacity degraded. This wise-sayer, instead of speaking wisdom as he did in his early days, became a pretender to profundity, the wiseacre of the plain, blunt man's contempt. Among my Fleet Street annals I remember a report that a newspaper tycoon, of great ability but little sensibility, broke the heart of a gifted member of his staff, a contributor of charming essays (rather too good for their surroundings) by calling his work, in public, 'wiseacre stuff'. It is possible to put a keenly cutting edge on to the disparaging syllables of wiseacre.

Wizard is another word of this kind which has lost distinction. The wizard, like the wiseacre, was once the truly wise, the sage unqualified. Milton gave highest honours to the wizards by calling the Magi so in his 'Ode on the Morning of Christ's Nativity'.

> See how from far, upon the eastern road,
> The star-led wizards haste with odours sweet.

Yet to Shakespeare, writing earlier, the wizard was already suspect.

> Peace, doting wizard, peace. I am not mad

indicates that the wizard, Dr. Pinch in *The Comedy of Errors*, is a trifle mad himself. The wizard mentioned by the Duke of Clarence in *Richard III* is not a philosopher, but a wiseacre.

What did Milton mean when he applied wizardry to landscape?

> Nor on the shaggy top of Mona high
> Nor yet where Deva spreads her wizard streams.

Since the friend mourned in *Lycidas* was drowned in the Irish Channel and Mona is the Isle of Man, this Dee is the Welsh and Cheshire member of that company. The adjective wizard in this case seems purely a compliment, as glamorous has become. And so, in our own time, it has continued to be, since it was for long the slang word for marvellous or superb, passing from R.A.F. lingo to that of the school-boy.

WORTH

WHAT a strong, simple, Anglo-Saxon monosyllable to describe the merit of a man! Consider this which I found in Lord Cockburn's *Memorials of His Time*, a vivid description of Fourth Georgian Edinburgh:

> The Whigs had only one opportunity of making a Scotch judge. They selected Charles Hay, a man famous for law, paunch, whist, claret, and worth.

Short words, but good.

Cockburn continues:

> Honest, warm-hearted, and considerate, he was always true to his principles and his friends. But these and other good qualities were all apt to be lost sight of in people's admiration of his drinking. His daily and flowing cups raised him far above the evil days of sobriety on which he had fallen, and made him worthy of having quaffed with the Scandinavian heroes. But there was no noise in his libations, no boisterous-

ness, no wrangling, not even disputation. The kindly stillness of his ordinary manner, instead of being disturbed, was deepened by potation; and a cask so well seasoned was not liable to be inflamed by anything so feeble as intoxication. His delight was to sit smiling, quiet, and listening; saying little, but that little always sensible, sated apparently with enjoyment, and only disturbed when he observed some unfortunate creature at table not taking as many or as full bumpers as himself.

All Scottish topers have not shown the same qualities of pacific and sweetly reasonable absorbency. Surely there is worth in the writing of those words. I suggest that the sentence, 'a cask so well seasoned was not liable to be inflamed by anything so feeble as intoxication' is a superb revelation of a judicial outlook upon the contemptible follies of the weak in head, the worthless ones.

WRITHEN AND WRITHLED

IN Kipling's poem on 'Sussex' in *The Five Nations*, we are told with as much melody as truth,

> No tender-hearted garden crowns,
>   No bosomed woods adorn
> Our blunt, bow-headed whale-backed Downs
>   But gnarled and writhen thorn.

Kipling's 'writhen' trees upon the Sussex hills are vivid to the eye, toughly invading and interrupting the smoothness of that curving line which Belloc deemed 'so noble and so bare'. Shakespeare, or whoever wrote *Henry VI*, Part I, had the same kind of twisty thing in mind when he used the word 'writhled'. But he applied it to a smaller matter.

> It cannot be this weak and writhled shrimp
> Should strike such terror to his enemies.

Were shrimps on sale in the fish-shops of his London so that he could note their writhled nature in a street stroll, or had he met the article alive and writhling while on a sea-side jaunt? But sea-side jaunts were unusual then. Shakespeare's marine contacts are strange and worth investigation.

ZENONIAN

A ZENONIAN attitude to life may be obstinate in two ways. The first Zeno was a philosopher of Elea who, in the fifth century B.C. disproved, as he thought, the possibility of motion. While I am naturally inclined to condole with the sage on the state of his bowels, the Zenonian assertion deserves, in other respects, some sympathy in our time of universal fidgets and of speeds in movement that reach the supersonic. It is certainly a trifle hard to prove his case since the whole of one's existence seems to consist of shifting things, words on to paper, ideas into heads, men into uniforms, and tourists into countries, as well as food into bodies and bodies to and from their work and play. However, I have previously quoted James Bridie's admirable argument that man's especial genius lies in his capacity for repose.[1] To that extent Bridie was a good Zenonian. 'Budge not' seemed common sense to him.

The other Zeno, 'the budge doctor of the Stoic fur', he who two hundred years after his namesake had thus disposed of motion, disposed, more or less, of pleasure, would have been no friend of the Scottish doctor, dramatist, and best of companions. But even the strictest of the Stoic tribe must admit the claims of kindness and gallantry. And Zeno did. It was not that he would try anything once, but that certain temptations called forth his sense of courtesy rather than proving his weakness. Montaigne has related that 'They report that Zeno never dealt with a woman but once in all his life, which he did for civility, lest he should over-obstinately seeme to contemne the sex'. The *vie amoureuse* of the earlier Zeno is not, I believe, known. He may, perhaps, in one of his major fits of negation, have denied the possibility of woman. For is she not volatile?

[1] See note on Carapace.

Not a French two-syllabled adjective, but a three-syllabled verb, coming from the language of the Machine Age. 'When finished, please zeroise the dial'. That is certainly more brief than 'put the dial back to nought'. It would fit in with words like alerted. 'When alerted please unzeroise the dial.' Zeroise could also pass for one of those euphemistic substitutes for massacre so dear to the political cant of the dictatorships. Instead of saying that reactionary elements have been liquidated the bulletin might announce that bourgeois objectivists have been zeroised. Objectivist is a recent addition to the lingo of Communist Orthodoxy. I presume that it means one who sees, or tries to see, realities plain and straight and is not to be upset by the subjectivism of propaganda. Thus objectivism ought to be the human ideal, but I gather from the neo-Marxist utterances that it marks the depth of human depravity and cries out for liquidation. If the verbose Marxians have not got on to zeroisation yet, they soon will.

ZEST AND ZYMURGY

If you have ever slipped on a piece of orange-peel you may well curse zest for the resulting sprain. It began life as orange or lemon-peel: since this was used for flavouring, zest became a word for piquancy and then for the gusto which relishes piquancy. Now, it serves for any kind of eagerness.

'Z' is a happy letter, as 'y' is so often a sad one. For though 'y' stands for youth it suggests to me the sadness of youth lost and not the glory of youth in being. It is the youth of which one thinks in one's sere and yellow leaf, lamenting dead yesterdays and yearning for the years that were. Years can sound almost as melancholy as tears and are close to yearn in connotation as well as in the dictionary. But the 'z's are full of vigour and fascination! The zephyrs bless us and make us zealous for zestful relish of the spring and lead on to the zenith of the summer. (I am conveniently forgetting the Zenonians.) There is many an exquisite line that lives in beauty by the grief that is in its 'y's.

> That time of year thou may'st in me behold
> When yellow leaves, or none, or few do hang.

'That time of life' would not ring the bell so movingly nor would 'faded leaves' affect me like the yellow ones.

'Z' makes no such dirge. One of the Greek words for life was Zoe. Of course life has its ugly manifestations, and some of these, such as Zopilote, a kind of carrion vulture, Zoril, a skunk, and Zoster, the disease of shingles, bring shame upon the 'Z' list. But to restore the aura of happiness which I have attributed to this letter, there are Zyme, which means any kind of fermentation, preferably alcoholic, and Zythepsary, a portentous and now almost obsolete name for a brewery. It presumably disappeared like the evaporating froth of zymous liquors, because it sounds too chemical and is unlikely to be comprehended by those engaged in zymurgy which is the practice or art of fermentation as in wine-making, brewing, distilling, etc. Zymurgous men, or, more classically, zymergs, use a simpler vocabulary on their way to and from the zythepsary. But the rhymers could use these terms and, muttering these words, I found rhyme upon my lips:

> You stagger and your step's awry
> With product of zythepsary:
> You are not of the wary 'uns,
> The hard-boiled zythepsarians,
> Who roll zymurgous barrels out,
> Yet never sway nor fall about,
> Nor take to rioting and crime
> But, fleeting peaceably the time,
> Absorb, enjoy, and master zyme.

A pleasing sentiment, I hope, with which to say farewell to the alphabet.